THE MIDDLE EAST TODAY

The Middle East Today is an accessible and comprehensive introductory textbook for undergraduate students of Middle East Studies, Middle East politics and geography. The book features a host of pedagogical features to assist students with their learning. These include detailed maps, case studies on key issues, boxed sections and suggestions for further reading.

The book highlights the current issues facing the Middle East, linking them to the rich political, geographical and cultural history of the region. The author examines the crises and conflicts, both current and potential, likely to dominate the region in coming years.

Key chapters focus on:

- stereotypes of the region
- the making of the modern state system
- contemporary Islamist thought
- the Arab–Israeli conflicts
- the struggle for economic and social development
- democracy and political transformation in the region

Designed both to introduce and to develop a deeper understanding of this rapidly changing region, *The Middle East Today* is an essential text for all students of Middle East Studies, Middle East politics and geography.

Dr Dona J. Stewart is the director of the Middle East Institute and associate professor of geography at Georgia State University. She is a specialist in the human and political geography of the Middle East and a former Fulbright scholar to Jordan. Her research interests also include urbanization and land-use change, especially in Egypt.

Michael Christopher Low is a doctoral student and Richard Hofstadter Faculty Fellow in the Department of History at Columbia University. He is author of *Empire and the Hajj: Pilgrims, Plagues and Pan-Islam under British Surveillance, 1865–1908* in *The International Journal of Middle East Studies*. He is a graduate of the Middle East Institute and Department of History at Georgia State University.

THE MIDDLE EAST TODAY

Political, geographical and cultural perspectives

Dona J. Stewart

Routledge
Taylor & Francis Group

LONDON AND NEW YORK

First published 2009 by Routledge
2 Park Square, Milton Park, Abingdon, Oxon OX14 4RN

Simultaneously published in the USA and Canada
by Routledge
270 Madison Ave, New York, NY 10016

Routledge is an imprint of the Taylor & Francis Group, an informa business

© 2009 Dona J. Stewart
Typeset in Garamond by Keyword Group Ltd
Printed by Edwards Brothers, Inc

British Library Cataloguing in Publication Data
A catalogue record for this book is available from the British Library

Library of Congress Cataloging in Publication Data
Stewart, Dona J.
The Middle East today : political, geographical and cultural perspectives /
Dona J. Stewart.
p. cm.
Includes bibliographical references and index.
ISBN 978-0-415-77243-3 (hardback : alk. paper) – ISBN 978-0-415-77242-6
(pbk. : alk. paper) – ISBN 978-0-203-88414-0 (ebook) 1. Middle East–Politics
and government–1979- 2. Middle East–Economic conditions–1979- 3. United
States–Foreign relations–Middle East. 4. Middle East–Foreign relations–United
States. 5. Geopolitics–Middle East. I. Title.
DS63.1.S75 2008
956.04–dc22
2008029204

ISBN10: 0-415-77243-5 (hbk)
ISBN10: 0-415-77242-7 (pbk)
ISBN10: 0-203-88414-0 (ebk)

ISBN 978-0-415-77243-3 (hbk)
ISBN 978-0-415-77242-6 (pbk)
ISBN 978-0-203-88414-0 (ebk)

CONTENTS

LIST OF TABLES

LIST OF MAPS

LIST OF BOXES

ACKNOWLEDGMENTS

A great many people helped this book become a reality, though any omissions and errors are mine alone.

I would like to thank my editor, Joe Whiting, and his editorial staff for their support and assistance throughout this process, which took longer than anticipated. I would also like to thank Ian Cool for his cartographic skills.

The staff of the Middle East Institute, Alta Schwartz and Letitia Williams, allowed me to escape from the office to write and, with their usual efficiency, handled many issues before they ever needed my attention.

Chris Low's contributions greatly improved the quality of this volume, and particularly its coverage of the non-Arab Middle East. Our long talks and debates over coffee were a welcome and rare escape from administrative duties.

This volume was really motivated by my students, and by a desire to provide an analysis of the region that would allow them to make sense of a part of the world that can seem hopelessly impenetrable.

Mallory, thank you for your understanding and tolerance when I could not be as available for you as I wanted to be.

Finally, I welcome suggestions for further improvement of this book and its approach.

PART I

INTRODUCTION TO THE REGION

1

THE MIDDLE EAST AND NORTH AFRICA: BETWEEN IMAGE AND REALITY

Think of the Middle East. Quickly, write down the first five words that come to your mind. Don't think too deeply; simply record the first words that you associate with the region. This is an exercise I have often done with my students. Analysis of the words typically associated with the Middle East, Arabs and Islam offers significant insight into the commonly held image of the region. The words also reveal much about the stereotype – even unconsciously held – that people have about the Middle East.

Table 1.1 contains the most common responses from my students in this exercise. Many of the responses reflect the region's predominant physical characteristics, such as desert, sand and the inevitable 'ship of the desert', the camel. Other responses reflect the region's primary export, oil, and the wealth associated with it. Violence and conflict figure prominently among the responses (this was true even before the events of September 11, 2001 in the United States). Two sources of conflict and violence most often mentioned are the Israeli–Palestinian conflict and violence associated with followers of militant Islam. Certainly al-Qaeda has gained a high profile, and Osama Bin Laden is more likely to be recognized by the general public than the leader of any country in the

Middle East. Finally, repression of women, symbolized in the West by the wearing of the 'veil', quickly comes to mind.

In truth these responses do accurately reflect some characteristics of the region; but, like most stereotypes, they offer an incomplete picture. For example, while much of the region is dry and dominated by deserts, major river systems such as the Nile and the Tigris and Euphrates create the fertile agricultural areas in which humankind first domesticated crops and created permanent settlements. Spending the winter in Amman, Jordan, means enduring much cold rain and even the occasional snow. In the mountains around Tehran, Iran, winter skiers take to the slopes.

While a few countries in the region are endowed with fabulous oil wealth, especially those in the Gulf, most countries are struggling with poor economic performance, significant external debt and a large number of unemployed young people. Though the veil is typically seen by Westerners as a sign of women's oppression in the region, only two countries, Iran and Saudi Arabia, have laws requiring women to cover themselves in public. In other countries women wear the veil voluntarily, though they may feel pressure to

Table 1.1 Words associated with the Middle East

oil war conflict holy lands ancient civilizations camel sand desert

Osama Bin Laden al-Qaeda mysterious wealthy Qur'an poor angry

veil Jerusalem terrorism Iraq repression Islam fanaticism

conform to societal norms. Finally, though fuzzy video images of terrorists beheading Western captives shock the Western public, few may realize that inhabitants of the region have also been victims of violence waged between their – often repressive – governments and Islamic militants in the years and even decades prior to 9/11.

Box 1.1

SHIRIN EBADI: AN ISLAMIC FEMINIST'S STRUGGLE FOR HUMAN RIGHTS IN THE ISLAMIC REPUBLIC OF IRAN

Michael Christopher Low

In 2003, Shirin Ebadi was awarded the Nobel Peace Prize in recognition of her tireless struggle on behalf of the rights of women and children, democracy, and freedom of speech in Iran. Despite being the first Iranian and the first Muslim woman to receive this honor, the Iranian government virtually ignored her achievement. Muhammad Khatami, Iran's president at the time, scoffed at the political motivations behind the prize, noting that it would have been more significant had it been awarded for a scientific or a literary achievement. Even more telling, Iran's state-run television refused to broadcast Ebadi's acceptance speech because she was not wearing the *hijab* and was therefore in violation of Iran's official dress code for women. Much to the chagrin of the Iranian government, however, Ebadi's Nobel Prize has made her the international face of Iran's struggle for democracy.

During the reign of the Shah, Ebadi was among the first female judges in Iran. Like millions of other women of her generation, however, Ebadi was marginalized in the wake of Iran's 1979 Islamic revolution. In 1980, despite her support for the revolution, she was stripped of her judgeship when Ayatollah Khomeini's turban-clad revolutionaries decreed that women could no longer serve as judges. Undaunted, Ebadi fought back. She became a lawyer and human-rights activist, devoting her life to exposing the hypocrisies and broken promises of the Islamist jurists, whose revolution had promised an alternative to the despotic rule of the Shah.

After the Islamic revolution, Iran's existing legal system was dismantled and replaced with an ideologically charged and highly patriarchal interpretation of Islamic law. Under these new laws, the *hijab* became mandatory. Men could now divorce their wives without offering any reason, while it became almost impossible for women to get a divorce. The testimony of two women became equal to that of one man. Any woman wishing to travel would need written permission from a male relative.

Unfortunately, as Ebadi points out, 'whenever women protest and ask for their rights, they are silenced with the argument that the laws are justified under Islam'. She dismisses such arguments as completely 'unfounded', while carefully noting that 'it is not Islam at fault, but rather the patriarchal culture that uses its own interpretations [of Islam] to justify whatever it wants'.

Despite the fact that Ebadi styles herself as an 'Islamic feminist' and 'continues to work within the framework of Islam', scouring religious texts in an attempt 'to come up with a progressive interpretation that provides maximum space for religious tolerance and women's rights', Ebadi's brave activism has often led to direct confrontations with the Iranian authorities. Nowhere is this fact more evident than in her legal representation of dissident journalists and intellectuals.

Box 1.1

SHIRIN EBADI: AN ISLAMIC FEMINIST'S STRUGGLE FOR HUMAN RIGHTS IN THE ISLAMIC REPUBLIC OF IRAN—CONT'D

Ebadi has represented the family of Zahra Kazemi, an Iranian-Canadian journalist who was killed while in police custody in 2003. Ebadi herself was imprisoned as a result of her work on another case involving a student who was beaten to death by paramilitary forces during a 1999 demonstration. In an even more chilling twist, while sifting through government documents in preparation for the trial of a case involving the premeditated murders of dissident intellectuals, Dariush and Parvaneh Forouhar, Ebadi stumbled across a government authorization for her own assassination!

Shirin Ebadi, 'The Progressive interview: Shirin Ebadi', interview by Amitabh Pal. *The Progressive*, September 2004: 35–9.

It is perhaps not surprising that the stereotypes are so simplistic and difficult to overcome. Even among the educated population in the West, knowledge of the region, its places and peoples remains poor. A survey conducted by the National Geographic Education Foundation in 2006 found that, among Americans aged 18–24, six in ten (63 percent) could not find Iraq or Saudi Arabia on a map of the Middle East, while three-quarters (75 percent) could not find Iran or Israel. In fact, 44 percent could not find even one of these countries (National Geographic Education Foundation 2006: 8). This survey was taken after three years of extensive media coverage following the US overthrow of Saddam Hussein's regime and occupation of Iraq.

BEFORE THE MIDDLE EAST: THERE WAS THE 'ORIENT'

Though today the term 'Middle East' is very common, it is a relatively new name, first used by American naval officer and geostrategist Alfred Thayer Mahan in reference to the area around the Gulf that made up a British 'zone of influence' in the late nineteenth century. At that time, parts of the region under French influence were known as the Near East. Both these terms were designed to distinguish the region from the Far East, composed of East and Southeast Asia. Because the term 'Middle East' traces its roots to Western imperialism, it can have a derogatory connotation. However, the term is used throughout the region; in fact, the largest Arabic daily newspaper, printed simultaneously in twelve cities, is the London-based *Asharq Alawsat*, or *The Middle East*.

In reality, however, despite the role of Western imperialism in creating the countries of the modern Middle East (the focus of Chapter 5), few people in the West had detailed first-hand knowledge of the place or its peoples. Instead, the Middle East and Asia were part of a much larger, if ill-defined, region stretching all the way to China and Japan, known as the Orient. The term 'Orient' derived from Latin, meaning 'land of the rising sun', hence 'East'. (The term 'Occident', referring to the West, but rarely used today, meant 'land of the setting sun'.)

The Orient was avidly studied by Western scholars, particularly during the era of Western imperial expansion in the eighteenth and nineteenth centuries. Departments of Oriental Studies were set up in numerous Western universities for the study of the Orient's languages, culture and history. Artists tried to capture the essence of the Orient in their paintings, compositions and literary works. Among the best-known are the operas *Aida* and *Madame Butterfly* and the musical *The King and I*. Agatha Christie's *Murder on the Orient Express* and *Death on the Nile* are examples of literary genres that embraced the Orient. These artistic works were avidly consumed by a European and American public enthralled by the exoticism of the Orient.

This construction of a place known as 'the Orient' had enormous ramifications for Western perceptions of the region. In his ground-breaking work *Orientalism*, Edward Said argued that Orient and Occident worked as oppositional terms, so that 'the Orient' was constructed as a negative inversion of Western culture. Furthermore, this view of the Orient helped to justify European imperialism during the eighteenth and nineteenth centuries by casting the 'Oriental' as uncivilized, backward and in need of Western supervision. The inhabitants of the Orient were placed low on the racial hierarchy in which Europeans held the highest position and justified their imperial ambitions.

Box 1.2

EDWARD SAID AND ORIENTALISM

Michael Christopher Low

In his ground-breaking work, *Orientalism*, the late Edward Said (1935–2003), a Palestinian-born professor of comparative literature at Columbia University, employed literary theory to scrutinize the intentions and assumptions of Middle East specialists, otherwise known as Orientalists. Said's work cast the opinions of these vaunted experts in a rather unfavorable light. In doing so, *Orientalism* has profoundly influenced the landscape of both European and American scholarship since its publication in 1978.

An entire generation of intellectuals has reassessed their attitudes toward previously accepted assumptions regarding the Orient in general and the Arabic-speaking Islamic world in particular. And, although Said's work is primarily a literary analysis of European imperialism in the Middle East, it has become one of the most influential perspectives in the variety of subjects that comprise the interdisciplinary field of Middle East Studies. As a result, it has become almost impossible to write anything about the Middle East without grappling with the controversial questions raised by Said's *Orientalism*.

Originally, Orientalism was simply a term for describing scholarship pertaining to the Orient and its languages and cultures. According to Said's polemical redefinition of the term, however, Orientalism is a regularized system of scholarship that contributed to the Western world's cultural, economic and political domination of the Orient. Said's analysis concluded that Orientalism, an allegedly objective system of Western scholarship, was in fact a highly developed web of racism and cultural stereotypes, and an institutionalized apparatus for interpreting or speaking for a mute, stagnant and ultimately inferior Orient.

In order to illustrate his point, Said crafted an 'intellectual genealogy', tracing the growth of Orientalism and its connections to Western imperialism.[i] Primarily focusing on British and French texts from the eighteenth and nineteenth centuries, Said contended that Western scholars, explorers, novelists, and colonial administrators used the discourse of Orientalism not only to gain authority over 'the Orient' but also as a way of defining themselves as Westerners. Thus, the West defined its own self-image by defining its Oriental 'other'.

Although it is undeniable that *Orientalism* has been responsible for stimulating a landslide of positive discussion and fruitful research regarding the Middle East and its interaction with the Western world, intense criticisms have lingered. In particular, critics have often taken exception to Said's monolithic conception of a culturally unified West. Still others have taken exception to Said's postmodern methodology, arguing that he selectively manipulated and distorted the past in order to create a politically convenient, pro-Palestinian narrative.[ii] They note that Said minimized the role of those writers and geographical areas that did not fit into his ideological argument, while exaggerating those that supported his contentions.

Box 1.2

EDWARD SAID AND ORIENTALISM—CONT'D

Said's militant and unsympathetic stance as well as his pro-Palestinian activism elicited polemical responses, most notably from Bernard Lewis, a professor of medieval Arab and Ottoman history at Princeton, who was sharply criticized in *Orientalism* for his negative view of the Arab world. However, it was Lewis's staunchly pro-Israel politics that placed him at the top of Said's list of postcolonial villains. For Said, Lewis's pro-Israeli positions and his role as consultant for the US government were evidence of the ongoing tradition of Orientalism in the contemporary world of American Middle East Studies. Ultimately, Lewis took exception to Said's reductive 'simplification' and his caricaturing of pioneering Orientalist scholars through the use of 'fashionable literary, philosophical, and political theories'.

Despite the criticisms of Lewis and many others, however, Said's perspective is now a major force in the field of Middle East Studies. Right or wrong, it is likely that his ideas will play an important, perhaps dominant, role in shaping the future of the field.

[i] Said, E. *Orientalism* New York: Pantheon Books, 1978; Vintage Books, 1994, p. 24.
[ii] Said's most ardent critic dedicated an entire chapter, 'The question of Orientalism', to similar questions in Lewis, B. (1993) *Islam and the West*. New York: Oxford University Press, p. 111.

The concept of Orientalism is important, both because of its impact on Middle East studies as a discipline and because of the power that Orientalist depictions of the region, in the media, academia and popular culture, continue to have over the public. Douglas Little, in his work *American Orientalism*, notes the continuing impact of Orientalism in daily American life, in films such as Disney's *Aladdin* whose theme song declared:

> Oh I come from a land, from a faraway place
> Where the caravan camels roam
> Where they cut off your ear
> If they don't like your face
> It's barbaric, but hey, it's home

Another example is the film *True Lies* in which Arnold Schwarzenegger's character battles the Crimson Jihad, a group of Arabs seeking nuclear weapons. In general, Arabs are negatively portrayed in film. All this, according to Said, creates an appallingly negative stereotype of the Arab. The Arab is represented as menacing, an oversexed degenerate, a colorful scoundrel and, most importantly, someone to be feared.

MISPERCEPTIONS OF ISLAM

Indeed, inaccurate or incomplete descriptions of the Middle East have been common in Western sources for centuries. As early as the medieval period (twelfth to fourteenth centuries), a distorted image of Islam was present in Europe. In medieval Europe, Muslims were commonly referred to as 'Saracens', a derisive term of uncertain origin; they were 'regarded as idolators who worshipped Muhammad; or else he was regarded as a magician or even as the devil himself' (Watt 1972: 73).

In his research into the medieval European view of Islam, Montgomery Watt identified four main characteristics:

(1) the Islamic religion is a falsehood and a deliberate perversion of the truth;
(2) it is a religion of violence and the sword;
(3) it is a religion of self-indulgence; and
(4) Muhammad is the Antichrist. (Watt 1972: 73)

Islam was compared, unfavorably, with Christianity, which was considered to be wholly true, free from carnal

---

Box 1.3

MOVIE TITLES INCLUDING THE TERM 'ARAB'

Negative depictions of the Middle East or Arabs in Western film is by no means a recent phenomenon. A search of the Internet movie database finds numerous film titles that use the term 'Arab', many dating from the early part of the twentieth century.

Arab Cortege (1896)
A Street Arab (1898)
Arab's Bride (1912)

The Arab (1915)
The Arab's Curse (1915)
The Barbarian (aka *The Arab*, 1933)
Sword of the Arab (1934),
Street of a Thousand Pleasures (aka *Arab Slave Market*, 1970)

Internet Movie Database, www.imdb.com

Box 1.4

BEYOND ORIENTALISM: THE MIDDLE EAST FIGHTS BACK!

Many in the Middle East have long been aware of the impact of the region's negative stereotype and not only its impact on how the region is viewed by outsiders but also its impact on the region's residents. Of particular concern is the impact of the negative portrayal of Arabs in the global media on young people and the effect of global consumerism. A few entrepreneurs have sought to create alternative choices for people in the Middle East.

Jalila, the heroine of a new Egypt-based comic-book series, fights to save the 'City of All Faiths' from evil. The buxom Jalila (alter ego: Dr Ansam F. Dajani) holds a doctorate in nuclear science, is able to control nuclear radiation and travel at near light speeds. Together with Aya, Zein and Rakan, she battles extremist groups seeking to control the city, including the United Liberation Force and Zios Army.

The creators of the series believe that there is a need for every society to have its own superheroes.

The Middle East Heroes comic-books are published in Egypt in both English and Arabic, though much of the studio work is done in the US and in Brazil. Their website (http://usa.akcomics.com/) contains character profiles and plot summaries.

The desire to offset the overwhelming presence of foreign brands in Middle Eastern markets, such as Coca-Cola and Pepsi, drove the creation of Mecca Cola. Created by a French entrepreneur of Tunisian origin, the cola is named for the holiest city in Islam. The company has pledged to donate 10 percent of its profits to support humanitarian projects in the Palestinian territories, and offers a purchasing alternative for the pro-Muslim customer.. The cola, which is sold throughout the Middle East and parts of Europe, bears the slogan 'No more drinking stupid, drink with commitment!' and a request that the contents not be mixed with alcohol.
(www.mecca-cola.com)

---

desires and rational. In these accounts Muhammad is often described as an impostor, able to fool people with his religion only with the aid of a former monk. Furthermore, his revelations were often attributed to epileptic episodes. These inaccuracies were used to incite fear and loathing within the European Christian public, and created support for European military incursions to the Holy Land during the Crusades.

Misperceptions about Islam and its followers have persisted well into the modern period, even among highly educated sectors of the Western public. Indeed, the term 'Muhammadan', a pejorative name for Muslims that implied that they worshipped Muhammad, was used routinely in textbooks and the media well into the twentieth century. For example, in 1907, US president Theodore Roosevelt offered the opinion that, while the US was obligated to help Westernize less developed regions of the world, 'it is impossible to expect moral, intellectual and material well-being where Mohammedanism is supreme' (cited in Little 2002: 15).

TRAVELERS IN THE HOLY LAND

Travel by the American upper middle class and elites on organized tours to the Holy Land became increasingly common in the nineteenth century. Their interest was propelled in part by what they knew of the region. As Little (2002: 11) notes:

> In 1776 what little the average American knew about the Middle East and its peoples likely came from two sources: the King James Bible and Scheherazade's Thousand and One Arabian Nights. Few Americans could have found Baghdad or Beirut on a map, and fewer still had climbed the great stone pyramids at Gize, or waded the holy waters of the River Jordan. But most Americans remembered the Gospel according to St. Matthew and the tale of Ali Baba and his forty thieves, most recalled the crucifixion and the crusades, and most regretted that the Holy Land was peopled by infidels and unbelievers, Muslims and Jews beyond the pale of Christendom.

For those who could not travel to the Middle East, the *National Geographic* magazine provided a window into the region, yet even this highly respected magazine presented views consistent with the imperialist context and reinforced prevailing stereotypes.

Linda Steet, in an analysis of the magazine's coverage of the region between 1888 and the late 1980s, documents the role of written text and photographs in creating misrepresentations of the region and its peoples. Typical language used to describe Arabs and their countries included: 'where centuries have seen no progress', 'living in primitive fashion', 'a gaily bedecked daughter of the desert', 'Algerian girls still weave magic carpets', all of which evoke images straight out of *The Arabian Nights* (Steet 2000: 50). Accompanying photos depicted girls said to belong to the harem and men identified as fierce Arab warriors. Then, as now, sensational imagery dominates articles on the Middle East. Shortly after 9/11, *Newsweek* ran a cover with the title 'Why They Hate Us'. The cover showed a photograph of a young turban-clad boy clutching a toy machine-gun; he seemed to be the embodiment of the West's long-held fears about the Middle East. The accompanying article discussed the 'roots of Muslim rage'.

RELATIONS BETWEEN ISLAM AND THE WEST: A CLASH OF CIVILIZATIONS?

Though the misrepresentations of the region, its religion and peoples have persisted for centuries, this alone is not enough to explain the current wave of anti-Western and anti-American opinion emanating from the region and the rise of groups willing to wage violent conflict with the West. Nor does it explain the deep distrust many Westerners have of the Middle East and its peoples.

One view on the conflict between the Middle East and the West argues that it is based on a fundamental and inexorable divide between the two cultures. Bernard Lewis, in an article entitled 'The roots of Muslim rage', notes that the West created a doctrine of separation of church and state in response to costly religious-driven European wars in the sixteenth and seventeenth centuries. This secularism reduced the power of religious institutions and created greater tolerance within Christianity, and contributed to great economic and scientific advancement in the West. Islam experienced no such separation.

At first, Muslims both admired and sought to emulate Western advances; according to Lewis (1990), 'This desire arose from a keen and growing awareness of the weakness, poverty, and backwardness of the Islamic world as compared with the advancing West'. He argues that the Muslim response to Western civilization today is one of hostility and rejection, fed by a feeling of Muslims' humiliation at the failure of their own civilization to progress. Lewis rejects the idea that policies such as imperialism or US support for Israel contribute to this conflict; rather the battle is between the secularism and modernism of the West and Islamic fundamentalists who seek to restore a rigid interpretation of traditional values.

His argument parallels that of Samuel Huntington, who predicted, following the breakup of the Soviet Union, that the source of future global conflict would not be based on economics or ideology, but would be between nations of different civilizations. Viewing religion as the most important aspect of civilization, Huntington's division of the world includes an Islamic civilization, a vast area stretching from Morocco to Pakistan, and parts of Southeast Asia (though the US and Europe are identified as Western civilization, not Christian). Conflict will occur along fault lines between civilizations where differing values clash. Like Lewis, he sees the conflict between the West and Islamic civilization fed by both an envy of Western success and the differences between a Western culture in which religions and politics are separate and a Muslim view which unites the two. In response to the argument that the West is not in conflict with the Islamic world overall, but only with Islamic extremists, Huntington contends that 1400 years of history, dating to the revelation of Islam, prove otherwise.

DEBATE WITHIN THE ISLAMIC WORLD

In essence, the differences between the views of Lewis, Huntington and Said reflect the debate among the public

---

Box 1.5

DELVING DEEPER: RE-EXAMINING THE 'ROOTS' OF THE 'CLASH OF CIVILIZATIONS'

Michael Christopher Low

As politicians in Washington and capital cities around the world watched the horrific events of September 11, 2001 unfold on their television screens, many openly wondered if they were witnessing the dawning of a new era in global politics. Since the end of World War II, foreign-policy thinkers and average Americans alike had come to operate under the assumption that the greatest threat to America's national security came from the Soviet Union, the spread of its communist ideology, and the grim prospect of nuclear war. By the early 1990s, the world was no longer characterized by a bipolar struggle between Washington and Moscow.

In an effort to grasp the new lines of conflict that emerged in the volatile post-1989 world, Samuel Huntington, a political theorist at Harvard University, proposed a radical departure from the Cold War paradigm in his *The Clash of Civilizations and the Remaking of the World Order*. Huntington boldly proclaimed:

> The great divisions among humankind and the dominating source of conflict will be cultural. Nation-states will remain the most powerful actors in world affairs, but the principal conflicts of global politics will occur between nations and groups of different civilizations. The clash of civilizations will dominate global politics.

Huntington's core arguments point toward an impending clash between 'the West' and the Islamic world. Especially in the wake of 9/11, Huntington's views have been transformed into a vision broadly shared in the more hawkish elements of the American

Box 1.5

DELVING DEEPER: RE-EXAMINING THE 'ROOTS' OF THE 'CLASH OF CIVILIZATIONS'—CONT'D

foreign-policy and intellectual establishment, and has even made its way into the general public's vocabulary. Thus, the Islamic world has replaced the Soviet Union as America and the West's most prominent enemy.

Such conclusions are unsurprising, especially when one takes a closer look at the intellectual roots of Huntington's thesis, which borrows heavily from the works of Bernard Lewis, influential Princeton professor and noted adviser to the US policy establishment. In fact, Huntington's celebrated phrase, 'clash of civilizations', is taken from the title of the final section of Lewis's 1990 article 'The roots of Muslim rage', which offers a concise yet overly reductive explanation for the causes of Muslim animosities toward the West. Lewis describes a yawning, almost inexorable gap between the culture of pluralism and freedom forged by the West's historical separation of Church and State and a contemporary Islamic world, characterized by religious intolerance, extremism, and a virtual unwillingness to accept the changes of modernity.

Though Lewis provides a provocative and insensitive depiction of Islam as a religion somehow predisposed to violence and *jihādist* extremism, he cautions foreign-policy observers that the 'clash of civilizations' should not be viewed as a struggle between Islam and the West. Rather, the real struggle is an internal one between moderate and extremist forces within the Islamic world. Moreover, Lewis warns that:

> we of the West can do little or nothing. Even the attempt might do harm, for these are the issues that Muslims must decide among themselves. And in the meantime we must take care on all sides to avoid the danger of a new era of religious wars, arising from the exacerbation of differences and the revival of ancient prejudices.

and the policy-makers between those who believe that conflict is inevitable and those who see it as avoidable if greater levels of understanding are achieved. Where both perspectives fall short, though, is in their tendency to view the Middle East as a monolith – to talk about 'the Orient' and 'Muslims' as a sort of single entity, not recognizing the heterogeneity in opinion within them. These theories lack any real analysis of the internal dynamics of Middle Eastern society and its impact on external relations with the West.

In his work *No god but God*, Reza Aslan speaks of a civil war within Islam. As proof, he notes that the London bombings of July 2006 targeted the most moderate Muslim neighborhood in London. This attack on Muslims, like those taking place in Turkey, Morocco, Saudi Arabia, Indonesia and Iraq, was as much an attack on modern, inclusive Islam as it was an attack against the 'West'. Indeed, though the US public first became aware

of the al-Qaeda-led Islamic war on the West after the September 11, 2001 attacks, the conflict between rigid interpretations of Islam and more moderate beliefs was openly raging within the region for well over a decade as '*jihādist*' sought to purify their own communities and expel those who did not meet their standard of belief or conduct.

For example, few in the West were aware of the plight of Naser Abu Zeid, an Egyptian professor of Islamic Studies whose research was accused of being 'un-Islamic'. In 1995 he was labeled an apostate (or one who has renounced Islam). As a non-Muslim he could no longer be married to his wife, and a Cairo court ordered their separation. They now live in exile in Europe. Similarly, in 1994, Egyptian Nobel author Naguib Mahfouz was attacked by an Islamist radical, leaving him unable to use his hand to write. At the same time, in Egypt, armed militants detonated bombs in subway stations and banks, killing and injuring the local population.

Aslan (2006: xxviii) says that it is no coincidence that the aforementioned London bombings took place only one day after 171 of the world's leading clerics, representing all sects within Islam, issued a legal ruling condemning all acts of terrorism committed in the name of Islam. For the violence between the West and Islam is rooted in 'an ongoing clash between those Muslims who strive to reconcile their religious value with the realities of the modern world, and those who react to modernism and reform by reverting – sometimes fanatically – to the "fundamentals" of their faith'.

Indeed, many Muslims also fear the impact of Islamic extremism in their own country. The Pew Global Attitudes survey conducted in July 2005 found widespread belief that Islamic fundamentalism posed a threat in Morocco (73 percent of respondents), Pakistan (52 percent), Turkey (47 percent), Indonesia (45 percent) and Lebanon (26 percent). Of the six Muslim countries included in the survey, only in Jordan was the perceived threat of Islamic fundamentalism low (10 percent).

Box 1.6

TALKING BACK TO TERRORISM: A VIEW FROM AMMAN

Michael Christopher Low

On the night of November 9, 2005, a series of coordinated bombings rocked Amman, the capital of Jordan. The explosions targeted three hotels frequented by Western military contractors and diplomats: the Radisson, the Grand Hyatt and the Days Inn. At the Radisson, two suicide bombers, a husband-and-wife team, entered the hotel ballroom, where Ashraf al-Akhras and his bride, Nadia al-Alami, were celebrating their wedding with some 300 Jordanian and Palestinian guests. While the woman was unable to detonate her explosives and was later captured by the Jordanian authorities, her husband, leaped on to a dining-room table and detonated his explosives, killing himself and nearly forty others, including the fathers of the bride and the groom. The second blast, less than half a mile from the Radisson, ripped through the Grand Hyatt, killing seven hotel employees and two guests. Finally, at the Days Inn, the fourth bomber entered a restaurant on the hotel's ground floor, where he unsuccessfully attempted to detonate his explosive belt. The bomber then ran outside in a panic before detonating his bomb, killing himself and several members of a Chinese military delegation. In all, the bombs resulted in 56 deaths and well over 100 injuries.

An Internet statement released the following day, purportedly from al-Qaeda in Iraq, claimed responsibility for the attacks. The posting proclaimed:

> Let all know that we have struck only after becoming confident that they are centers for launching war on Islam and support the crusaders' presence in Iraq and the Arab peninsula and the presence of the Jews on the land of Palestine.

In particular, the posting blamed Jordan's King Abdullah II for allowing Amman to become 'a backyard for the enemies of faith – the Jews and the crusaders'. Despite al-Zarqawi's anti-Western rhetoric, however, the vast majority of the victims of the attacks in Amman were not Christian Americans or Israeli Jews, but Muslim Jordanians and Palestinians.

Thus, in the wake of al-Zarqawi and al-Qaeda in Iraq's web posting, Jordanian anger boiled over. Hundreds of Jordanians took to the streets to denounce the terrorist attacks. King Abdullah noted that while 'suicide bombings may be common in some parts of the Middle East', Jordan is a different matter. These attacks 'will only strengthen the resolve of Jordanians to keep terrorism from breaching its borders'. King Abdullah's sentiments were furiously expressed in the chants of anti-terror protesters, who shouted 'Burn in hell, Abu Musab al Zarqawi!'

A WORD OF CAUTION: A CONFUSION OF LABELS

This chapter has focused on the way in which the Western image of the Middle East has been created historically and on the varied explanations for the current conflict between the West and the Middle East and the broader Islamic world. These themes, especially Western–Middle Eastern/Islamic relations, will be explored in great depth throughout this volume. Unfortunately, the media and even scholars off-handedly use a variety of terms when discussing the region, often interchangeably, causing confusion for anyone trying to achieve a more nuanced understanding. Terms like 'fundamentalist', 'militant', '*jihādist*' and 'Islamist' should be used with care, and their meaning understood.

A Muslim is simply anyone who follows the religion of Islam. As in every religion, some Muslims may be more devout than others, attending mosque regularly and following dietary restrictions against alcohol and pork. Others may not regularly observe such religious rituals.

Islamists, sometimes called Islamic fundamentalists, seek to create societies, even states, which follow more strict interpretations of Islamic law and practice. They are willing to use innovation and modern technology (such as computers and television) to achieve that goal. Most Islamic fundamentalists are non-violent and seek to exercise power through reform in their own society, often through achieving electoral influence.

Militant Islamists, or '*jihādis*', are Islamists who are willing to use violence in pursuit of their goals, especially the establishment of an Islamic state or re-establishment of a larger Islamic caliphate. This is the stated goal of al-Qaeda. Their violence may be used against Westerners but is more often directed against existing governments in the region they view as un-Islamic. The ideological beliefs of many militant Islamic groups are based on the intellectual thought known as 'salafism', which advocates a return to Islam as it was practiced in the first few centuries after the death of Muhammad. For this reason, the term 'salafists' may also be used to refer to militant Islamic groups. (For more on this, see Chapter 7.)

Finally, Muslim secularists are Muslims who want the Islamic world to accept the separation of church and state in the manner of Western industrial democracies. Religion would be a personal and private, rather than a state, matter.

SUMMARY OF MAIN POINTS

- The lack of first-hand information about a place or culture produces a reliance on stereotypes created by media and others.
- The concept of Orientalism argues that a comprehensive negative stereotype of the Middle East and North Africa was created to serve the interests of the West.
- Some scholars believe that conflict between the Middle East and the West is inevitable and based on cultural differences.
- Muslims and Muslim governments have also been the target of violence by militant Islamists.
- There is a debate within Muslim society around differing interpretations of the faith; violence toward the West is one outcome of this debate.

QUESTIONS FOR DISCUSSION

1 If students in the Middle East were asked to repeat the exercise that opens this chapter and name five words they associate with the United States or Great Britain, what do you think those words would be? Why?

2 What is the role of stereotype? Does it have an impact on government policies? How?

3 What role does the media play in shaping the view of the Middle East and the Islamic world?

4 What evidence is there to support the civilization clash between the Christian West and Muslim East? What evidence is there to refute this argument?

5 What kinds of issues are currently being debated within the Muslim world? Are they different from debates in other parts of the world?

SUGGESTIONS FOR FURTHER READING

Books and articles

Aslan, R. (2006) *No god but God: The Origins, Evolution and Future of Islam*. New York: Random House. The discussion of contemporary Islam and the role of Muslim identity in the West and the Islam world in this short history is particularly useful for understanding the conflict within Islam today.

Horowitz, T. (1991) *Baghdad without a Map and Other Misadventures in Arabia*. New York: Penguin Books. Written by a reporter for the *Wall Street Journal*, it recounts his experiences throughout the region, with great stories and local color.

Humphries, R. S. (1999) *Between Memory and Desire: The Middle East in a Troubled Age*. Berkeley, Calif.: University of California Press. See especially Chapter 4, 'The shaping of foreign policy: the myth of the Middle East madman'.

Huntington, S. P. (1997) *The Clash of Civilizations and the Remaking of the World Order*. New York: Touchstone. Details Huntington's theory of civilization-based conflict.

Lewis, B. (1990) 'The roots of Muslim rage'. *The Atlantic Monthly*, 266: 47–60. Puts forward Lewis's central argument on the sources of violence within Muslim communities and toward the West.

Lewis, B. (1993) *Islam and the West*. New York: Oxford University Press.

Little, D. (2002) *American Orientalism: The United States and the Middle East since 1945*. Chapel Hill, NC: University of North Carolina Press. Discusses the roots of American stereotypes of the Middle East; particularly interesting insights on representations of the region and Arabs in popular culture.

Lockman, Z. (2004) *Contending Visions of the Middle East: The History and Politics of Orientalism*. Cambridge: Cambridge University Press. A good introduction to Orientalism and its impact. See particularly Chapter 6, which discusses Said's book, *Orientalism*.

National Geographic Education Foundation (2006) *National Geographic–Roper Global Literacy Survey*: http://www.nationalgeographic.com/foundation/news_resources.html#reports.

Pew Global Attitudes Project (2005) 'Islamic extremism: common concern for Muslim and Western publics', July 14: http://pewglobal.org/reports/display.php?ReportID=248.

Said, E. (1978) *Orientalism: Western Conceptions of the Orient*. London: Routledge & Kegan Paul. Said's groundbreaking work on the process of constructing a false representation of the 'Orient'.

Soueif, A. (2004) *Mezzaterra: Fragments from a Common Ground*. New York: Anchor Books. This book is a collection of essays, many written by Middle Easterners living both in the region and in the West. Topics include: Muslim reactions to 9/11, the occupation of Palestine, and the decision to wear the veil.

Steet, L. (2000) *Veils and Daggers: A Century of National Geographic's Representation of the Arab World*. Philadelphia, Pa: Temple University Press. Filled with images and quotes from this popular magazine, the book gives concrete examples of the 'Orientalist' view of the Middle East.

Watt, W. M. (1972) *The Influence of Islam on Medieval Europe*. Edinburgh: Edinburgh University Press. A concise investigation of interaction between Europe and the Islamic world during the medieval period. Includes a section on Muslim contributions to European scientific thought.

Many media outlets in the region, including newspapers and television stations, have English websites, which are useful for understanding Middle Eastern perspectives on current events.

Television

Al-Jazeera – www.english.aljazeera.net

Note: the website www.aljazeera.com is NOT affiliated with the Qatar-based Al-Jazeera satellite news network.

Newspapers

Jordan Times (Jordan) http://www.jordantimes.com

Al-Ahram Weekly (Egypt) http://www.ahram.org.eg/weekly/

Gulf Daily News (United Arab Emirates) http://www.gulf-news.com

Haaretz Daily (Israel) http://www.haaretzdaily.com

The Daily Star (Lebanon) http://www.dailystar.com

Yemen Times (Yemen) http://www.yementimes.com

Iran Daily (Iran) http://www.iran-daily.com

Asharq Al-Awsat (London-based) http://www.asharqalawsat.com/english/

Turkish Daily News (Turkey) http://www.turkishdailynews.com.tr/

Khaleej Times (UAE) www.khaleejtimes.com

Kuwait Daily News (Kuwait) http://www.kuwaittimes.net

2

THE GEOGRAPHY OF THE MIDDLE EAST AND NORTH AFRICA

DEFINING THE MIDDLE EAST

So far in this discussion of the Middle East, its geographical boundaries have not been specified. This approach is intentional, for it is important to realize that the 'Middle East' is a subjective construction – not a geographic 'fact'. The construction of the region, in the public and academic mind, is based on factors such as geographic characteristics, shared historical experiences, and religious and linguistic patterns. Moreover, the conception of the region is fluid and has changed over time.

In defining the geographical limits of the region, a number of criteria could be utilized. One possibility is to include those countries which are predominantly Arab and hold membership in the political body the Arab League (Table 2.1). While this does include countries traditionally considered to be the 'core' of the Middle East and the Arab world, such as Egypt and Syria, it also includes the island nation of Comoros, Djibouti in the Horn of Africa and Mauritania in West Africa, which do not share much of the Arab world's common history. More importantly, key non-Arab states, Turkey, Israel and Iran, are not members of the Arab League, but are important countries in the region. A shared historical past under the Ottoman Empire would incorporate many of the Arab states as well as Turkey and Israel, but exclude

Iran and the parts of the Arabian peninsula that never came under Ottoman control. In sum, no single criterion defines the countries included in the Middle East; rather the countries in the region have extensive connections, both historical and current, with neighboring areas. Such contacts have contributed to the enormous complexity and vitality of the region.

In this volume, the Middle East and North Africa (MENA) region includes members of the Arab League, with the exception of Mauritania, Comoros and Djibouti, plus Iran, Israel and Turkey (Map 2.1). Since 9/11, Afghanistan has sometimes been included on maps of the Middle East, reflecting the importance of Islam in south Asia and the role that Afghanistan's recent history has played in creating the leaders of militant Islamic movements such as al-Qaeda. Though the Middle East makes up the core of the Islamic world, the most populous Muslim country, Indonesia, is located in Asia.

Within the Middle East, countries can be divided into some regional subgroupings. Again, these subgroupings are determined by a set of subjective criteria. The Gulf states, which border the Persian (Arab) Gulf, include many of the region's major oil producers, though not all of these countries have vast oil wealth. Included in the Gulf states are: Saudi Arabia, Oman, Qatar, Bahrain, Kuwait and the United Arab Emirates. With the

Table 2.1 Member states of the Arab League

The Hashemite Kingdom of Jordan
United Arab Emirates
Kingdom of Bahrain
Republic of Tunisia
Democratic and Popular Republic of Algeria
Republic of Djibouti
Kingdom of Saudi Arabia
Republic of Sudan
Arab Republic of Syria
Republic of Somalia
Republic of Iraq
Sultanate of Oman
State of Palestine
State of Qatar
Federal Islamic Republic of Comoros
State of Kuwait
Republic of Lebanon
Socialist Peoples Libyan Arab Jamahiriya
Arab Republic of Egypt
Kingdom of Morocco
Islamic Republic of Mauritania
Republic of Yemen

Source: www.arableagueonline.org

exception of Saudi Arabia and Oman, these states once formed the Trucial Coast, under British control. For historical and cultural reasons Iraq and Iran, though they border the Gulf, are generally not considered Gulf states. Countries in the Gulf are characterized by conservative social values and governmental systems headed by monarchies.

The Levant includes the countries of Lebanon, Syria, Jordan and Israel. The origin of the term is obscure but may come from the French verb *lever*, 'to rise', as these countries are in the east, where the sun rises. These countries were the subject of intense imperialist control, which shaped their modern borders. Today, the Israeli–Palestinian conflict dominates politics in the Levant while also having a negative impact on the subregion's economic development.

Egyptian rule over Sudan from 1899 to 1955 drew that country, the northern part of which is largely Arab and Muslim, into relations with the Middle East. These connections remain, and in many ways Sudan has closer relations with Middle Eastern countries than with those in sub-Saharan Africa.

North Africa, or the Maghreb (Arabic meaning 'western', indicating the place of the setting sun), includes Morocco, Algeria, Tunisia, Libya and the disputed territory of Western Sahara. Though the French colonial experience is a recent common bond between Algeria and Morocco, they have deep historic ties. Libya and the Western Sahara experienced colonialism under Italy and Spain respectively.

Though geographically distant from the core of the Middle East and culturally distinct, Afghanistan and Pakistan are influenced by Islamist thought originating in the Middle East. Both the Taliban and al-Qaeda are militant Sunni groups with a connection to Saudi Arabia. Increasingly, militant groups claiming affiliation with al-Qaeda are operating in the Middle East, especially in Iraq.

Finally, a number of countries share cultural characteristics and historical ties with Africa as well as with the Middle East, and may be considered the 'African Fringe'. Djibouti, Mauritania and Comoros are all located within or contingent to Africa, their populations have many cultural characteristics more commonly associated with Africa, yet they are members of the Arab League.

PHYSICAL GEOGRAPHY

Climate

Geography textbooks once described the Middle East as the 'dry world', a reference to the region's aridity and deserts. This name, however, is misleading, for true desert is found only in the Empty Quarter (Rub al-Khali) of the Saudi Arabian peninsula and the Saharan desert. Though the region is predominantly arid, other climate zones are present. Various landforms, seas and river systems also mitigate the overall arid characteristics of the region. Nevertheless, precipitation, rather than temperature, is the major factor in climatic variation within the Middle East and North Africa.

According to the Köppen–Geiger climate classification system, much of the Middle East is classified as desert, specifically hot low-latitude desert climates (BWh). These areas have annual average temperatures above 64.4F (18C). They may receive up to 14 in (35cm) of rain, though some areas receive no rain at all (Map 2.3).

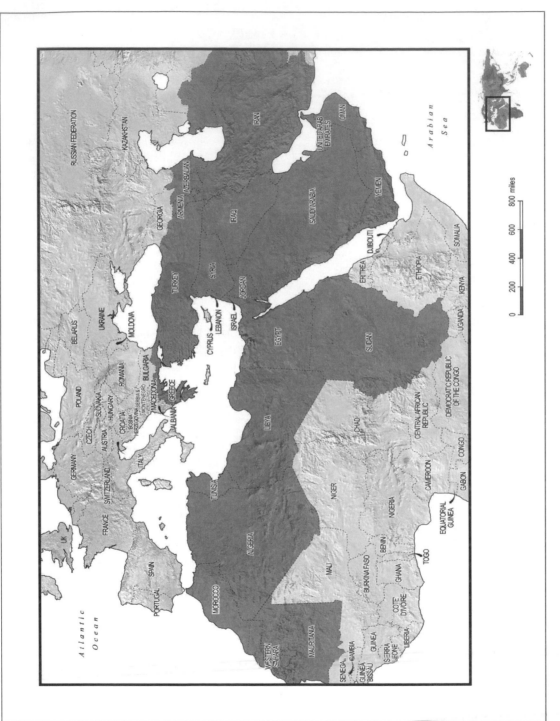

Map 2.1 The Middle East and North Africa

Box 2.1

REDRAWING THE MAP: WHAT IS THE ISLAMIC WORLD?

Michael Christopher Low

Contrary to the common view held by most Americans, the Arabic-speaking Middle East is not an accurate synonym for the Islamic world. Although the Middle East, particularly Arabia, is rightly considered to be the historical and geographical core of Islamic civilization, the region is merely one part of the diverse global Islamic community, otherwise known as the *umma*, a concept with which devout Muslims from across the world identify more strongly than any regional identity. *Umma*, a nebulous yet fundamental concept in Islamic thought, originally mentioned in the Qur'an, has over the centuries come to explain how Muslims from different ethnic, linguistic and regional backgrounds are united by their faith and common values into a single trans-national, trans-regional community (Map 2.2).

Despite the fact that religion is the most important commonality linking Muslims around the world, the map of the Islamic world drawn by most American and Western observers is generally defined by the political borders of nation-states. Thus, the Islamic world often appears as a collection of nation-states whose population contains a majority of Muslims. As a result, when one looks at a typical map of the Islamic world, it would appear that most Muslims live in an enormous, contiguous swathe of Muslim-majority countries stretching across the Middle East and North Africa. However, in reality, the Islamic world includes significant populations spread across not only the Middle East and North Africa, but also South and Southeast Asia, as well as sizable minority communities in the rest of Africa and Asia, Europe and North America. In fact, the three most populous Muslim countries in the world, Indonesia, Pakistan and Bangladesh, are located outside the Middle East in South and Southeast Asia, while yet another South Asian nation, the predominantly Hindu India, boasts the fourth-largest Muslim population in the world.

Just as contemporary conceptions tend to use political boundaries to define the territorial extent of the Islamic world, medieval Muslim jurists and rulers also attempted to define their world in similar terms. They coined the term *dar al-Islam*, referring to the 'abode of Islam', as opposed to the *dar al-harb* or 'abode of war'. These terms sought to demarcate the limits of their civilization from what they considered the moral disorder and 'barbarism' of non-Muslim lands. The defining characteristic of the territory deemed to be part of the *dar al-Islam* was the presence of a Muslim ruler, under whose authority it was presumed that Islamic law and culture would be propagated. While the *dar al-Islam* was once a coherent territory, comparable to the medieval concept of Christendom or the imagined boundaries separating the Occident and the Orient, over time Muslims have increasingly found themselves living in predominantly non-Muslim lands such as China, India, Europe, North America and sub-Saharan Africa. Moreover, in the wake of the conquest of much of the Islamic world by European powers during the colonial era and the postcolonial influx of Middle Eastern and South Asian immigrants into Europe and North America, this model seems to have been stretched almost beyond recognition. Many Muslims living in the Middle East now find themselves living in Muslim-majority countries undergoing rapid and sometimes violent changes wrought by globalization and Western secular influences. Ironically, caught in the clash between extremely polarized visions of militant Islam and Westernized notions of modernity in their home countries, many Muslims fleeing the economic and political insecurity of their homelands have actually discovered greater freedom to practice Islam in the West than under their own governments in the Islamic world.

Given the growing Muslim minorities now thriving in Europe and North America, Tariq Ramadan (2004) notes that the old lines between the West and the

---

Box 2.1

REDRAWING THE MAP: WHAT IS THE ISLAMIC WORLD?—CONT'D

Islamic world, Occident and Orient, and *dar al-harb* and *dar al-Islam* are no longer capable of adequately representing the way that imperialism, migration and globalization have altered the realities in which people live. For Ramadan and Muslims like himself, living in the commingled environment of the West, it is natural to 'consider themselves both Muslims and completely European or American'. Therefore, it would be unthinkable for these individuals of mixed identity to continue drawing the old lines between the Islamic and non-Islamic worlds.

Ramadan T., (2004) *Western Muslims and the Future of Islam*. New York/Oxford: Oxford University Press.

The Empty Quarter (Rub al-Khali) dominates the interior of the Arabian peninsula. It is one of the world's largest sand deserts, with dunes more than 1000 ft (330 m) high. Stunningly beautiful, these dunes are also dangerous as they can migrate in response to prevailing winds. The Rub al-Khali extends for 600 miles (1000 km) along the east–west coast of the Arabian peninsula and is 300 miles (500 km) wide. Throughout the Middle East, smaller deserts, such as the Syrian Desert, contribute to the region's overall aridity.

In North Africa, climatic areas around the vast Saharan desert are also classified as desert (BWh). Incredibly high temperatures are found here; on September 13, 1922, the highest recorded temperature in the shade of 136F (58C) was recorded in Al 'Azi'ziyah, Libya. The very name 'Sahara' is an English pronunciation of the Arabic word for desert. At 3,500,000 square miles, the Sahara is almost as large as the United States. The Sahara contains extensive areas of dunes, known as ergs or a 'sand sea'. The Grand Erg Oriental in the central Sahara exceeds 4000 ft (1200 m) in depth and covers 75,000 square miles (192,000 square kilometers).

A different type of desert, formed by salt deposits, can be found in central Iran. Though the Great Salt Desert (Dasht-e Kavir) and the smaller Dasht-e Lut may look like a frozen lake, they are uninhabitable.

In transition zones between the desert and the Mediterranean, and in upland plateaux, steppe climates, of both low-latitude hot (BSh) and mid-latitude cold (BSk) types are found.

Around the Zagros and Elburz mountains in Iran and the Taurus and Pontic mountains in Turkey, the cold steppe can be found. Rainfall in these areas is highly variable, ranging from 7.9 to 15.7 in (20–40 cm). A hot low-latitude steppe is located around the edges of the Sahara and the Rub al-Khali.

Along the coast of the Mediterranean the dry and steppe climates give way to a Mediterranean-influenced (CSa) zone. The Mediterranean summer dry climate is characterized by a hot, dry summer and a cooler, wetter winter. The majority of precipitation is received during winter months; indeed, winters in Lebanon and Israel can be wet and miserable.

The Middle East and North Africa region is the most water-scarce region of the world, containing only 1.4 percent of the world's renewable fresh water. Water scarcity can be measured in terms of the per capita amount of renewable fresh water. Water-scarce countries are those with less than 1000 cubic meters of renewable fresh water per person. Of the world's fifteen water-scarce countries, twelve of them are located in the Middle East and North Africa. Rapid population growth and urbanization have exacerbated water shortages. Countries are utilizing a variety of measures to maximize use of existing resources. Systems of *qanats* (or *kareez* in Iran), or series of interconnected vertical tunnels in mountainous areas, using gravity to transport water to arid areas, have been in use for thousands of years. More modern approaches include desalination of sea water (Population Reference Bureau 2002).

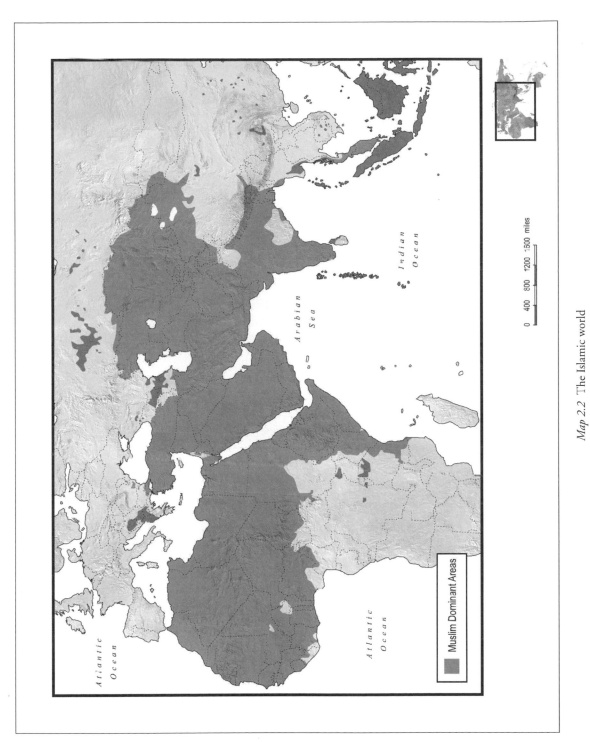

Map 2.2 The Islamic world

Muslim Dominant Areas

0   400   800   1200   1500 miles

Box 2.2

THE DISPUTE OVER THE WESTERN SAHARA

The disputed territory of the Western Sahara is a colonial creation. In 1884 the major European powers met at the Berlin Conference to set the rules for the division of Africa amongst themselves. Spain seized the area, subduing the local inhabitants. The Western Sahara remained a Spanish protectorate until World War II. After the war, as decolonization spread throughout the region, the desire for independence grew in the Western Sahara. Spain resisted the calls until 1974 when she agreed to conduct a referendum on the question of independence. Spain's decision was, in part, a response to a rising nationalist movement in the territory, headed by a group called the Polisario Front, which had begun to fight the Spanish authorities in 1973.

With Spain's withdrawal imminent, neighboring Morocco and Mauritania both sought to exercise their claims to sovereignty over the territory. Algeria, long Morocco's rival, sought to counter their claims and provided support to the Polisario. Meanwhile, the International Court of Justice affirmed the territory's right to self-determination. Following Spain's withdrawal, Morocco occupied the northern two-thirds of the territory, Mauritania the remaining southern portion. Both met opposition from Polisario. Mauritania withdrew from the Western Sahara in 1979, in response to continuous pressure from the Polisario. Over the next twenty years Morocco, in control of the entire territory, fought with the Polisario, gradually gaining the upper hand. In 1991, the two parties signed a ceasefire overseen by the United Nations.

The terms of the ceasefire called for a referendum to be held, giving residents of the territory the choice between independence or integration and rule by Morocco. Originally scheduled for 1992, the referendum was never held, caught up in disputes over who was qualified to vote. Attempts by the UN and the US to develop a referendum process acceptable to both sides have failed. Increasingly, Morocco does not seem to view independence as an option. Since 2005 pro-independence demonstrations inside the Western Sahara have met with harsh reaction from Moroccan security forces, though the ceasefire has held and the Polisario has not taken up arms.

Morocco's interest in the sparsely populated Western Sahara is spurred by the area's economic resources that include huge deposits of potash and some iron ore. More significant may be the territory's potential resources. The likely presence of offshore petroleum resources has recently attracted the interest of international oil firms. The discovery of oil off the shore of Mauritania, in an area geologically similar to the Western Sahara, and the increase in oil exploration off the shore of Morocco have driven further interest. In 2001, Morocco signed two deals with firms to scout for petroleum resources in territory off the coast of the Western Sahara; this caused objections by the Polisario Front's government-in-exile, the Saharan Arab Democratic Republic (SADR). Though the United Nations found the contracts for reconnaissance to be legal, it warned that exploration could not be undertaken until the political situation was resolved. In response SADR also signed an agreement with foreign firms to assess offshore oil and gas potential.

LANDFORMS AND WATER

The Middle East and North Africa occupies the area where the African and Asian land masses meet. The slow movement of the African land mass, over time, and the interaction between tectonic plates created the region's mountains and uplands.

In northwest Africa the Atlas Mountains run through Morocco, Algeria and Tunisia. This 1500-mile (2400 km) range separates the Mediterranean from the

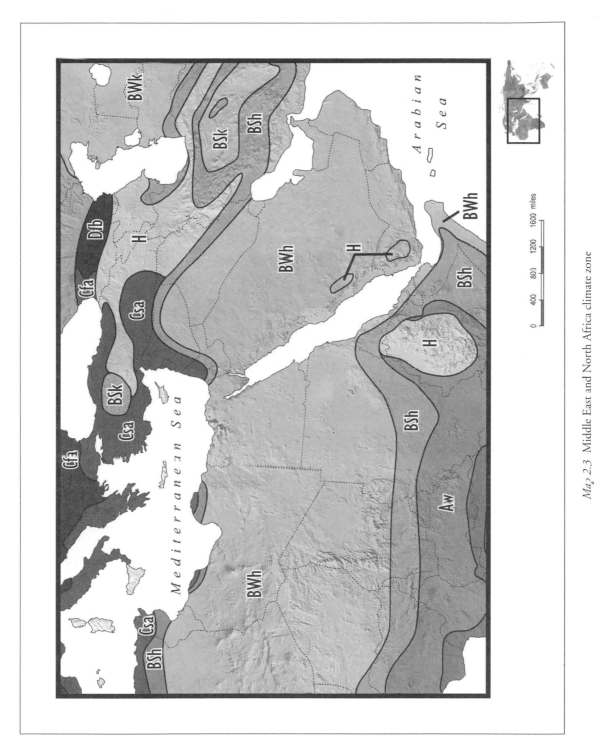

Map 2.3 Middle East and North Africa climate zone

Box 2.3

WATER SCARCITY IN THE MIDDLE EAST

The Middle East has less than 2 percent of the world's total renewable water resources. Within the region, available water resources are unevenly distributed. The Maghreb and the Arabian peninsula suffer severe water scarcity, receiving less than 10 mm of precipitation per year. Some countries, such as tiny Kuwait, have no renewable water resources of their own.

The region has the lowest per capita internal renewable resources in the world (IRWR), averaging 1577 cubic meters per year, compared with a global average of over 7000 cubic meters per year. Ten countries have annual IRWR rates of less than 500 cubic meters. Only Turkey has an IRWR above 2000 cubic meters.

A number of countries depend on water resources originating in other countries for 90 percent of their renewable water resources. They include countries dependent on exotic rivers fed by rains falling beyond their borders, such as Egypt, Sudan, Syria and Iraq. Kuwait and Bahrain both rely on groundwater from Saudi Arabia.

Water scarcity is a contributing factor to conflict in the Middle East. Historically, Egypt and Sudan fought over the Nile river. Control over the Tigris and Euphrates river system has caused conflict between Iraq and Turkey, exacerbated by upstream dam construction in Turkey. Control over the Jordan river basin is perhaps the most contentious water issue as it is deeply embedded in the overall Arab–Israeli conflict.

Despite the small size of the Jordan valley and its riparian system, its water resources are extremely complex, partly because four countries share them: Lebanon, Syria, Jordan and Israel. The Jordan river basin is made up of two main sources of surface water, the Jordan river and the Yarmouk river, as well as numerous streams such as the Zarqa. The Jordan river flows north to south and is fed by three springs originating in Syria and Israel. The Yarmouk river, which forms the border between Jordan and Syria, converges with the Jordan river inside Jordanian territory and then flows into the Dead Sea. Attempts to work out a regional water-sharing plan have failed, and the use of water by one state diminishes availability for others.

Another major issue is the disparity in water consumption between Israel and the Occupied Territories. The Mountain Aquifer, which supplies 25 percent of Israel's water needs, is fed by rains that fall on the mountains of the West Bank. Israel has adopted policies to limit Palestinian access to this water, including restrictions on the drilling of new wells. As a result, the Occupied Territories face a severe water shortage. Total per capita water use in the West Bank is 22 cubic meters a year, the equivalent of 60 liters per person a day. This is far below the World Heath Organization's recommended minimum consumption of 100 litres per person per day. Per capita consumption in Israel is five times greater, at 120 cubic meters a year (330 litres per person a year).

http://www.fao.org/ag/agl/aglw/aquastat/regions/neast/index10.stm
http://www.btselem.org/english/Water/Consumption_Gap.asp
Amery, H. A. and Wolf, A. T. (eds) (2000) *Water in the Middle East*. Austin, Tex.: University of Texas Press.

Saharan desert. The Atlas Mountains were formed by the process of uplift when the African and European land masses collided. Its highest peak, Jbel Toubkal, reaches 13,665 ft (4167 m). The Atlas Mountains are rich in mineral resources, such as iron, lead, mercury and silver.

Uplift also caused the creation of the Anatolian plateau and the surrounding mountain ranges, the Pontics along the Black Sea and the Taurus along the Mediterranean coast. The headwaters of the Tigris river have their origin in the Taurus Mountains, which can reach elevations of 4000 meters (12,000 feet).

This zone of intense geological interaction continues to the east in Iran. North of Tehran, the Elburz Mountains are home to snowy winters. With peaks reaching to 5604 meters (18,385 feet), the range boasts numerous ski resorts. The longer Zagros range runs 1500 km (932 miles) from western Iran to the Strait of Hormuz, at the entrance to the Arabian (Persian) Gulf. Formed by the collision of the Eurasian and Arabian plates, the Zagros contain salt deposits and salt domes, often indicators of buried petroleum resources.

Much of Turkey and Iran lies in a geologically active area and is the site of frequent earthquakes, such as the one that hit the ancient city of Bam in 2003, killing 26,000 people and destroying historic structures.

While the collision of tectonic plates formed the region's mountains, the separation of the African and Arabian plates characterizes the geography of the Arabian peninsula and neighboring areas. Running 5000 km from Syria to Mozambique, the Great Rift Valley can be 30–100 km wide, forming key sites such as the Beqaa valley in Lebanon, the Jordan river and the Red Sea. As the Arabian plate pulls away from the African plate, the Arabian peninsula shifts northeastward (Map 2.4).

RIVER SYSTEMS AND SEAS

The region's riparian systems are crucial for human habitation of the region; indeed, settled human civilization first developed in the fertile crescent formed by the valleys of the Nile, Tigris and Euphrates rivers.

The Tigris, 1500 km long, originates in the Taurus Mountains of Turkey and flows southeast into Iraq. The Euphrates, too, has its origins in Turkey and flows into Iraq. These two rivers form a fertile valley, leading to the Greek name for the area, Mesopotamia, meaning 'land between the rivers'. These two rivers meet in southern Iraq, forming a 200-km waterway known as the Shatt al-Arab, which flows into the Arabian (Persian) Gulf. Iraq and Iran, and their predecessor states, have long fought for control of the Shatt al-Arab, especially during the Iran–Iraq War.

The longest river in the world, the Nile stretches for 4184 miles (6695 kilometers) from its headwaters in Sudan and Ethiopia to its giant fan-like delta at Alexandria, Egypt. The Nile is known as the 'life blood' of Egypt; though the country's agriculture is entirely dependent on the river, Egypt contributes nothing to its flow, making it an exotic river. Historically, the annual flood of the Nile river deposited rich silt across the flood plain, creating fertile conditions for agriculture and allowing the development of a complex civilization along its shores. Egyptian attempts to control the river's floodwaters began in the mid-nineteenth century. Since 1970, the massive Aswan High Dam has controlled the Nile's flow. Behind the dam, the artificial Lake Nasser holds 173 cubic kilometers of water, allowing it to be released gradually, producing electricity, but retaining the rich alluvial sediments.

The Jordan river (156 miles/251 kilometers) flows through the Great Rift Valley, emptying into the Dead Sea. The river's course drops rapidly as it descends to the level of the Dead Sea, 400 meters below sea level. Israel, Jordan and Syria all draw water from the river; the large water demands have reduced the level of its flow and have created contamination problems. The Jordan river has important religious significance as both the location of a number of miracles and the place where Jesus was baptized. The Dead Sea is the lowest point on earth (417 meters/1373 feet) and one of the most saline bodies of water. Its waters are too salty to support any forms of life; the dissolved mineral salts in the water give it greater buoyancy, so one floats on it without effort. The Dead Sea, which forms part of the border between Israel and Jordan, is also a major tourist resort.

The Red Sea was formed by continental drift as Arabia moved away from Africa. The Red Sea is roughly 1200 km (1900 miles) long and 190 miles (300 km) wide at its widest point. Though its average depth is 500 m (1640 ft), it reaches a maximum depth of 8200 ft (2500 m) in the central median trench. The Red Sea is an extremely rich marine habitat, with extensive coral life. The overdevelopment of tourism sites and industry along the Red Sea in recent years has threatened much of the coral and marine habitat.

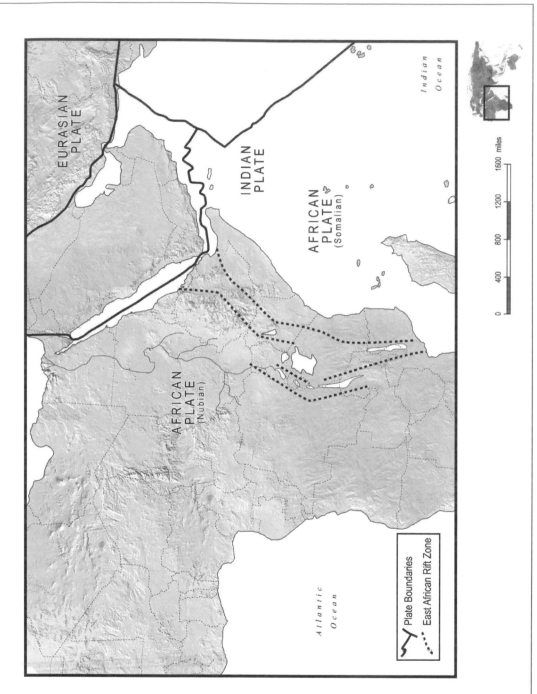

Map 2.4 The Great Rift Valley

Box 2.4

CREATING NEW LAND: ISLANDS IN THE UAE

Flush with oil money, the United Arab Emirates is literally reshaping the physical geography of the Gulf, creating a series of new islands. One of the largest projects, called 'The World', will create 300 man-made islands to accommodate private residences, resorts and recreation. The 'Thailand' island, for example, will contain a five-star resort, with design elements inspired by traditional Thai architecture. The islands, which replicate a map of the world, cover an area 5.4 miles (9 km) by 2.6 miles (6 km). Many of the islands are quite small, ranging from 250,000 sq ft (23.2 thousand square meters) to 900,000 sq ft (83.6 thousand square meters), and will be developed by private companies. The project should be completed in 2008, at a cost of over $14 billion.

The Palm Islands, off the coast of Dubai, are the world's largest man-made islands. In the shape of giant palm trees when viewed from space, they will contain 60 luxury hotels, 5000 luxury homes, 5000 apartments, theme parks, restaurants, malls, cinemas and sporting facilities. The islands are linked to the mainland by bridges. The largest of the islands, the Palm Deira, covers an area 8.4 miles (14 km) by 5.1 miles (8.5 km). Much of this project has already been completed.

The construction of the islands, and their impact on local marine life, is of significant concern to environmentalists. Large-scale dredging and shifting of sand was required to create the islands, reshaping the underwater environment and having a negative impact on coral reefs, oyster beds and underwater vegetation. The construction has also produced much silt, clouding the water, and affecting the overall health of the marine environment. Furthermore, one development, Palm Jebel Ali, is located within the Jebal Ali marine reserve, and management of the reserve has been turned over to the private developers building the island.

http://realestate.theemiratesnetwork.com/developments/dubai/.
http://guide.theemiratesnetwork.com/living/dubai/the_palm_islands.phpworld_islands.php.

The body of water between the Arabian peninsula and Iran, known to the Arabs as the Arabian Gulf and to Iranians as the Persian Gulf, is relatively shallow, with a maximum depth of 90 meters (295 ft) and an average depth of only 50 meters (164 ft). Vast petroleum deposits lie under its waters, and its ports form a major global shipping hub. Entry into the Gulf is through the Strait of Hormuz, which is only 21 miles wide; ships pass through two channels only one mile wide. The strait, and its control over access to this crucial international waterway's petroleum resources, is of key strategic importance.

POPULATION DISTRIBUTION

The total population of the Middle East and North Africa is approximately 445.6 million people, or 6.3 percent of the world's population. This relatively low population is a result of the region's aridity and the challenges it presents to human habitation.

The MENA occupies approximately 10 percent of the world's land area. The largest countries are Sudan (967,500 sq mi/2,505,825 sq km), Algeria and Saudi Arabia. At the other extreme, the tiny Gulf state of Qatar is only 776 square kilometers (299 square miles).

Population is concentrated in areas with greater water availability, especially around river valleys and oases. Significant population concentrations can also be found along the coast of the Mediterranean and Red seas and the Arabian Gulf. Egypt's population of 78.8 million is centered around the fertile Nile river valley and delta. This area includes the capital city, Cairo. Turkey's population of 70.4 million is heavily concentrated along the coasts of the Black Sea, the Aegean Sea and the Marmara Sea that connects the two in the large city of Istanbul. Iran's population of 68.6 million is

Table 2.2 Population and land area of MENA countries

Country	Population 2004 (thousands)	Land area (sq km)	Land area (sq ml)	Population density in urban areas (per sq km)	Population (percentage)
Algeria	32,853.8	2,381,740	919,595	14	49
Bahrain	726.6	665	257	1023	100
Egypt	74,032.8	1,001,450	386,662	74	43
Iran	67,699.8	1,634,800	631,200	41	68
Iraq[a]	21,600.0	437,072	168,754	N/A	67
Israel	6,909.0	20,770	8,019	318	91
Jordan	5,411.5	92,300	35,637	61	82
Kuwait	2,535.4	17,820	6,880	142	96
Lebanon	3,576.8	10,400	4,015	350	87
Libya	5,853.4	1,759,540	679,362	3	86
Morocco	30,168.0	446,550	172,414	68	55
Oman	2,566.9	212,460	82,031	8	71
Qatar	812.8	11,437	4,416	74	100
Saudi Arabia	24,573.1	1,960,582	756,985	11	86
Sudan	35,522.0	2,505,810	967,499	15	36
Syria	19,043.3	185,180	71,498	104	50
Tunisia	10,021.9	163,610	63,170	65	65
Turkey	72,636.0	780,580	301,384	94	59
UAE	4,533.1	82,880	32,000	54	74
West Bank/Gaza	3,626.0	6,220	2,402	N/A	57
Yemen	20,974.6	527,970	203,850	40	26

Source: World Development Indicators (2005), total population and population density figures, *CIA World Factbook* online (2006), for land area, Population Reference Bureau (2006), for urban population figures.
[a] Last year data available for Iraq, 1995.

concentrated in the country's eastern half, especially in the area around the capital, Tehran.

Despite the stereotypical image of Middle Easterners living in tents, most of the people in the Middle East and North Africa live in cities. The region is highly urbanized, boasting cities of various size and heritage. The region's urban history dates back thousands of years, to the period when humans began to engage in settled agriculture and gave up constant migration. The ancient Mesopotamian city of Ur in modern Iraq had a population of 65,000 by 2000 BCE; Babylonia was the first city in the world to reach a size of 200,000. Today, the Cairo metropolitan area boasts a population of over 15.2 million, earning it the designation of mega-city. While cities such as Jerusalem, Damascus and Fez contain architectural gems that reflect thousands of years of Islamic history, the gleaming new skylines of the United Arab Emirates

embrace modern architecture fused with Islamic design elements.

CULTURAL CHARACTERISTICS

The Middle East and North Africa contains a rich mosaic of ethnicities, languages and religions. All of these factors are important elements in politics and in both national and individual identity formation. Ethnicity can best be described as 'a social or group identity that an individual ascribes to himself or herself and that is also accepted by others' (Bates and Rassam 2001: 91). Ethnic categories are often based on differences in language, religion and cultural practices between groups. A shared history, such as descent from a particular ancestor or group, is a common feature of ethnic identification. In the MENA, language, ethnicity and religion can form both overlapping and divergent patterns; the influence of global culture, through television and the Internet, adds a further layer to issues of identity. However, some generalizations about the region can be made, but cultural identities can be much more intricate than the following discussion suggests. Bear in mind that ethnic identities are culturally, not biologically, determined and therefore are not 'fixed'. An individual may have more than one ethnic identity, for example, as both Kurd and Turk, but choose to utilize only one of them, or to utilize each one in different circumstances. Most of the states in the region are officially Arab, though they may contain many other ethnicities. But clearly Arab culture dominates, and forms a foundation for a common regional bond.

Arabs are by far the largest ethnolinguistic group, though there is considerable diversity within this group. They are also politically dominant in most countries in the region, with the exception of Israel, Turkey and Iran, but even here they comprise a large minority population. Arabs share a strong linguistic bond – the Arabic language. Though various spoken dialects of Arabic exist – the Arabic spoken in Morocco is very different from that heard on the streets of Kuwait – the written word is common to all. Arabic is also religiously important as it is the language of the Qur'an. Arabs, whether Muslim or Christian, have a shared linguistic heritage of rule by successive Islamic empires. This period created a distinct Islamic culture, reflected in art, architecture and scientific achievements, found not only in the Arab Middle East but also in Iran and Turkey.

NON-ARAB ETHNIC GROUPS

This section provides a brief overview of some of the major non-Arab ethnic groups. However, the region's ethnic complexity is much more varied than the discussion below allows.

Berber

Indigenous Berbers inhabit much of North Africa; their history in the region long pre-dates the arrival of Islam and Arab populations. Today they are located primarily in Algeria, Morocco and Libya, but Berber communities can be found throughout North Africa and even into sub-Saharan Africa. Approximately 14–25 million Berbers speak a language of Afro-Asiatic origin. While most of the population of Algeria and Morocco are of Berber ancestry, the term today is usually reserved for those Berbers living in mountainous areas or the oases of the Maghreb and retaining traditional aspects of Berber culture. Major groups include the Kabyles of northern Algeria (approximately 4 million) and the Chleuh of southern Morocco (8 million).

The status of Berbers within the Arab-dominated states of the Maghreb can often be an issue of contention. With Arabic as the official language in these states, Berbers have had to learn that language as well as their own. Berber is considered a 'national' language in Algeria, though Arabic remains the official language; Berber has no official status in Morocco. Berber attempts to retain their culture and to seek economic and educational rights have sometimes led to political tensions with North African governments.

The origins of the term 'Berber' are unclear, but may come from a Greek word that entered into English usage as 'barbarian' or from Arab references to the inhabitants of this area as 'El Babar'. Indeed, the North African coast was referred to by Europeans as the Barbary Coast until the late nineteenth century. Berbers, however, refer to themselves as the Amazigh or Imazighen people, a term meaning 'free men'.

Iranians (Persian)

The modern state of Iran contains a rich mixture of ethnic groups, many of which share a common cultural heritage linked to ancient Persia and descent from the Aryan tribes that settled in the area in the second millennium BC. Persians (51 percent) and Azeris (24 percent) are the largest ethnic groups in Iran; minority ethnic groups include: Galaki and Mazandarani (8 percent), Kurds (7 percent), Arabs (8 percent), Baluchi (2 percent), Turkomen (2 percent), as well as Armenians, Georgians, Assyrian, Circassians, Pashtuns and others. This ethnic diversity is a result of the region's history, in which Persian-influenced empires such as the Sassanid and Safavid exercised control over large areas, including

Box 2.5

ZOROASTRIANISM

Zoroastrianism is a monotheistic religion that developed in the area of ancient Persia. Written references document its existence by 600 BCE, though it is thought to have originated earlier. Once the dominant religion in Greater Persia, its influence waned after the fall of the Persian Empire and the gradual spread of Islam in the area. However, aspects of Persian/Iranian culture can be traced to Zoroastrianism. The Iranian New Year, Nowruz, traces its origins to Zoroastrianism. Today there are approximately 200,000 followers worldwide, located primarily in Iran, India, Pakistan and the cities of North America, Canada and the United Kingdom. Followers in India are known as Parsis (or Parsees).

Many of the ideas of Zoroastrianism are thought to have influenced the Abrahamic religions: Judaism, Christianity and Islam. Zoroastrianism was founded by Zoraoster (also spelled Zarathustra), who proclaimed Ahura Mazda as the creator and sole God.

The universe, and everything in it, is locked in conflict between truth and order (*asha*) and chaos and disorder (*druj*). Humans are active participants in this conflict and must engage in appropriate actions to keep chaos at bay. The concepts of moral choice (free will), duty and responsibility figure prominently in Zoroastrianism. Other tenets include the belief in equality of all, regardless of race, gender or religion; respect and kindness for all living things; and environmentalism. Time is divided into three periods: the first was characterized by perfection; in the current time period, evil is active; in the third, yet to come, perfect goodness will be restored.

Worship practices include five daily prayers. Worshippers often pray before a fire; considered both radiant and pure, it is the symbol of Ahura Mazda. The belief in heaven, hell and final judgment is central. There are a large number of Zoroastrian religious texts; collectively they are known as the Avesta. The soul is thought to leave the body on the fourth day after death. Formerly, the dead were placed on open towers, the bodies left to vultures, as the earth was considered too sacred for the dead. Today, both burial and cremation are common. Traditionally, adherents married within the religious community; however, intermarriage with people of other faiths is increasingly taking place owing to the community's small size.

modern Iraq, Armenia, Afghanistan and parts of Syria, Turkey, Pakistan, Arabia and Central Asia.

The majority of Iranians speak Farsi (Persian) or a related Iranian language. A shared history of Persian culture also binds together Iran's diverse population. From the second millennium AD, Persia strongly influenced the cultural development of the region and the world beyond. Persian was the language of intellectuals and government officials before the rise of Arab (and Arabic-speaking) empires after the coming of Islam. The influence of Persian literature and poetry, and key achievements of Persian scientists during the Islamic Golden Age, assured the continued significance of Persia and Persian culture. This shared historical experience of Persian culture forms a common basis for Iran's diverse populations.

Turkic peoples

The term 'Turkic' refers to a large group of people in Northern and Central Eurasia that speak a Turkic language. Azerbaijan, Kazakhstan, Kyrgyzstan, Uzbekistan, Turkmenistan and Turkey all have majority Turkic populations. Most Turkic peoples are Sunni Muslim, though some Christian communities exist. Turkic peoples arrived in the Middle East between the fifth and tenth centuries BCE, when large numbers migrated from Central Asia.

Though a majority of Turkey's population is of Turkic origin, approximately 15–30 percent are ethnically Kurdish, though they hold Turkish citizenship and may refer to themselves as Turks. The desire among Turkish Kurds for autonomy or independence is a major challenge to the idea of a common 'Turkish' identity.

Kurds

Approximately 30 million Kurds live in Turkey, Iran, Syria and Iraq. They speak Kurdish as their native language, but Turkish, Persian and Arabic are also widely spoken. The Kurds have long sought to create an independent Kurdish homeland, Kurdistan, made up of the territories with large Kurdish populations. This has caused tension between the Kurds and governments in Iraq, Iran, Syria and Turkey. Most Kurds are Sunni Muslim, though a substantial minority are Shia; some Kurds are Christian.

Kurds make up approximately 20 percent of the population in Iraq. Under the regime of Saddam Hussein they were systematically persecuted. In 1988 the Iraqi government adopted a policy called *Anfal* ('Spoils of War') which led to the deportation of thousands of Kurds from the north of the country to south and central Iraq, destruction of Kurdish villages, and large numbers of civilian casualties.

RELIGIOUS DIVERSITY IN THE MENA

Religion is a significant factor in cultural differentiation in the Middle East. The region is home to the three monotheistic faiths: Judaism, Christianity and Islam. Each has left an impression. All three faiths exist today as historical events, such as the Ottoman *millet* system, ensured the survival of religious pluralism in the region. There is also considerable diversity within religions; Lebanon, for example, has at least eighteen confessional groupings, or distinct religious communities. Below are some of the region's major confessional groups, though many smaller groups also exist.

Islam

Islam is by far the most prominent religion in the MENA. Islam is divided into two main branches, Sunni and Shia.

This division in Islam dates to a dispute over who should succeed the prophet Muhammad as leader of the Muslim community after his death in 632 CE. Sunni Muslims account for about 85–90 percent of the world's Muslims. They are also the majority in the MENA. Within the general categories of Sunni and Shia there are further subdivisions. The discussion below provides a brief introduction to the considerable diversity within Islam.

Within Sunni Islam there are four major schools of religious thought (*fiqh*), which create law and commentary on religious practice, each founded by a particularly renowned religious scholar. The Hanafi school, prominent in Egypt, Iraq, India, Turkey and the West, is the most open to modern ideas and the most liberal. The Hanbali school, followed in Saudi Arabia, is the most conservative. The other two schools are the Maliki, followed in North and West Africa, and the Shafi'i, prevalent among Kurds. These schools of thought co-exist, and there is considerable intellectual discourse amongst legal scholars.

Shia sects

Jafari (Twelvers) are the largest group (about 80 percent) within the Shia community. All Shia believe that 'Alī should have succeeded Muhammad, and therefore do not recognize the judgments of the three caliphs that preceded 'Alī's succession as caliph. Twelvers also believe in imams, divinely appointed guides in religious and social matters. 'Alī was the first of the imams, of which there have been twelve. The twelfth imam is believed to be in hiding, and will reveal himself on the Day of Judgment. The Twelver perspective is predominant among Shia in Iran, Iraq, Lebanon and Bahrain (Map 2.5).

Ismailis broke with the Twelvers over the issue of the succession of the sixth imam: while the Ismailis accepted the eldest son, the Twelvers accepted a younger son as the rightful successor. Similarly, Zaydis disagree with Twelvers over the succession of the fifth imam.

Alawis consider themselves Twelver Shia but are also a distinct group. The name Alawis refers to their reverence for 'Alī, the cousin and son-in-law of the prophet Muhammad. The origin of the Alawis is disputed, but

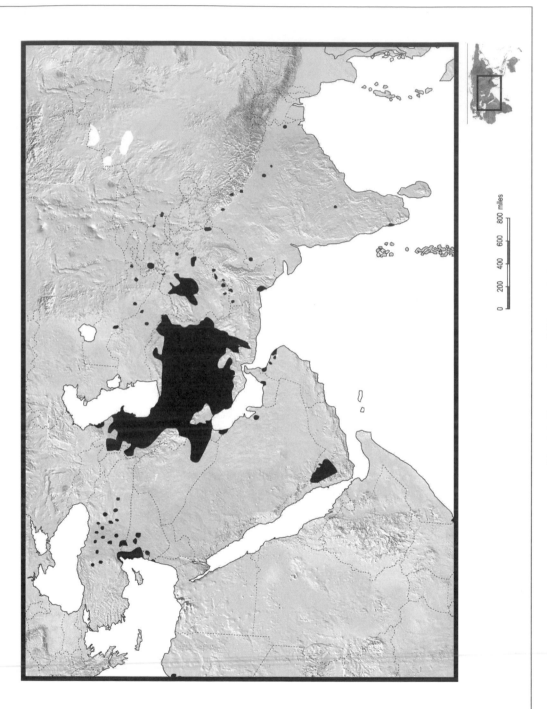

Map 2.5 Concentrations of Shia populations

by the tenth century they were present in Aleppo, Syria. Syria remains the location of most Alawis, a minority population who were given autonomy during the French colonial period. Significant numbers of Alawites are also found in Lebanon and Turkey. In 1971, Hafez al-Assad, an Alawi, became president of Syria, a position which can only be held by a Muslim. Al-Assad's presidency, and that of his son Bashar al-Assad, is interesting, as many Muslim religious authorities do not consider the Alawi to be Muslim.

Alawites believe that 'Alī is Muhammad's true successor; indeed, he was the last incarnation of God on earth. The Alawites worship secretly and do not accept converts; and their religious texts are closely guarded, passed down from scholar to scholar. Therefore, little is known about the sect's specific theology.

The Druze are an offshoot of the Ismaili branch of Islam, but also significantly influenced by other religious and philosophical perspectives. Most Druze do not consider themselves Muslim. Historically they faced much persecution and keep their religious beliefs secret; they practice *taqiyya*, or 'dissimulation', concealing their own religious beliefs and outwardly accepting those of the community in which they live. As the Druze do not accept converts, its practitioners are born into the religious community. Traditionally, intermarriage into other religious communities was discouraged but does now take place. Prayer is usually conducted privately, among family and friends. Druze place a high value on respecting the elderly and protecting and serving one's community.

The Druze symbol is a five-colored star, with each color representing cosmic principles believed by the Druze, including: green (intelligence/reason), red (soul), yellow (word), blue (precedent) and white (immanence). In addition to prophets such as Moses and Abraham, the Druze revere the teachings of classical Greek philosophers such as Plato. Materialism is also discouraged.

Today, most Druze live in Lebanon, where they make up about 5 percent of the population, and played a major role in the Lebanese civil war. Druze can also be found in surrounding countries of Syria, Turkey and Israel. Approximately 20,000 Druze live in the United States.

Sufism, or mystical Islam, focuses on dedication to God and divine love. Sufis may be either Sunni or Shia; followers of Sufism study in small groups under a more learned spiritual leader. Sufis have made a considerable contribution to Persian literature; the poet Rumi is perhaps the best known. Sufis have been persecuted and Sufism banned in parts of the region for their mystical beliefs.

Maronite Christians

Maronites are Christians who followed a Christian hermit, Maron, in the fifth century AD. This community continued to grow after the death of Maron. The Maronites fully backed the decisions made at the Council of Chalcedon, which determined that Jesus was both human and divine. When the Maronites were violently attacked by those believing the monophysite position, which determined that Jesus had only one divine nature, they took refuge in the mountains of Lebanon.

Isolated, the Maronites established their own church hierarchy, including a patriarch, separate from the Byzantine Empire. However, at a later period the Maronites fought alongside the Crusaders and were loyal to the Catholic pope. Maronites follow Catholic doctrine; but Aramaic is their liturgical language, and they retain an independent church hierarchy, headed by its own patriarch, who resides in Lebanon.

Under French control in Lebanon, the Maronites were favored politically. The National Pact created in 1943 determined the political system of newly independent Lebanon, giving the presidency to the Maronites. Today, their power has been reduced somewhat as a result of the Taif Agreement that ended the Lebanese civil war.

Copts

The term Copt refers to native Egyptian Christians, who have followed Christianity since the first century AD, when it was brought to the region by the apostle Mark. The majority of Copts belong to the Coptic Orthodox Church, which is headed by a patriarch in Alexandria. Other Copts belong to the Coptic Catholic Church and the Coptic Protestant Church. The Coptic Orthodox Church has been an independent body, headed by an Egyptian patriarch, since the Council of Chalcedon in AD 451 in which a schism occurred within the Byzantine Empire (or Eastern Roman Empire) over the nature of Christ. Many of the eastern and African churches held the monophysite position, that Christ was wholly divine. When the Council of Chalcedon, attended by over 500 bishops, declared that Christ had two natures, human and divine, churches such as the Egyptian Orthodox Church rejected the council's authority.

Assyrian Christians

Assyrian Christians include Christians who belong to a number of Christian denominations, most notably the Chaldean Church (of Babylon), the Antiochian Orthodox Church, the Assyrian Evangelical and Pentecostal churches, and the Syriac and Catholic orthodox churches. The common bond among the Assyrians, however, is their descent from the ancient Akkadians. The Assyrians speak a modern form of Syriac, an Aramaic language, and consider themselves to be the indigenous inhabitants of Mesopotamia.

The largest concentrations of Assyrians are in Iraq (800,000) and Syria (500,000), with much smaller numbers in Iran, Turkey, Jordan and Lebanon. Many Assyrians live outside the Middle East; the US has the largest concentration (83,000), followed by Sweden (35,000).

Small pockets of Protestant Christians exist in the Middle East; some are the result of missionary activity by both United States and British churches. In the eighteenth and nineteenth centuries, Protestant churches set up many educational institutions, including the precursor to the American University of Beirut. Today, evangelical Christian churches send missionaries, often working 'undercover', to attempt to convert the 'wayward Muslims'. Still other Christians (Protestant and others) come to Israel, and especially to Jerusalem, seeking the opportunity to live in the 'Holy Land'.

There are many Christian groups in the MENA, many of which date back to the earliest days of Christianity as well as more recently developed denominations. The groups described here are only part of a much more complex Christian presence.

Jews

Judaism was the first of the monotheistic religions to develop in the Middle East. Today it is important to distinguish between the terms 'Israeli' and 'Jew', and the differing meanings of the term 'Jew'. 'Jew' is both a religious affiliation and an ethnic identity; traditionally a Jew is a person whose mother is Jewish or who converts in accordance with Jewish law. It is possible to be a secular Jew and not practice Judaism. 'Israeli' refers to a citizen of Israel. While most Israelis are Jewish, some are Christian and Muslim. This includes Israeli Arabs, who are Arabs who remained inside the borders of the state of Israel when it was created. Some Israeli Arabs consider themselves Palestinians. Though most Jews in the Middle East live in Israel, small communities of Jews exist in other countries, including: Tunisia, Yemen and Iran.

A number of denominations exist in Judaism; differences are based on issues of what beliefs a Jew should hold and how to live a Jewish life. The major divisions are Orthodox, Conservative and Reform Judaism. Orthodox Judaism is the most conservative and traditional in perspective and holds the belief that Jewish law (the Torah) was divinely inspired and is unchanging. Conservative Judaism was developed in Europe and the United States in the 1800s. It places emphasis on practicing Judaism in modern life, including critical interpretation of Jewish law to reflect modern conditions. Reform Judaism (also known as Liberal Judaism) is founded on Enlightenment-era principles that reject compulsory adherence to Jewish ceremony over an individual's personal interpretation of Jewish tradition.

Israel's diverse Jewish population reflects intense migration of Jews from Europe, the former Soviet Union, the United States, Africa and North Africa. They practice many forms of Judaism in addition to those described above.

HISTORICAL GEOGRAPHY

The Middle East was a pivotal location for much of human history. In Mesopotamia ('the land between the rivers'), now modern Iraq, the first written language was developed by the Sumerians. Here, too, populations became settled, engaging in agriculture and building the first sizable habitations. Laws were first codified, bureaucracy developed and monotheistic religions established. In the ancient world, the Mediterranean and the Middle East was the key crossroads for trade between the Europe

Box 2.6

THE SILK ROAD

The 'Silk Road' is not a single route or road but a series of interconnected overland and sea trade routes that connected the known world for over a thousand years. The route passed through rugged parts of Central Asia, including the Gobi and other deserts, to link the Mediterranean and Europe with China, spanning a distance of 5000 miles (8000 km).

Though archaeological evidence, such as the presence of silk in an ancient Egyptian tomb, suggests that trade took place possibly as early as 3000 BCE, the development of a large-scale East–West trade route was spurred by Alexander the Great's conquest in central Asia. In 329 BCE he established the city of Alexandria Eschate ('Alexandria the Furthest') located in what is today northern Tajikistan; the city would become a key stop on the trade route. For three centuries after Alexander's campaign the Greeks maintained a presence in central Asia, and pushed further eastward, forming significant trade relations with their eastern neighbors and through them having eventual contact with China. The rise of the Han dynasties in China, which sought commercial contact with the West and with India, further drove the development of extensive trade links. By the first century BCE the 'Silk Road' was formed.

The consolidation of territory under the vast Roman Empire in 30 BCE provided further impetus for the growth of trade. India, Southeast Asia, China, the Middle East, Africa and Europe were now linked for trade and communication. The Roman obsession with silk, imported in large quantities, in exchange for Roman gold, created a desire for direct contact with China. The Romans had first discovered silk in 53 BCE during a military campaign against the Parthians, who continued to be the prime intermediary in Rome's silk trade. At one point the Empire tried to prohibit the wearing of silk, to curtail the vast amounts spent on the commodity, but the efforts were to no avail. In addition to silk, furs, ceramics, jade, bronze, lacquer and iron came from the East. In exchange the West offered gold, precious metals, ivory and glass, which China did not yet have the technology to manufacture. All along the route, goods passed through the hands of many merchants and intermediaries, until finally transiting the vast continent.

Not only merchandise was transported along the Silk Road. People also carried ideas, innovations and artistic practices, along the way encouraging a diverse cultural communication. In this way, Buddhism originated in northern India in the first century BCE and spread across central Asia and into China, finally reaching Korea in the fourth century and Japan in the sixth. When the Nestorian Christians were outlawed by the Roman Empire in 432 BCE, they fled east, eventually bringing this form of Christianity to China. Islam eventually spread along the Silk Road, and Arabic became a primary language of trade. With the end of the Roman Empire in the fifth century and the rise of Islam in the seventh century, trade on the Silk Road declined. However, the westward expansion of the Mongols (1215–1360) reinvigorated trade and reopened trade links between China and the now predominantly Muslim Mediterranean.

Though he was not the first to travel the route, Marco Polo's description of his travels is the most widely known. In 1271, at the age of 17, he set off with his uncle, a merchant, to travel the route. He visited the court of the leader, Kublai Khan, in what is now Beijing and visited the famed summer palace, known as Xanadu. Before returning to Italy, he traveled extensively throughout China. Between 1325 and 1354 the Muslim traveler Ibn Battuta followed the route, embarking from the city of Tabriz in modern Iran.

A variety of technologies were transferred to the West. The most important among them include printing and papermaking techniques, gunpowder, the astrolabe and the compass. The Europeans would use these innovations to establish large empires and undertake new voyages of exploration.

Box 2.6

THE SILK ROAD—CONT'D

The Silk Road entered a permanent decline after breakup and disintegration of the Mongol Empire at the end of the fourteenth century; no further silk was traded along the route after 1400. European states seeking a new sea route to the Far East sponsored large expeditions and spurred the growth of navigational technology.

X. Liu, and L. N. Shaffer, (2007) *Connections across Eurasia: Transportation, Communication, and Cultural Exchange on the Silk Roads.* New York: McGraw-Hill.

Box 2.7

THE *DESCRIPTION DE L'EGYPTE*: IMPERIALISM, EGYPTOLOGY AND THE ORIENTALIST REDISCOVERY OF THE MIDDLE EAST

Michael Christopher Low

'Soldiers, from the height of these pyramids, forty centuries look down upon you....' On July 21, 1798, these weighty words fell from the lips of Napoleon Bonaparte as he prepared his troops for the battle of the Pyramids. In many ways Bonaparte's words were prophetic, aptly summarizing how France's ill-fated Egyptian campaign would ultimately be redefined and overshadowed by the archaeological conquests that came in its wake. The primary objective of Bonaparte's audacious military expedition was to threaten British interests in the Mediterranean and India. It was amid the violence of this Anglo-French imperial rivalry that modern Egyptology was born and the Middle East was 'rediscovered' by European Orientalists.

Ironically, French soldiers stumbled upon the famous Rosetta Stone – the very same inscriptions that would eventually be used to decipher hieroglyphics – while digging military fortifications. When Admiral Horatio Nelson's fleet sank some 200 ships at Abu Qir (Aboukir), however, Bonaparte hastily abandoned his doomed Egyptian expedition and returned to France to have himself crowned emperor. Thus, in 1801, the Rosetta Stone was seized by Britain as part of the spoils of war, touching off more than a century of Anglo-French Egyptopological gamesmanship. Yet in the end it would take a Frenchman, Jean-François Champollion, to decipher the Rosetta Stone and unlock the secrets of the pharaohs.

Realizing that the *Description* could be used to repackage his military failures as an academic and cultural victory, Napoleon endorsed the work as a state project in 1802. During the Egyptian campaign, some 170 members of the Commission des sciences et arts had accompanied Bonaparte, the leading members of which belonged to the Institut d'Egypte. The commission included some forty-five engineers and geographers, a dozen mechanics and balloonists, a dozen physicians and pharmacists, and thirty geometers, astronomers, chemists, zoologists, botanists and mineralogists. There were an additional fifteen draftsmen, painters and architects, and even a handful of men of letters, antiquarians, musicians and political economists. And, perhaps most important of all, ten Orientalists served as translators; and in 1799 the term *orientaliste* first appeared in its modern French meaning of one who studies or paints the Orient.

Though the famous Abd al-Rahman al-Jabarti, the great professor of al-Azhar whose *Ajaib al-Athar* detailed Egyptian history from the seventeenth century to the French occupation of Egypt, piled scorn upon

Box 2.7

THE *DESCRIPTION DE L'EGYPTE*: IMPERIALISM, EGYPTOLOGY AND THE ORIENTALIST REDISCOVERY OF THE MIDDLE EAST—CONT'D

Napoleon and the invading French, he, too, recognized the talents of Napoleon's army of Orientalists. Upon visiting the scholars of the Institut d'Egypte, he proclaimed:

> They have a great interest in the sciences, mainly in mathematics and knowledge of Languages and make great efforts to learn the Arabic language and the colloquial. In this they strive day and night. And they have books especially devoted to all types of Languages, their declensions and conjugations as well as their etymologies. They possess extraordinary astronomical instruments of perfect construction.

The results of their collective labors was a voluminous work, consisting of four folio volumes of text on antiquities, two folios on the modern state and two on natural history, and a further five folio volumes of plates covering the same subjects. Eventually ushered to its completion by Edmé François Jomard, a geographer who had helped map Cairo, Alexandria and the surrounding countryside for the expedition, the *Description* was finally published in 1810.

Despite its importance in reintroducing Egypt and the Middle East into the European imagination, the *Description* also helped lay the foundation for the kind of European arrogance that would characterize Orientalist scholarship until well into the twentieth century. As Edouard de Villiers du Terrage, one of Napoleon's young engineers, described his experience in Egypt, he juxtaposed now familiar images of Egypt's ancient ssplendor with its modern-day squalor, 'Oriental barbarism' with 'European enlightenment':

> An Arab village, made up of miserable huts, dominates the most magnificent Monument of Egyptian architecture and seems placed there to attest to the triumph of Ignorance and barbarism over centuries of light which in Egypt raised the arts to the Highest degree of splendour. We were pleased to think that we were going to take back to our country the Products of the ancient science and industry of the Egyptians; it was a veritable Conquest we were going to attempt in the name of the arts.

G. Néret, (ed.) (2001) *Description of Egypt*. Köln: Taschen.

D. M. Reid, (2002) *Whose Pharaohs?: Archaeology, Museums, and Egyptian National Identity from Napoleon to World War I*. Berkeley, Calif.: University of California Press.

and Asia. The Silk Road extended 5000 miles (8000 km) connecting the great civilization of China to Europe by way of the Middle East; control of this overland trade route gave rise to large and prosperous Middle Eastern cities (Map 2.6).

As a result, for much of its history the region's absolute location was truly the center of the known world. The silk route facilitated not only trade but also the transfer of knowledge and scientific invention, which scholars in the Middle East improved and expanded upon. So, while

European cities languished in the so-called 'Dark Ages', a period when knowledge was stifled, cities in the Muslim world flourished. In the thirteenth century Cairo boasted a population of over a half a million people, making it one of the largest cities in the world and vastly exceeding that of any European city at the time (Abu Lughod, 1989).

To the east, a rich and diverse Persian-influenced culture flourished. Persian rulers fostered an environment in which scientific inquiry, philosophy, arts and medicine flourished, helping to create the Islamic Golden Age.

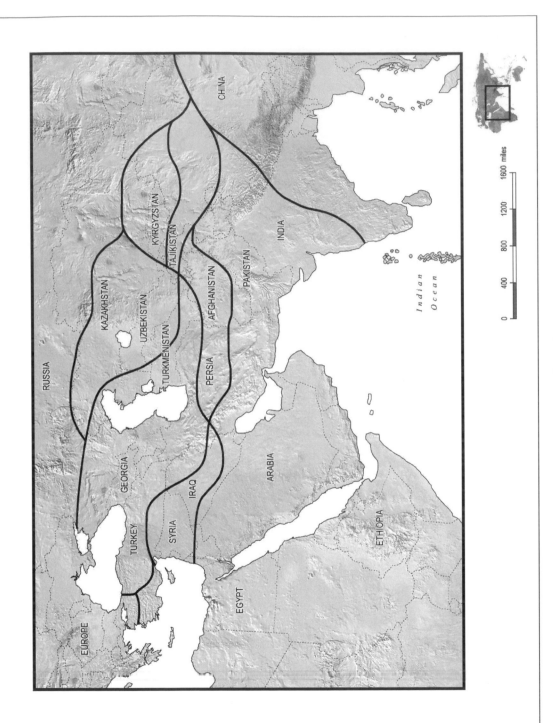

Map 2.6 Silk Road routes

Persian became the language of government, and Persian bureaucrats created administrative practices that influenced the region for centuries.

In the fifteenth century, increases in navigation technology, which enabled sea travel beyond the horizon, and the subsequent discovery of the New World, radically altered the absolute location of the Middle East and its economic prospects. With ships no longer needing to hug the coastline, the Mediterranean and the overland routes connected to it ceased to be the most efficient means of transport. After the discovery of the Americas, transatlantic trade grew rapidly, and the Middle East was further marginalized. Furthermore, a scientific and artistic revolution, the Renaissance, had taken hold in Europe, laying the foundations for the Industrial Revolution. In the new age of exploration and scientific discovery the Middle East region would find itself growing more and more peripheral on the world stage. No longer controlling much of the world's economy, by the eighteenth century the now powerful European states began to exercise economic and political control over the region, ushering in a period of colonialism, the impact of which still marks the Middle East today.

SUMMARY OF MAIN POINTS

- The construction of the Middle East and North Africa region is based on a set of subjective criteria, often based on historical precedence.
- The Islamic world extends far beyond the Middle East and North Africa.
- The physical geography of the region is quite varied, including deserts and key river systems.
- Population density in the region is closely related to the presence of water or coastline.
- Though predominantly Arab and Muslim, the region contains a mosaic of religions and ethnicities.
- Earlier in its history the Middle East was the center of the known world, and economically and politically dominant.

QUESTIONS FOR DISCUSSION

1   What do you think of this book's definition of the Middle East and North Africa? Would you define the region differently? How?
2   How has the 'everyday' definition of the Middle East changed in response to events such as the September 11 attacks and the subsequent war on terrorism?
3   How do the Arab world and the Islamic world overlap? Diverge?
4   How does climatic variability, within an overall dry region, impact on settlement patterns and economic activity?
5   What challenges does geological instability pose for the region?
6   What are the impacts of cultural and ethnic diversity on the Middle East and North Africa?
7   How have so many different religions co-existed, largely peacefully, in the region for so many centuries?

SUGGESTIONS FOR FURTHER READING

Abu Lughod, Janet L. (1989) *Before European Hegemony: The World System AD 1250–1350*. Oxford: Oxford University Press. Describes the known world before the discovery of the New World and European industrialization, when the Middle East, India and China controlled the global economy. See especially chapter 7 on Cairo.

Amery, Hussein A. and Wolf, Aaron T., (eds) (2000) *Water in the Middle East*. Austin, Tex.: University of Texas Press. Provides an overview of the scarcity of water resources in the Middle East and, in particular, its role in past, current and potential future conflicts.

Anderson, E. (2000) *The Middle East: Geography and Geopolitics*. London: Routledge. Overview of the region's physical, human and political geography. See especially Chapter 5 on oil and water resources.

Bates, D. G. and Rassam, A. (2001) *Peoples and Cultures of the Middle East*. Upper Saddle River, NJ: Prentice Hall. An insightful, and accessibly written, socio-anthropological analysis of the region. Particularly relevant today are the sections on communal identity and ethnic groups.

Cutler, I. (2001) *Mysteries of the Desert: A View of Saudi Arabia*. New York: Rizzoli International Publications. Stunning photographs of Saudi Arabia's deserts as well as of some of its people.

Esposito, J. L. (2005) *Islam: The Straight Path*. Oxford: Oxford University Press. An introduction to Islam, including its historical development in the region.

Fernea, E. (1995) *Guests of the Sheikh: An Ethnography of an Iraqi Village*. New York: Anchor Books. This classic ethnography, first published in 1965 and based on two years living in southern Iraq, offers deep insights into traditions of rural Arab society.

Held. C. C. (2006) *Middle East Patterns: Places, Peoples and Politics*. Boulder, Colo.: Westview Press. A comprehensive geography of the region (not including North Africa). Includes an extensive section on the region's physical geography and country studies.

Manners, I. 'The Middle East: a geographic preface'. In D. Gerner and J. Schwedler (eds) *Understanding the Contemporary Middle East*, 2nd edn. Boulder, Colo.: Lynne Rienner Publishers. A brief introduction to the region's geography, including a section on the role of urbanism in the region's historical development.

Nasr, V. (2006) 'When the Shiites rise'. *Foreign Affairs*, 85: 58–74. Argues that the end of Saddam Hussein's regime has empowered Shiites in Iraq and beyond its borders, to the dismay of many in the region.

National Geographic Society (2003) *National Geographic Atlas of the Middle East*. Washington, DC: National Geographic Society. Provides both thematic and country-specific maps of the region. Does not include North Africa.

Ramadan, T. (2004) *Western Muslims and the Future of Islam*. New York/Oxford: Oxford University Press.

Scheindlin, Raymond P. (1998) *A Short History of the Jewish People: From Legendary Times to Modern Statehood*. Oxford: Oxford University Press. A concise history spanning 3000 years, including the origins of the Israelites and the establishment of the state of Israel. See Chapter 4, 'The Jews in the Islamic world'.

Thesiger, W. (1958) 'Marsh dwellers of southern Iraq'. *The National Geographic Magazine*, February, pp. 205–49. A classic article by the famed explorer of the Middle East provides a vivid picture of the 'Marsh Arabs', whose culture and way of life was virtually eliminated during the Saddam Hussein era.

PART II

EMERGENCE AND EVOLUTION OF THE REGION

3

THE CONTEMPORARY STATE SYSTEMS

The modern state system in the Middle East and North Africa is relatively young; most states achieved independence in the mid-twentieth century. The creation of these states was profoundly affected by the influence of European forces including colonialism and two world wars (see Chapter 5). Yet, despite the often tumultuous history leading to the creation of these countries, the modern state system has been remarkably stable for the last half century (Map 3.1).

With the exception of north and south Yemen, which unified in 1990, there have been few substantial border modifications in the post independence period. Similarly, many of the regimes in power have held it consistently since independence; while this has often not fostered widespread civil society involvement in politics, it has maintained stability. The last decade has witnessed the death of many of the region's often iconic post-independence leaders, including Sheik Zayed bin Sultan al Nahayan of the United Arab Emirates (d. 2004), King Hussein bin Talal of Jordan (d. 1999), Hafez al-Assad of Syria (d. 2000) and King Hassan II of Morocco (d. 1999). The transition to a new generation of leaders, all descendants of the deceased heads of state, has been largely uneventful as they have continued to follow the paths laid down by their predecessors. Anticipation that the end of the bipolar world order, in which the United States and the Union of Soviet Socialist Republics each sought influence in the MENA to serve their own goals, would have a major impact on the region's stability has also remained largely unrealized (Map 3.2).

Despite this stability in state structures and regime longevity, governments in the region are under significant pressure from societal actors. This includes the growing power of Islamist parties, most of which are non-violent, seeking a greater role in governance through the ballot box. Secular and religious pro democracy advocates in many countries are pushing for a greater role for civil society in the political process. At the same time, the threat of militant Islam, and its potential to radicalize the large youth population, remains a concern.

A notable exception to the stability of the MENA overall has been the continuing Arab–Israeli conflict (see Chapter 9). The three wars between the Israeli and Arab states (1948, 1967, 1973), and the resulting occupation of the West Bank and the Golan Heights (and, previously, the Gaza Strip), continue to undermine the stability of the Levant, at great cost to its economic development (Map 3.3). Today the instability within Iraq, and its descent into civil war, has unleashed separatist forces which threaten the territorial cohesion of Iraq and are causing deep concerns around the region. A divided Iraq, and the ascent of Shia political power, gives Iran greater

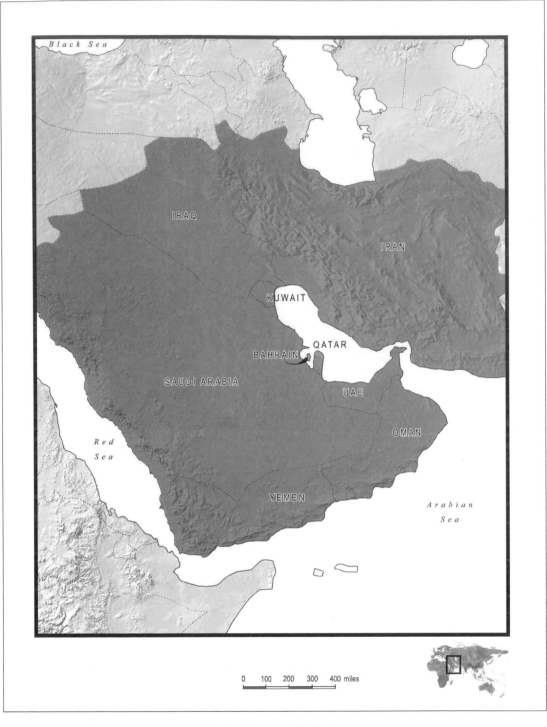

Map 3.1 The Arab Gulf region

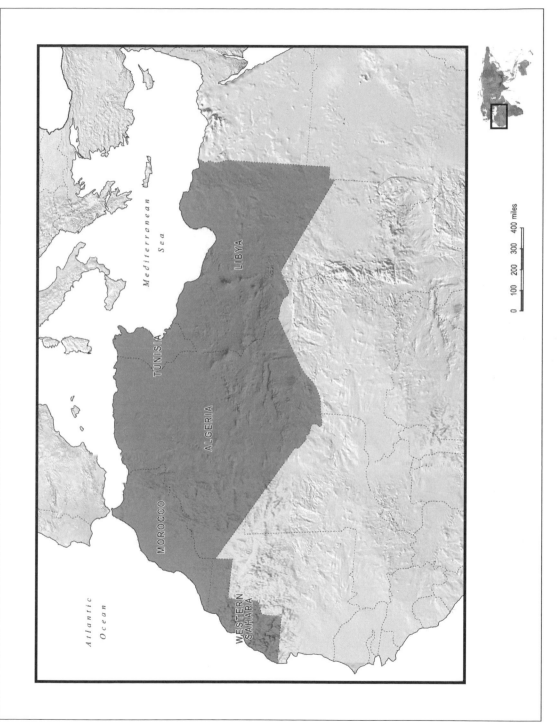

Map 3.2 North Africa

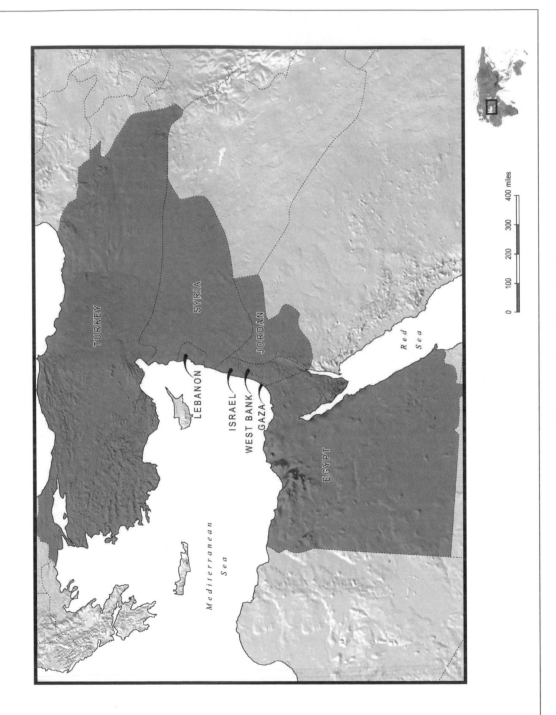

Map 3.3 The Levant and Anatolian peninsula

strategic importance, to the concern of Sunni states such as Saudi Arabia and Jordan. This has also heightened concerns in Israel, the usual target of Iranian saber-rattling. These challenges to the current state system are discussed in more detail in Chapter 10.

CHALLENGES TO THE STATE SYSTEM

Though the political system is remarkably stable, the individual states face many challenges. Some of these challenges stem from the countries' colonial history and their struggle for independence, while others are the result of post-independence economic and social challenges. Some general observations of state challenges can be made, though various states exhibit these characteristics at different levels.

The boundaries of most Middle Eastern states were imposed largely by external forces, namely the European countries that carved out spheres of influence for their own control after the end of World War I. In doing so, they often split ethnic groups between states or included within one state a volatile mix of ethnic groups with historic rivalries. Iraq is an excellent example of this phenomenon. Iraq was formed by combining the former Ottoman provinces of Mosul, Baghdad and Basra by the British, who desired control of the country's rich oil resources. In this partition, however, the Kurds found themselves divided among Turkey, Iran, Syria and Iraq. Similarly, the large population of Shia Muslims is separated from large Shia populations in Iran and Saudi Arabia. Iraq therefore contains a volatile mix of Sunni Muslim Arabs, Shia Muslim Arabs and non-Arab Kurds, as well as numerous other smaller ethnic groups. This ethnic fragmentation creates significant centrifugal forces that discourage integration of the state and its population. Similarly, the French creation of Syria out of a larger Ottoman province, which stretched to the sea, cost Syria access to a port, separated peoples that had been together for centuries and created a volatile confessional mix in Lebanon. Such ethnicity-based centrifugal forces can be found throughout the region, and were often intensified by colonial policies that placed minority groups in political power, which many retain today.

States in the MENA also face challenges of weak institutional development or institutional dualism within their governmental systems. Many states had little governmental infrastructure in place upon reaching independence when colonial systems were withdrawn. Newly independent states found themselves grappling with essential state functions such as tax collection, provision of social services, law enforcement and transportation infrastructure development for large and growing populations. In many instances, the actual 'presence' of the state beyond the capital is quite low. At the same time, states grapple with bureaucracies that have two sets of institutional systems to address one function. For example, an Islam-based judicial system for domestic and family law may exist alongside a Western-based system that addresses commercial and legal aspects of the law. This 'institutional dualism' is the result of an institution being established during the colonial period, or even before when countries underwent modernization programs, while at the same time 'traditional' institutions were retained.

In the decades since independence these states have dealt with enormous economic and social challenges, including both those of low economic development and extremely rapid development associated with oil revenues. Largely agriculture dependent, with little or no industrial development, many states had few revenues to meet the needs of rapidly growing populations. In the independent period farmers from the countryside flocked to the urban areas, usually the capital, in search of work. Middle Eastern cities, burgeoning with this rural–urban migration, became extremely large urban areas, though with strongly rural characteristics as the migrants struggled to support themselves with few available jobs. The state struggled, usually unsuccessfully, to maintain economic growth and job creation at levels equal to population growth.

In the Arab/Persian Gulf region, a huge influx of income from oil exports drove the construction of ultra-modern cities while creating a welfare state. In a few short decades, cities such as Dubai and Riyadh rose from the desert, characterized by gleaming skyscrapers and shopping malls, built by imported expatriate labor, from India, Pakistan, the Philippines, Indonesia and South Asia. Citizens of Gulf countries often hold undemanding jobs within the government bureaucracy or do not have to work at all, and are provided with very high levels of social and educational benefits. Government expenditure is very high, and can be difficult to sustain during periods of low oil prices. With a rapidly increasing population, these benefits have become more costly to maintain; at the same time the need to diversify economically, in preparation for the eventual depletion of petroleum supplies, became evident.

At present, many governments in the MENA are facing new challenges from non-state actors. Broadly, these are of two types: militant Islamist groups that seek to overthrow the existing government and groups, both Islamist and non-Islamist, which seek greater civil society participation in the political process. Countries such as Yemen, Jordan, Egypt, Tunisia and Morocco have witnessed bombing campaigns as well as direct attacks on government forces by groups, some of which share ideological elements with al-Qaeda, intent on undermining the government. At the same time, non-violent groups, such as the Kifaya movement in Egypt, have sought to expand opportunities for public participation in government. Each of these, though in different ways, has posed a challenge to existing government regimes.

TYPES OF POLITICAL SYSTEMS

There is considerable variability within the governmental systems of the MENA, which include monarchies and parliamentary systems of various types. The section below provides an overview of the major types of systems and the states associated with them. When examining these systems it is important to look at not only the governing structures in place, such as a legislature, but also at the actual functions the structure performs. The short descriptions below provide only an introduction to the complex political systems of the MENA.

Monarchies

Eight states in the MENA are best described as monarchies, where the head of state is a hereditary ruler, typically with extensive power to implement the country's internal politics and conduct foreign affairs. In the MENA monarchs carry various titles: king,

sheikh, emir and sultan. With the exception of Morocco and Jordan, all of the region's monarchies are in the Arab/Persian Gulf. In some states the monarch's power is limited by a constitution; in others he (and it is always a he) has absolute rule. A number of the monarchies, especially in the Arab/Persian Gulf region, have recently instituted changes, including elections to legislative bodies, to increase civil society participation and democratization (for more details, see Chapter 10).

Saudi Arabia is a hereditary monarchy ruled by the al-Saud family. State law stipulates that the monarch must be one of the sons or grandsons of Abd al-Aziz al-Saud, who unified the tribes of Saudi Arabia and became the first king in 1926. Succession does not pass from father to son; rather a successor is chosen by consensus within the ruling family. The current monarch, King Abdullah, replaced his half-brother King Fahd (ruled 1982–2005) following his death. The Saudi royal family is very large, and its members hold key positions in the government.

A council of ministers is appointed by the king and serves in an advisory capacity and issues legislation. Though there is no constitution, the ruler is expected to implement policy consistent with Islamic law and local tradition. To the Western eye, the most apparent manifestation of rule by *sharia* is the concealment of women in long black enveloping *abayas*, restrictions on women's driving, and criminal penalties that include amputations for theft and public flogging. These interpretations of the *sharia* are based on the prevailing form of Islam in the kingdom, Wahhabism, an ultra-conservative form of Sunni Islam (see Chapter 7). The ideas of Wahhabism, founded by Muhammad ibn Abd al-Wahhab (1703–87), played a crucial role in the formation of the Saudi state, and interdependence between the Saudi royal family and the religious establishment has existed ever since.

Recent years have seen growing strife between elements within the al-Saud family that favor political liberalization and less conservative social norms and the religious establishment and members of the royal family closely aligned with it. Along with this tension, attacks by al-Qaeda-linked militants on foreigners, many of them Muslim expatriates, in the kingdom have undermined internal security. At the core of al-Qaeda's grievances against the royal family is its historically close relationship with the United States, and especially the stationing of US troops inside the kingdom.

In 2005 the kingdom held its first ever elections for city-level (municipal) councils. Women were not allowed to vote.

Tiny *Qatar* is ruled by the Khalifa family. The emir, Hamad bin Khalifa al-Thani, is chief of state. His brother, the prime minister, is head of government, though he is not elected by the people. A cabinet, the Council of Ministers, is appointed by the monarch.

In 1999, Qatar made steps toward democratization, holding its first municipal elections. In 2005 a new constitution came into effect that called for a forty-five-member parliament, or *Majlis as-Shura*, with thirty members to be elected by the citizenry and fifteen appointed by the monarch. Elections are scheduled for early 2007.

Though Wahhabi Islam is dominant in Qatar, it takes on a more tolerant form here than in Saudi Arabia. Women, for example, are allowed to both drive and vote. Qatar is also notable for its promotion of independent media; it is the major underwriter for the al-Jazeera network. Doha, its capital and only city, is developing a growing international profile, creating an 'education city' with campuses established by Carnegie Mellon University, Georgetown University and Texas A&M University.

Oman is ruled by Sultan Qabus ibn Said as-Said, who holds the titles of both sultan and prime minister. Succession is determined by the royal family following the death of a sultan, though the current leader, who has ruled since 1970, overthrew his father. A cabinet, appointed by the sultan, assists with governing Oman.

Oman has a bicameral *majlis* (legislative assembly). The upper chamber, *Majlis al-Dawla*, has fifty-eight members, appointed by the monarch. The lower chamber, *Majlis as-Shura* (Arabic for 'consultation'), has eighty-three seats. These members are elected by universal suffrage of all Omani citizens who have reached the age of 21. In the last election, held in October 2003, two women were elected to the *Majlis as-Shura*. The *Majlis al-Shura* has a limited ability to propose legislation, but its role, and that of the *Majlis al-Dawa*, is largely advisory.

Bahrain is a constitutional monarchy, headed by the al-Khalifa family; the current ruler is King Hamad bin Isa al-Khalifa. In recent years Bahrain has undergone substantial political liberalization led by the ruling family. The parliament consists of a lower house, the Chamber of Deputies, elected by universal suffrage, and an upper house, the Shura Council, appointed by the king. Each body of the legislature has forty members. The Shura Council includes six women as well as representatives of the indigenous Christian and Jewish communities (Christians account for approximately 9 percent of the population). Parliamentary elections were last held in 2006 (see Chapter 10). There are numerous political parties, most based on either Sunni or Shia Islam. Though the Shia are numerically dominant, Sunnis hold more political power. These parties tend to have a conservative social agenda, which is often more conservative than that of the monarchy.

Kuwait is a constitutional monarchy ruled by the al-Sabah family. It has the most active parliament in the Gulf region. The parliament, or National Assembly (*Majlis al-Umma*), consists of fifty elected representatives who serve four-year terms. Members of the cabinet (up to fifteen) also serve in the parliament. A number of political parties exist, some with a religious agenda, though many candidates run as independents. Suffrage in Kuwait is limited only to Kuwaiti citizens and those who have been naturalized for at least thirty years. Since 2005, women have had the right to vote.

The legislature has considerable power to draft legislation and play a role in governmental decision-making. The parliament has been known to reject decrees issued by the monarch, and often advocates more socially and economically conservative policies than those put forward by the emir. The legislature can also question cabinet ministers. Though the emir appoints the prime minister, the parliament has the ability to dismiss the prime minister as well as cabinet members. In a highly unusual move, the parliament voted to remove an ailing emir from his throne in January 2006. In addition, the national assembly must affirm the selection of a crown prince, following the death of an emir.

Though Kuwait enjoys considerable political liberalization by the standards of the Gulf, the extent of this liberalization should not be overestimated. The emir has the power to disband the legislature, and has done so in the past. Constitutionally, the emir is considered 'immune and inviolable', and therefore criticism of him or of the ruling family in the media is prohibited.

The *United Arab Emirates* presents an interesting case as it is a federal constitutional monarchy; the country is made up of a federation of seven small emirates who merged in 1971. The members of the UAE federation are: Abu Dhabi, Ajman, Dubai, Fujairah, Ras al-Khaimah, Sharjah and Umm al-Quwain. These emirates are quite varied: while Dubai is a major world trading center, Abu Dhabi is a petroleum giant; and others, such as Fujairah or tiny Ajman, have much lower levels of economic development. Similarly, while Dubai embraces a frenetic nightlife, no alcohol is allowed in Sharjah.

The UAE's constitution provides for a president and vice-president, who each serve five-year terms. Unofficially, the presidency is a hereditary position held by a member of the al-Nahayan family, which heads the Abu Dhabi emirate. Sheikh Zayed bin Sultan al-Nahayan served as president of the UAE from its formation until 2004; currently his eldest son serves as president. The president and vice-president are elected by the Federal Supreme Council, made up of the seven leaders of the emirates.

The governmental structure is reflective of power-sharing between the two largest emirates: Abu Dhabi and Dubai. The position of vice-president and prime minister is traditionally held by a member of Dubai's ruling family, the al-Maktoom clan.

The Supreme Council also elects the Council of Ministers, which serves an advisory function. A forty-member legislature, though it has only the power to review, not change or propose legislation, contains representatives of all the emirates. In December 2006 the UAE held its first elections ever to fill half of the seats in the Federal National Council (*Majlis Watani Ittihad*). Voting was limited to 6689 members of the electoral college, appointed by the emirs. There are no political parties in the UAE. On the whole, the UAE has been the slowest of the Gulf monarchies to implement a political liberalization plan.

Jordan has been a constitutional monarchy since 1952, shortly after its independence from Britain. The country's official name, the Hashemite Kingdom of Jordan, refers to the royal family's descent from the Banu Hashem clan within the Quraysh tribe, to which the prophet Muhammad belonged. This descent from the prophet is a primary source of legitimacy for the monarchy.

The king appoints the prime minister and also the cabinet in consultation with the prime minister. The legislature, the National Assembly (*Majlis al-Umma*), contains an upper house, the Senate, and a lower house, the House of Representatives. The fifty-five-member Senate is appointed by the monarch for five-year terms. The House of Representatives (also called the Chamber of Deputies) is a 110-member body elected by vote of male and female citizens aged 18 or over. Six seats are reserved for women, nine seats are reserved for the minority Christian population and three for members of the Chechen/Circassian ethnic group. The National Assembly can overrule the monarch's veto on legislation with a two-thirds majority vote.

Jordan has numerous political parties, many of which are loyal to the monarchy and others which oppose his policies. The major opposition party is the Islamic Action Front, which has accused the government of adopting electoral procedures designed to favor groups that traditionally support the monarchy and limit the influence of Islamists. The influence of Islamists, and of their conservative social agenda, is a growing tension within Jordanian politics and society. Another source of tension is that approximately 50–55 percent (no official census exists) of the population are Palestinians, many of whom live in refugee camps. In addition, a recent influx of large numbers of refugees from Iraq, perhaps totaling a million (Jordan's total population is 5.3 million), has caused price increases and heavy demands on government services such as schools and healthcare.

Morocco is a constitutional monarchy; the current king, Mohammad VI, has ruled since 1999. His leadership has been more progressive than that of his predecessor, his father Hassan II. In particular he established an Equality and Reconciliation Commission to investigate and rectify political persecutions conducted prior to his reign. Morocco has also adopted a family code granting greater rights to women.

Box 3.1

MOROCCO: THE EQUALITY AND RECONCILIATION COMMISSION

Human rights records throughout the region tend to be poor. Dissenters are often intimidated and imprisoned without due legal process.

In Morocco, steps have been taken to rectify past human rights abuses and prevent future occurrences. During the reign of King Hassan II (1961–99), who dissolved parliament in favor of his own direct rule, abuses were severe and numerous. Opponents were jailed, some in secret internment camps, killed or 'disappeared' by the government. The abuses reached their height between the 1960s and 1980s, the so-called 'Years of Lead'.

Hassan's successor, Mohamed VI, is more modernizing and has sought to alter Morocco's human rights records. In January 2004 he established the Equality and Reconciliation Commission to address human rights violations during his father's reign. After a two-year investigation the Commission awarded compensation to 9280 victims of violence. The Commission also found that 322 people had been killed by security forces during protests and 174 while in prison. The Commission acknowledged the existence of secret prisons, which had held 85 detainees. The Commission did not reveal the identities of individuals who had committed acts of torture nor hold them responsible. Morocco also passed new laws against the use of torture.

Despite this progress, however, concerns remain over the country's human rights record. New antiterrorism laws, in response to attacks on Moroccan hotels, facilitate arbitrary arrest and imprisonment. Human rights organizations assert that torture is consistently used to obtain confessions from suspected terrorists.

US Department of State. Bureau of Democracy, Human Rights and Labor (2005) *Morocco: Country Report on Human Rights Practices*, released March 8, 2006.

United Nations Development Programme. *Human Rights Index for Arab Countries*. Morocco http://www.arabhumanrights.org/en/countries/index.asp?cid=12.

The legislature is bicameral. The upper house, the Chamber of Counselors, contains 270 seats; members are elected for nine-year terms. Elections are held every three years, when a third of the body is up for election. These members are chosen through a system of elections held by local councils, professional organizations and wage-earner groups. The lower house, the Chamber of Representatives, contains 325 members, elected by popular vote of citizens over age 18. Thirty of the seats are reserved for women. These representatives serve five-year terms. Morocco has dozens of political parties; as no party receives a majority in the parliamentary election, they form coalitions in order to govern. Both the prime minister and the cabinet are appointed by the monarch. Morocco's legislature does have some authority over budgetary issues and approval of legislature, and may dismiss the government through a vote of no confidence.

'Presidential' and authoritarian systems

In the following 'presidential systems', a president, rather than a monarch, is the head of government. However, presidential systems in the MENA tend to be very different from those in republics in the West. While the apparatus for civil society participation may be present, such as parliaments, constitutions and elections, a closer analysis finds presidents serving 'for life' in systems dominated by a single political party that they control. Legislatures tend to be weak. In some cases, the 'president' is simply a title used by the authoritarian ruler.

Egypt is a classic example of a presidential republic dominated by a long-serving executive. Egyptian president Hosni Mubarak became president in 1981 following the assassination of then president Anwar Sadat. Mubarak, as vice-president, took office. Since 1981 martial law has been in effect in Egypt, which triggers suspension of many of the civil rights guaranteed by the constitution.

Until 2005, the Egyptian president was nominated by the People's Assembly, and affirmed by the electorate by referendum. In May 2005 a constitutional amendment established multi-candidate elections for presidency. Mr Mubarak easily won the first such election in September 2005 with 88.6 percent of the vote against an independent candidate, Ayman Nour (see Chapter 10). Despite the change in electoral practice, there are strong indications that Mubarak's son, Gamal Mubarak, is being groomed to succeed his father. This speculation is fueled by the fact that Mubarak has never appointed a vice-president.

The legislature is composed of two houses. The People's Assembly (*Majlis al-Sha'ab*) contains 454 seats; 444 of these are elected by popular vote for five-year terms; the other ten members are appointed by the president. The other chamber, the Advisory Council (*Majlis as-Shura*), contains 264 members; 176 are elected while eighty-eight are appointed by the president. Its function is only consultative.

Though Egypt has technically a multi-party system, all parties must be approved by the government. The National Democratic Party dominates political life; in the 2005 elections it won 311 seats in the People's Assembly. The government's main opposition, the Islamist Muslim Brotherhood, is banned as a political party, though it runs candidates as independents. Islamists, especially the Muslim Brotherhood, are playing an increasing role in Egypt's electoral politics (see Chapter 10).

In *Tunisia*, the president, Zine El Abidine Ben Ali, has ruled since 1987, supported by the dominant party, the Democratic Constitutional Rally (RCD). Changes to the constitution have raised the number of five-year terms Ben Ali can serve from two to five; he was most recently re-elected in 2004. Though the election technically has multiple candidates, Ben Ali regularly wins 95 percent of the vote. The prime minister and the cabinet are appointed by the president.

Tunisia has a bicameral legislature. The Chamber of Deputies (*Majlis al-Nuwāb*) contains 189 seats; members are elected by popular vote for five-year terms. All citizens over the age of 20, except active-duty military, can vote. The Democratic Constitutional Rally currently holds 152 of the 189 seats.

The upper house of the legislature, the Chamber of Councillors (*Majlis al-Mustashārīn*), was established by changes to the constitution in 2002 and formed in 2005. Eighty-five of its 126 members are elected by professional associations, trade unions, mayors and municipal counselors. The remaining forty-one are appointed by the president. All members serve six-year terms.

Tunisia has tight restrictions on freedom of speech and severely limits opposition politics. The Islamic fundamentalist party al-Nahda (Renaissance) is outlawed. As a result of Tunisia's economic stability and high level of development relative to neighboring countries, Ben Ali receives widespread popular support.

Algeria specifically bans political parties based on religion, ethnicity, language or race differences. This policy is an attempt to control political aspirations of Islamist groups and Algeria's ethnic minorities, especially the Berbers. Though more than forty parties exist, the National Liberation Front (FLN), with roots in wresting Algeria's independence from France, dominates.

The president, currently Abdelaziz Bouteflika, can serve two five-year terms, and is elected by universal suffrage of those aged 18 or above. The president appoints both the prime minister and the cabinet. Algeria's bicameral parliament consists of a National People's Assembly (*a-Majlis Ech-Chaabi al Watani*) and the Council of Nations, or Senate. The National People's Assembly has 389 seats; its members are elected by popular vote to five-year terms. A third of the Senate's 144 members are appointed by the president; the remainder are elected by indirect vote of municipal and regional representatives. Senators serve six-year terms.

Algeria is recovering from a brutal civil war touched off by the first multi-party elections in 1991. These elections followed decades of one-party rule in which all parties except the FLN were outlawed. In December 1991 the

Box 3.2

PRESS RESTRICTIONS: TUNISIA AND THE WORLD SUMMIT ON THE INFORMATION SOCIETY

Many, if not most, of the governments in the Middle East and North Africa restrict the freedom of the press to varying degrees. The holding of the UN-sponsored World Summit on the Information Society (WSIS) brought an unwelcome spotlight on Tunisia's restrictions on the press and access to information in books and on the Internet.

The goal of the World Summit on the Information Society was to promote global access to information and bridge the 'digital divide' separating rich and poor countries. In November 2005, the second conference in the WSIS series was held in Tunisia.

Concern had been raised prior to the conference over Tunisia's human rights record and heavy-handed restrictions on freedom of the press and of assembly. Specifically, critics cited the restriction of the free circulation of books; each title must be approved by the Ministry of the Interior prior to publication. Banned books included those dealing with human rights and democracy.

Government control over access to the Internet was a further cause for alarm. All Internet service providers in the country were nationalized in 2004; the government now regulates the content of websites and blocks those of which it does not approve. Banned websites include those relating to human rights, as well as hotmail. The government also monitors so-called 'over-active' Internet-users. Tunisia is ranked last in terms of cyber-freedom.

The mere viewing of certain websites is punishable with imprisonment; hundreds have been put in jail for viewing websites the government says promote terrorism. In December 2003 the government passed the 'Law on Terrorism', which has been used broadly as a means to suppress dissent. Internet and telephone communications of journalists, opposition members, human rights activists and Islamists are monitored. Journalists and critics of the government are subject to intimidation, harassment and imprisonment.

In advance of the summit, the government banned gatherings of representatives from Tunisia and foreign associations attempting to organize a 'Citizens' Summit' to address issues on the WSIS agenda. Conference attendees who had made reservations at hotels and restaurants to hold meetings found that the venues were 'no longer available'. During the summit journalists and human rights advocates were harassed; a French journalist was stabbed by unknown individuals shortly after he reported on local human rights protestors.

US Department of State. Bureau of Democracy, Human Rights and Labor, *Country Report on Human Rights Practices,* Tunisia, 2005, released March 8, 2006: http://www.state.gov/g/drl/rls/hrrpt/2005/61700.htm.

Tunisia: Alongside a World Summit the police ban a gathering of international and Tunisian associations. Human Rights Watch. November 14, 2005. More information at: http://hrw.org/doc/?t= mideast&c=tunisi.

---

religion-based Islamist Salvation Front won the first round of the elections, prompting the military to cancel the second round and forcing then president Benejedid to resign. Civil war broke out, with violence between government troops and Islamic militants. More than 160,000 people were killed, including many civilians. The Algerian experience is an example of the way in which returning *muhajadeen* from Afghanistan have played a role in radicalizing local Islamist groups. (This issue is addressed in greater depth in Chapter 7.) Conflict subsided in 1998; the following year the current president was elected.

In *Yemen*'s presidential system, the president is elected for a seven-year term. There must be at least two candidates, both endorsed by parliament. All citizens over the age of 18 have the right to vote. The current president is Ali Abdullah Salih; he was originally elected in 1999 and is the first president to hold office since North Yemen and South Yemen unified in 1990. Abdullah Salih had served as president of North Yemen from 1978 to 1990. The president appoints the vice-president, the prime minister, deputy prime ministers and the cabinet.

Yemen has a two-house legislature. The House of Representatives has 301 members, elected by popular vote. Multiple political parties exist, but the General Peoples Congress (GPC) is dominant and holds an absolute majority in the House of Representatives. Opposition politics is often led by the Islah Party, which has a strong tribal and Islamist identity. Members serve six-year terms. The 111 members of the Shura Council are appointed by the president.

The *Syrian* president, Bashar al-Assad, presides over a parliamentary system dominated by the Ba'ath (meaning 'renaissance') party. Bashar al-Assad assumed power in 2000 following the death of his father, Hafez al-Assad, who held power between 1971 and 2000. As candidates for president, both men ran unopposed in referendums to confirm their rule. As in Egypt, a state of emergency has been in effect since 1963 and is used to justify the government's far-ranging security powers that repress any political opposition.

Political power in Syria is tightly held by the president and a close circle of advisors who hold government positions, including the cabinet, or Council of Ministers, appointed directly by the president. The Ba'ath Party (officially known as the Arab Ba'ath Socialist Party) dominates political life; its role in ruling Syria is guaranteed in the constitution. The president, who serves a seven-year term, is also the secretary general of the Ba'ath Party. The principles of Ba'athism, a political philosophy founded by a Syrian Christian and a Syrian Sunni, emphasize secularism, socialism and Arab unity.

The legislature is the unicameral People's Council (*Majlis al-Sha'ab*), directly elected by all citizens aged 18 or over. The Ba'ath Party holds two-thirds of the seats in a coalition with a number of approved minor parties. Members of the People's Council serve four-year terms,

though the body has little authority. Eighty-three seats are reserved for workers and peasants.

Colonel Mummar al-Qadaffi, the leader of *Libya*, does not use the title of president; rather he is the 'Brother Leader and Guide of the Revolution', a reference to the revolution he led in 1969 that overthrew King Idris. Since the revolution al-Qadaffi has exercised absolute power in Libya, adhering to an ideology that blends Islamist and socialist thought, published in his 'Green Book'.

Libya's revolutionary roots are reflected in the governmental structure. A Revolutionary Command Council contains the surviving members of the original twelve leaders of the revolution. A cabinet, the General People's Committee, is elected indirectly through 'people's committees' at the local and regional levels. The head of government is the secretary of the General People's Committee, who serves as prime minister.

Officially, Libya is a *jumhūriyya*, or a 'republic of the masses'. Local People's Congresses exist in each of 1500 urban districts, in thirty-two regional-level congresses and in the National General People's Congress. The General People's Congress serves as a legislative branch, though it has very little actual authority. Political parties are not allowed.

In effect, all power is held by Colonel al-Qadaffi, who runs a strong security apparatus to minimize opposition. Libya has had difficult relations with the West. In 1992, UN sanctions were imposed following Libyan involvement in the explosion that brought down Pan Am flight 103 over Lockerbie, Scotland. These sanctions were lifted in 2003 following Libya's decision to eliminate its program to produce weapons of mass destruction and a settlement in the Lockerbie case. Currently, Libya is trying to normalize its relations with the West. A recent rise in Western tourists is one manifestation of this effort.

Parliamentary systems

A handful of states in the MENA have more fully developed parliamentary systems in which members of the parliament as well as a head of government (typically a prime minister) are directly elected by the populace. The role and function of the parliaments vary, but they generally exercise more authority than those under presidential systems.

In *Lebanon* the parliamentary system is modified to guarantee representation of the major confessional (i.e. religious) groups in the country. This confessional system reflects the tension that religious differences have played in Lebanon's politics. Changes were made to Lebanon's political system under the Taif Accord that ended Lebanon's civil war. Under this system the president must be a Maronite Catholic Christian, the prime minister a Sunni Muslim, the deputy prime minister an Orthodox Christian and the speaker of the parliament a Shia Muslim. The role of the president is largely ceremonial; the prime minister functions as the head of government.

The parliament contains 128 seats, equally divided between Christians and Muslims. Elections are held every four years; however, they could not be held during much of Lebanon's civil war. The parliament nominates the prime minister, who is officially appointed by the president. Lebanon's parliament has the authority to approve laws and expenditure for the state.

Lebanon has many political parties. Parties tend to be affiliated with a particular confessional group, though secular parties also exist, or a single charismatic leader such as the former prime minister Rafik Hariri, who was assassinated, possibly with Syrian involvement, in 2005.

Hezbollah, which is classified by the United States as a terrorist organization, is also a political party in Lebanon; it holds fourteen seats in the parliament. Presently there is much instability in Lebanese politics as a result of rising Shia power, a protest movement known as the Cedar Revolution following the Hariri assassination and military conflict with Israel in summer 2006 (see Chapter 11).

Turkey may be the most democratic and secular political country in the region. Its secularism and its commitment to democracy are guaranteed in the constitution, which also specifies the indivisibility of the Republic and the Turkish nation. These principles are a reflection of modern Turkey's creation out of the remains of the Ottoman Empire and the influence of Mustafa Kemal, who sought to create a modern, secular Turkey, free from ethnic separatism (to the detriment of minority rights). This tradition of secularism, highly unusual for the region, means that women cannot wear the *hijab*, or Islamic headscarf, in government jobs or institutions, including schools. As a parliamentary democracy, the president, elected by parliament for a seven-year term, is largely ceremonial. Governing authority is held by the prime minister, who is aided by a Council of Ministers.

A 550-member unicameral legislative body, the Grand National Assembly of Turkey (*Turkiye Buyuk*

Box 3.3

THE TAIF ACCORD: REBALANCING LEBANESE POLITICS

The Taif Accord, signed in Saudi Arabia on October 22, 1989, ended the Lebanese civil war (1975–90), though fighting continued for another six months. In doing so, it rebalanced Lebanese politics, shifting power away from the majority Christian population that had been given privileged status under the 1943 National Pact, which set the country's governing structures. In the decades after independence, Lebanon's Muslim population grew rapidly owing to both higher rates of natural increase than the Christian population and a large influx of Palestinian refugees. Though no census

had been conducted since 1932, it seems clear that the Christians no longer had a majority.

Specifically, the Taif Accord reduced the authority of the presidency, held by a Maronite Christian, and increased the powers of the Sunni prime minister. The size of the legislature was increased to 108, and evenly divided between Christians and Muslims. Similarly, the cabinet was divided between the two faiths.

The Accord also called for the reassertion of Lebanese sovereignty in southern Lebanon, which had been

Millet Meclisi), is elected by popular vote for five terms. Women in Turkey received the right to vote in 1934. Turkey has a multi-party system, though only parties that receive 10 percent of the vote are represented in parliament. In the last election there were over fifty political parties, though approximately ten of them receive the bulk of popular support.

Currently, the dominant party in the parliament is the Justice and Development Party (AKP). The victory of the AKP in the 2002 parliamentary elections was notable as the AKP can be described as a 'moderate' Islamic party. It does, however, respect Turkey's secular democratic tradition; its policies focus on support for the urban and rural poor and on economic growth. The current prime minister, Recep Tayyip Erdogan, is a former mayor of Istanbul.

The military plays a high-profile role in Turkey and is charged with protecting the constitution and ensuring the unity of the state. In this way it acts against religious extremism and ethnic separatism, and is a very trusted institution. In attempts to combat religious extremism and ethnic discord Turkey implements harsh restrictions on speech that supports 'separatism', such as statements on rights of the minority Kurdish population or that implicate Turkey in the death of Armenians during World War I. These press restrictions complicate Turkey's ongoing efforts to achieve membership in the European Union.

Like Turkey, *Israel* is a parliamentary democracy, but religion plays a large role in politics. Israel is explicitly the homeland for the Jewish people – a designation sometimes at odds with the minority rights of the Israeli Arabs who make up approximately 20 percent of the population.

Israel has a rich and varied system of political parties, which reflect the diversity of Israeli society in which secular and religious Jews from a variety of national origins seek political expression. The primary political body is the 120-seat Knesset, elected every four years. Seats in the Knesset are allocated according to the proportion of the vote that each party receives. As no single political party achieves the majority of the Knesset, all governments have been coalition governments. The head of the coalition serves as the prime minister, who is the head of government and rules, with the assistance of the cabinet, selected by the prime minister and approved by the Knesset.

In the most recent elections (May 2006), the Kadima party won the largest share of the vote (22 percent), and formed a coalition with Labor (15 percent), GIL and Shas. Over thirty parties put forward candidates in that election; twelve parties gained enough seats to be represented in the Knesset. Because of the need for the winning party to form a coalition to control the majority of seats necessary to govern and pass legislation, smaller parties such as the religiously conservative Shas

Box 3.4

TURKEY: THE STRUGGLE FOR SECULARISM AND AGAINST EXTREME NATIONALISM

In Turkey, the current struggle over two major issues, secularism and the limits of nationalism, will have great significance for the country's future.

Secularism has been a defining characteristic of the modern Turkish state, first articulated under the leadership of Mustafa Kemal, also known as Ataturk. This secularism has been secured both by the country's legal structure and by the historic willingness of the military to step in and guarantee this principle.

In May 2007, Turkey erupted in widespread pro-secularism demonstrations. Millions of people marched to oppose the ruling Justice and Development Party, a moderate Islamist party, from appointing one of their own as president. The military also issued a warning regarding their readiness to defend secularism.

In response the party reaffirmed its commitment to the secular ideals of the Turkish Republic, moved up legislative elections and withdrew its candidate for the presidency. The party, however, continues to promote a conservative social agenda that supports wearing of the Islamic headscarf, religious schools and restrictions on the sale of alcohol.

A move away from secularism could undermine Turkey's membership discussions with the European Union.

Restriction on freedom of speech, particularly that which 'harms the nation', is a further complication in Turkey's effort to demonstrate its commitment to human rights. Journalists and writers have been intimidated and prosecuted, often in connection with statements that acknowledge the existence of the genocide of a million Armenians in Turkey between 1915 and 1923. The government of Turkey has long denied that the deaths constitute genocide.

In 2006, Orhan Pamuk, Turkey's best-known novelist, was put on trial. His works include *The Black Book* and *My Name Is Red*. The charge was 'insulting Turkishness' for his statements regarding the mass killings of Armenians in Turkey during World War I. The charges were later dismissed. Later that year Pamuk was awarded the Nobel Prize for Literature, further raising his status as a public figure in Turkey.

Mr Pamuk is now living in the US, with some observers claiming that he is in exile out of concern for his safety. In January 2007 an ethnic Armenian journalist who had labeled the killings of Armenians as genocide was killed by a Turkish nationalist. The killer also issued threats against Mr Pamuk.

In her novel *The Bastard of Istanbul*, the author Efif Shafak claimed that Armenians were massacred. Her work also crossed the line regarding sexual taboos and usage of certain language. She, too, was charged, but acquitted, of 'Insulting Turkishness'. The novelist, a professor at the University of Arizona, fears for her safety.

Both of these issues, secularism and the rise of extreme nationalism, threaten internal political stability in Turkey as well as the country's bid for European Union membership.

Bilefsky, D. (2006) 'Turks seething over French bill; dispute taints pride over Nobel honor'. *International Herald Tribune*, October 16.

Bosman, J. (2007) 'Novelist endangered by her book'. *New York Times*, February 10.

and United Torah Judaism or special-interest parties are able to exercise greater political influence than their share of the vote would indicate. If a coalition falls apart, as it did in both 1999 and 2001, the government falls and early elections are required.

Traditionally, two parties have dominated Israeli politics: the left-wing Labor Party and the right-wing Likud. Both are secular in orientation. The current ruling party, Kadima, was an offshoot of the Likud, created by Ariel Sharon; its platform explicitly embraced the concept of territorial concessions to the Palestinians in order to resolve the Israeli–Palestinian conflict, such as the Gaza disengagement plan. Tzipi Livni is currently the acting Prime minister. If she is able to successfully form a coalition government she will become the second female prime minister of Israel. The Knesset also elects a president, who serves a largely ceremonial role for a seven-year term. The current president is Moshe Katzav.

The Knesset has broad governing powers, including the power to enact legislation, as long as it does not contradict Israel's Basic Law. Currently Israel does not have a constitution, though a draft is in preparation. Israeli law has numerous sources, including Anglo-American law, European law and Jewish law.

Iran has officially been an Islamic republic since the Islamist-led revolution in 1979 that overthrew the US- and UK-backed Pahlavi dynasty (see Chapter 6). Religion, and the religious establishment, controls Iran's political system. The most powerful figure is the Supreme Leader, currently Ayatollah Ali Khamenei. Literally translated as 'sign of God', an *ayatollah* is an expert in the interpretation of Shia law. As commander-in-chief, he controls Iran's military and intelligence system. The Supreme Leader is chosen by an Assembly of Experts, a group of eighty-six highly respected clerics (religious leaders) who serve eight-year terms, giving the religious establishment extensive control over political authority.

The Supreme Leader influences politics through the appointment of six of the twelve members of the Council of Guardians, which is responsible for interpreting Iran's constitution, the 'Fundamental Law' (*Qānūn-i Asāsi*), and may veto parliament and parliamentary candidates. He also appoints the head of the judiciary.

The president of Iran is elected by universal suffrage every four years. Candidates must be approved by the Council of Guardians, and must support the ideals of the Islamic revolution. The president oversees the day-to-day governing of Iran, including setting a legislative agenda and representing Iran in the foreign policy arena. The president appoints a twenty-one-member Cabinet of Ministers, although candidates for the posts of minister of defense and of intelligence must be approved by the Supreme Leader, who controls the military.

Iran's unicameral legislature, the Islamic Consultative Assembly (*Majlis Shura-ya Melli*), contains 290 members, who serve four-year terms. All candidates for the *Majlis*, as well as all legislation, must be approved by the Council of Guardians.

In the 1990s a political reform movement grew in Iran, backed by widespread popular support. A reformist president, Muhammad Khatami, as well as a moderate parliament were elected. During this period of political openness, Iran increased its overtures to the West; but in the aftermath of 9/11 the West adopted a hard-line policy toward Iran, dubbed a menber of the 'Axis of Evil' by the American president. By 2004, the conservatives had re-established control over the reform movement.

States in transition

At present, Iraq and the *Palestinian Territories* (West Bank and Gaza) must be considered 'states in transition'; their status will be discussed in greater detail in later chapters.

Though the creation of an independent Palestinian state has been the focus of peace-making since 1991, an agreement that would establish permanent peace between Israel and the Palestinians has not yet been achieved. At present the Palestinian Authority, the Palestinian governing body for the West Bank and Gaza, is deeply divided between supporters of Hamas and supporters of Fatah. The result is a further breakdown of the already weak government institutions inside the Occupied Territories. Though the Gaza disengagement gave the Palestinian Authority control over Gaza, Israeli military presence remains. In the West Bank, Israeli soldiers man checkpoints and roadblocks. In both territories Israel is able to control the passage of individuals as well as of goods in and out, with negative economic consequences for the Palestinians.

The construction of the separation barrier (i.e. fence or wall) further isolated the West Bank economically and had an impact on a future peace settlement. In sum, despite the Gaza disengagement, the West Bank and Gaza remain dependent territories occupied or controlled by Israel and have not achieved sovereignty or statehood.

Iraq, too, is in transition. In 2003 the United States led a coalition to overthrow the regime headed by Saddam Hussein (see Chapter 11). Hussein had ruled as 'president' since 1979, though the political system was highly authoritarian. Aside from the Ba'ath party, no political parties were allowed, and dissenters were dealt with harshly and usually eliminated. Hussein was a member of the Sunni minority, who exercised rule over the majority Shia as well as over the Kurds.

Following the war, the US led the creation of a new political system in Iraq. Constitutionally, Iraq is a democratic federal republic. In its multi-party system, candidates are elected to serve in a 275-member National Assembly. Political parties are based largely on religious or ethnic affiliation. The National Assembly elects the presidency council and the prime minister. In the most recent, and only, elections for the National Assembly, held in December 2005, Shia-affiliated parties won 113 seats. These parties chose Nuri al Maliki to be prime minister. The National Assembly also selects the presidency council, which must make decisions unanimously. The current president of Iraq is Jalal Talabani, a Kurd; one vice-president is Sunni, the other Shia.

Though Iraq now technically has a government, it has been unable to establish control over the country as a whole, or even over the capital, because of attacks by Sunni militants, many of whom poured into Iraq following the ouster of Hussein. Regular clashes between Sunni militants and Shia militias further undermine the security situation. The rise of sectarian strife has taken a high toll on the civilian population, with estimates of civilian dead exceeding 65,000 in June 2007 (www.iraqbodycount.org).

In sum, though 'sovereign', Iraq remains occupied by US troops (albeit at the 'invitation' of the US-backed government), with growing violence, now being dubbed civil war, and concerns about the break-up of Iraq,

growing Shia and Iranian influence, and destabilization of the region overall (see Chapter 11).

CONTINUITY AND CHANGE IN POLITICS

The political systems in the MENA are simultaneously characterized by continuity and change. For example, monarchies such as Bahrain and Kuwait, as well as presidential systems like Egypt, have established continuous rule for decades. And yet none of these systems has been static; all have had, to varying extents, to adapt to changing circumstances. In some cases change in the governmental systems is driven from the top down, through the decision to implement reforms or scale back public participation; in other cases, the government has had to respond to societal pressure for change.

The coming decades are likely to witness greater changes in the region's political systems in response to the debate over the role of religion in politics and new demands by civil society. Though the Iranian revolution stands as a stark reminder of the capacity for drastic change within a single country's government, it seems likely that change will take place within the current systems, rather than through the overthrow of existing regimes and the establishment of new forms of government. Such changes will likely be in response to societal pressures that have been building up within these societies, in some cases for more than a decade.

SUMMARY OF MAIN POINTS

- States in the MENA face enormous challenges as a result of their historical development and economic and social conditions.
- Despite these challenges, the state system has been remarkably stable in the last half century.
- The governmental systems of Middle Eastern countries are quite varied and are undergoing change in response to societal pressures.
- It is necessary to examine the actual functioning of a political system to understand where true

QUESTIONS FOR DISCUSSION

1 How would the challenges that states face differ between the Middle East and the United States and/or Europe?

2 What historical factors have influenced the development of the contemporary state system in the MENA?

3 This chapter has organized the region's states into 'types', such as presidential and parliamentary. Are there other possible ways to categorize these states?

4 Based on this brief introduction, which types of state system(s) offer the greatest opportunities for civil society participation?

5 In what ways does religion affect the structure of political systems in the region?

SUGGESTIONS FOR FURTHER READING

Anderson, L. (1986) *The State and Social Transformation in Tunisia and Libya, 1830–1980*. Princeton, NJ: Princeton University Press. Traces the development of Tunisia and Libya from the pre-colonial to independence.

Central Intelligence Agency (2007) *CIA World Factbook*: https://www.cia.gov/cia/publications/factbook/index.html. Provides regularly updated descriptions of political systems in each country, including current head of state.

Derbyshire, J. D. (2000) *Encyclopedia of World Political Systems*. Armonk, NY: Sharpe Reference. Provides brief overviews of governmental systems in a comparative format.

Doran, M. (2004) 'The Saudi paradox'. *Foreign Affairs*, January/February. Discusses the growing crisis within Saudi Arabia and the tension between reformist elements and the religious establishment.

Dresch, P. (2005) *A History of Modern Yemen*. Cambridge: Cambridge University Press. A socio-political history of modern Yemen, both before and after unification.

Herb, M. (1999) *All in the Family: Absolutism, Revolution and Democracy in the Middle East Monarchies*. Syracuse, NY: State University of New York Press. A deeply insightful analysis of the governing systems in the Gulf monarchies.

Hinnebusch, R. (2001) *Syria: A Revolution from Above*. London: Routledge. Focuses on the formation and development of Syrian politics under Ba'athism.

Hudson, M. (2001) 'The Middle East'. *PS: Political Science and Politics*, 34: 801–4. An introduction to major themes investigated by political scientists working on the Middle East, including the role of the state, civil society and democratization, the role of religion and identity politics.

Keddi, N. (2006) *Modern Iran: Roots and Results of a Revolution*. New Haven, Conn.: Yale University Press. Traces the development of modern Iran in the nineteenth and twentieth centuries, including the 1979 Islamic revolution.

McDermott, A. (1988) *Egypt from Nasser to Mubarak: A Flawed Revolution*. London: Croom Helm. Examines the development of Egypt's presidency since independence.

Owen, R. (2004) *State, Power and Politics in the Making of the Modern Middle East*, 3rd edn. London: Routledge. Provides an overview of the contemporary political system in the region and its emergence.

Springborg, R. and Bill, J. A. (1999) *Politics in the Middle East*, 5th edn. London: Longman. Overview of the region's politics and political systems.

4

HISTORICAL FOUNDATIONS

The origins of the modern Middle East and North Africa can be traced directly to the development and spread of Islam in the seventh century. Islam created not only a new religious community, but also vast and complex empires. The institutions and achievements of these empires created a legacy that still influences the modern era (Map 4.1).

THE PRE-ISLAMIC MIDDLE EAST

The Middle East has a long and rich pre-Islamic history. In ancient times, the Middle East, in the area known as Mesopotamia, was home to the first settled human civilizations. Around 7000 BCE, settled agricultural developments appeared along the fertile floodplains of the Tigris and Euphrates rivers.

By 3000 BCE trade flourished, and sizable cities began to form. In the ancient Mesopotamian city of Sumer, language was first written, which later developed into cuneiform. The Sumerian city Ur, located in modern Iraq, was thought to be the world's largest city in 2000 BCE, with a population of 65,000. To the west, in Egypt, a civilization ruled by pharaohs lasted for over 3000 years, leaving behind temples and pyramids at which the world still marvels today. Here, too, a complex

writing system, hieroglyphics, developed which may indeed be as old as, or older than, cuneiform.

In addition to writing, these ancient civilizations created systems that would have a lasting impact on humanity, including money, bureaucracy, long-distance trade, legal codes, and styles of art and architecture. Critical religious concepts, such as the belief in one god, and the linkage between religion and politics in the form of divine or divinely inspired rulers, also formed at this time.

The ancient Middle East was characterized by a series of successive and often overlapping empires, including Sumerians, Babylonians, Assyrians, Hittites, Elamites and ancient Israelites. Contact between these empires ensured that the region had a rich exchange of peoples and ideas as merchants, soldiers, scholars, religious leaders and others moved from place to place within this dynamic center of human contact. As the ancient period came to an end, much of the Middle East became incorporated into the Roman Empire, its rich agricultural land fed Rome's European subjects, and an extensive trade network criss-crossed the Mediterranean coast. Greek and Latin culture left its imprint in the form of architecture, such as the Roman amphitheaters found throughout the region, and, more importantly, in the

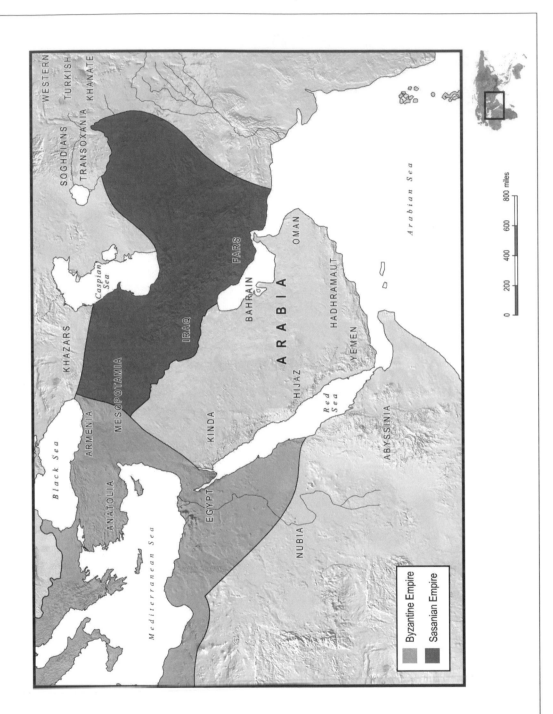

Map 4.1 The Middle East on the eve of Islam

ideas of Greek and Latin scholars that were known throughout the region. Arab scholars would later save, and expand upon, much of the knowledge recorded in their classic texts.

On the eve of Islam, long after the ancient empires had given way to new ones, the western half of the world was controlled by two forces: the Byzantines and the Sasanians. In 395 the Roman Empire was split into eastern and western halves. The eastern portion, known today as the Byzantine Empire, was based in Constantinople (Istanbul). Though the western empire, based in Rome, fell in 476 CE, the Byzantine Empire, in decline, lasted until the coming of the Ottoman Empire in 1453.

The Byzantine Empire was a multi-ethnic empire of Greek-speaking peoples who followed the empire's official religion, Greek Orthodox Christianity. By the time of Islam's appearance, the Byzantines controlled Italy, Greece and the Balkans in Europe, as well as the Anatolian peninsula, the Levant, Egypt and the coast of North Africa as far as modern Tunisia.

To the east, the Sasanian Empire controlled what is today Iran, Iraq, Afghanistan, Armenia and parts of Turkey, Syria, Central Asia and Arabia. The empire encompassed Persian-speaking peoples of many ethnicities. On the eve of Islam the Sasanians were the latest in the series of empires, including the Achaemenids, which had established a 1200-year tradition of rule through a hereditary absolute monarch. The Persian-based Sasanian Empire, and its culture, left a lasting impact on the region long after the empire converted to Islam. Many aspects of what is today considered Islamic civilization have their roots in this empire.

Sasanian achievements included the formation of a strong centralized government and associated bureaucracy that controlled a vast territory unified by adherence to Zoroastrianism. Though they fought the Byzantines, the Sasanians embraced Greek medicine and philosophy, providing refuge to persecuted Greek scholars. Decorative arts flourished: textiles, tapestries, as well as paintings and sculptures created by the Persians, were prized well beyond the borders of the empire.

Unsurprisingly, the Byzantines and the Sasanians, as previous empires had done, constantly fought each other for control of territory. Warfare became particularly intense in the century (540 CE–629 CE) before the coming of Islam. Soon both empires would come into conflict with an empire based on a new religion – Islam.

THE COMING OF ISLAM

In the town of Mecca, in the western Arabian province of Hijaz, a religious movement began that redefined the region and created new and more powerful empires. The Arabian peninsula is largely desert with little water except a few oases. Its inhabitants included the Bedouin, pastoralists who raised camels, sheep or goats, or grew grain or dates in the desert oases. The towns, small compared to those in the empires, were home to traders and craftsmen.

Of these, Mecca was the most important center of trade. Here the Bedouin, though less numerous than the townspeople, dominated the political structure. Their lifestyle was strongly marked by a distinctive culture which emphasized a code of honor and loyalty to one's kin group or tribe. The Bedouin illustrate one of the most important features of society in the Middle East and North Africa, both before and after the advent of Islam: the significance of family ties. Kinship groups formed the nucleus of society, regardless of the rise and fall of empires, and contained traditions to decide critical issues involving the allocation of resources, adjudication of disputes and protection from outsiders. In Mecca, the Quraysh tribe exercised political and religious control, and monitored the town's commercial activity. Their command over territory outside the towns allowed them to control the road that was the lifeblood of Mecca's commercial activity.

The dominant religious practice in pre-Islamic Arabia focused on polytheistic nature-objects and good and evil spirits. Family, kin groups and villages worshipped local gods, who were often embodied in natural features such as rock formations or trees. Some of these gods were quite well known and were the objects of pilgrimage from surrounding areas. The Ka'aba, in Mecca, was an important site for religious pilgrims, and a source of the town's income. The idea of one universal God was also known, having been introduced in ancient Israel (Judaism) and in Persia (Zoroastrianism). Christianity was also known among the Bedouin as two confederations of

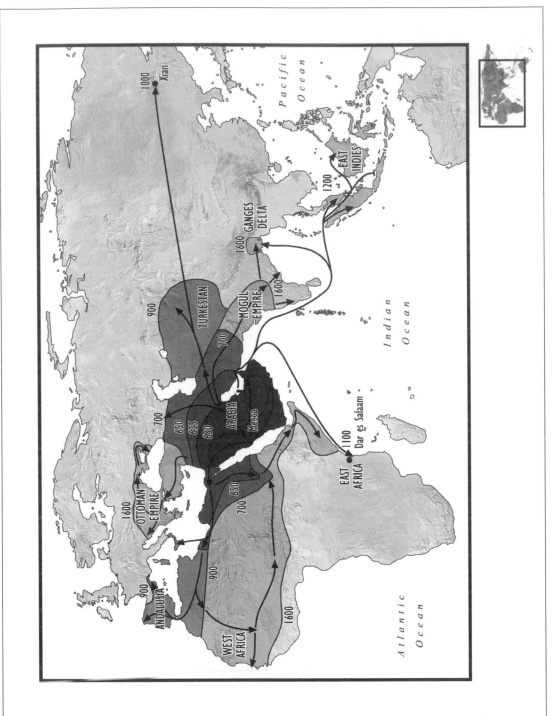

Map 4.2 The expansion of Islam

Christian Bedouin in the north of the peninsula served as clients for the Sasanian and Byzantine empires.

THE REVELATION OF ISLAM

According to tradition, the word of God (Allah) was revealed to Muhammad, between 610 and 632 CE, by the angel Gabriel. Muhammad ibn Abdullah was born in Mecca around 570 CE. His early life is unremarkable. Born into the Hashemite clan (a subtribe of the Quryash), he was orphaned as a child and raised by an uncle. He was respected for his skill in trade, and at a young age he married a wealthy widow, Khadijah.

As he neared 40, Muhammad's behavior changed. He left Mecca to meditate in the hills outside the city.

It is during one of these solitary vigils that Muhammad is said to have first heard God's message. On this night, known as the Night of Destiny, Muhammad was summoned to be God's messenger and to receive the word of God.

Over the next twenty-two years, until his death, Muhammad continued to receive revelations, which were later collected into a single work, the Qur'an ('Recitation'). This new religion became known as Islam ('submission'), its followers known as Muslims ('one who submits'). Islam emphasized devotion to a single god, Allah. For Muslims, the Qur'an, as it contains the word of God, is divine and unchangeable. The Qur'an is a source of guidance on appropriate behavior for a Muslim, including one's duty toward the weak

---

Box 4.1

THE FIVE PILLARS OF ISLAM

Michael Christopher Low

The five pillars of Islam, also known as *Arkān al-Islam* or *Arkān al-dīn*, consist of the five basic requirements considered obligatory for all Muslims. The Qur'an presents these requirements as a framework for both individual and communal worship and as a means of sustaining both the individuals and the community's commitment to the faith. Both Sunnis and Shias agree on the essential details involved in these five practices. The five pillars are:

Shahāda: witnessing the oneness of God and the prophethood of Muhammad

The *shahāda* involves two declarations. The first, 'There is no god, but God', is an affirmation of *tawhīd*, the belief in the unity of God, or monotheism. The second, 'Muhammad is the messenger of God', is an affirmation of one's submission to God through the acceptance of His message as revealed through the Prophet Muhammad. This declaration of faith marks one's entrance into the larger community of believers (umma) and is required of all converts to Islam.

Salāt: performing the five prescribed daily prayers

The performance of five daily prayers serves as public, physical evidence of the believer's continual submission to God and adherence to Islam. These prescribed prayers are to be performed just before dawn (*salāt al-fajr*), at noon (*salāt al-dhur*), in the mid-afternoon (*salāt al-'asr*), just after sunset (*salāt al-maghrib*), and in the evening (*salāt al-'ishā'*) between an hour after sunset and midnight. Prayers are to be made in a state of ritual purity (*wudū'*), achieved by either the performance of ablutions or a bath. Prayers must also be performed in the direction of the *qibla*, facing the Ka'ba in Mecca. Each set of prayers includes a prescribed cycle of movements, bows and prostrations, and a set formula of canonical prayers. From the initial utterance of *Allahu Akbar* ('God is greater than all else') and the recitation of the first chapter of the Qur'an, *Sūrat al-Fātiha*, to the concluding affirmation of the *shahāda*, this entire cycle is known as a *rak'a*. After the completion of the prescribed number of canonical prayer cycles, worshippers are then free to petition God directly.

Box 4.1

THE FIVE PILLARS OF ISLAM—CONT'D

Zakāt: contributing alms to provide assistance to the poor in the community

The third pillar is an alms tax, typically paid to a religious official, a representative of one's local mosque, or to a representative of the Islamic state. The alms tax is traditionally set at 2.5 percent or one-fortieth of the value of all liquid assets and income-producing holdings owned by the believer. These funds are used to feed the poor, encourage Islamic missionary activities, ransom captives, support travelers and pilgrims, support those undertaking religious works, and defend the faith. The alms tax is a reminder of one's broader social and charitable responsibilities to the Islamic community.

Sawm: fasting during the month of Ramadan

The fourth pillar is the observation of a fast from sunrise to sunset during the month of Ramadan, the ninth month of the lunar Islamic calendar. During this period, the faithful are to abstain from food, drink and sexual activity during the daylight hours. By deliberately sacrificing one's bodily desires for the sake of God, the fast is considered to be not only an act of purification, but also an affirmation of ethical awareness. This very real experience of pain and hunger over the course of the month-long fast is also a reminder of the sufferings endured by the poor. While personal self-sacrifice is one element of the fast, on a broader level the shared experience of suffering during the fast is also a powerful communal symbol, which unites the entire Islamic world.

Hajj: performing the pilgrimage to Mecca at least once in a lifetime

The fifth pillar is the pilgrimage to Mecca. All adult Muslims are obliged to perform the *hajj* at least once in their life, so long as they are physically and financially able. Each year during the first ten days of the month of *Dhū al-hijjah*, some two million Muslims descend upon Mecca and its environs to participate in a series of sacred re-enactments, physically and spiritually linking each pilgrim to their spiritual forebears. The nine essential rites of the *hajj* are: donning the *ihrām* (unsewn cloth symbolizing the humility and equality of all believers); the performance of the *tawāf*, or circumambulation of the Ka'ba; standing at the plain of Arafat; spending the night at Muzdalifa; throwing stones at three symbols of Satan at Jamra; sacrificing an animal in Mina; repetition of the circumbulation of the Ka'ba; drinking water from the well of Zamzam; and the performance of prayers at the Station of Abraham. These rituals underscore the unity of the global Islamic community and mark the zenith of one's spiritual life as a Muslim.

and orphaned. It also details how Muslims will be judged by God on the Day of Judgment. In addition to the Qur'an, which is the literal word of God, Muslims also look to Muhammad's life as an example of appropriate deeds and actions. The fundamental beliefs of Islam are embodied in the five pillars.

Muhammad's wife, Khadijah, was the first convert to the new religion. Over time a small community of followers developed including craftsmen, slaves, a few members of the Quraysh and other tribes. Soon Muhammad, who spoke out against worshipping idols such as those in the Ka'aba, and his followers posed a challenge to the existing religio-political power of the Quraysh tribe.

In 622, Muhammad and the Muslim community (umma) left Mecca for Yathrib (Medina) a hundred miles to the north. This event is known as the *hijra*, and it marks the beginning of the Muslim calendar. Muhammad had been invited to mediate in a costly blood feud amongst the town's tribes; in return he and his community were offered protection.

In Medina, Muhammad became known for his arbitration skills and he gained influence over the surrounding areas. Conflict with the Quraysh turned to open warfare, and Muhammad proved his skill in battle against a superior foe and disrupted the crucial caravan trade to Mecca. During this time, his followers grew, and by 630 CE the Quraysh had surrendered to Muhammad and his Muslim army. Muhammad was now the dominant political and religious leader in Arabia, extending his control over a wide area. Muhammad's success radically changed the traditional social order in the Hijaz, directly threatening the previously dominant Quraysh and their polytheistic religious system. This social revolution, which unified society, also undermined the traditional role of Mecca, which had served as a sanctuary (or *haram*) during the numerous clashes between tribes.

THE DEATH OF MUHAMMAD AND THE SUCCESSION

In 632, Muhammad died, leaving the Muslim community with no leader and no established mechanism for choosing a new one. The new leader was not to be a prophet, as Muhammad was, but the religious and political leader of the umma. The choice of Muhammad's successor would eventually cause a permanent schism in the Muslim community. Muhammad's companions, especially those followers who had converted to Islam early and had endured the community's *hijra* to Medina, elected Abu Bakr, Muhammad's father-in-law, to succeed Muhammad. Though other factions of the Muslim community accepted this decision, the issue would later resurface.

Abu Bakr's reign was quite short, lasting from 632 to 634 CE. He was succeeded by Umar (634–44), 'Uthman (644–56) and finally 'Ali (657–61). Collectively, these four leaders are known as the 'Rightly Guided Caliphs' (*Rashidun*). Their period of rule is looked upon by the Muslim community as a period of true Islamic rule in which the caliph was both the political and religious leader. During this period, the Muslim Arab armies enjoyed great success in their territorial conquests, defeating the Sasanians in 637. They soon challenged Byzantine control over territories in the Middle East,

taking Damascus in 635 and Egypt in 641. Despite the Muslims' success, the community was not without internal discord. Indeed, internal power struggles led to the death of Umar, 'Uthman and 'Ali.

Upon the death of 'Uthman, a power struggle re-emerged, amounting to a civil war within the Muslim community. 'Ali ibn Abi Talib (656–61), son-in-law and cousin of Muhammad, and second convert after Khadijah, claimed leadership. His claim was challenged by the governor of Muslim Syria, Mu'awiyah. They fought on the banks of the Euphrates river in modern Syria, though there was no clear winner. 'Ali set up a rival caliphate in Kufa, though he continued to lose support until his murder, possibly orchestrated by Mu'awiyah, in 661. This event created a permanent schism in the Muslim community between the minority who saw 'Ali as the rightful successor, the Shia (followers of 'Ali, Sh'atu 'Ali), and those who followed Mu'awayah, Sunni ('people of the tradition').

Despite this internal schism, Islam spread rapidly during this period. Its spread was facilitated by the Muslims' military success, especially against the weakened Byzantine and Sasanian empires. Moreover, as the monotheistic ideas of Islam were not alien to former subjects of Greek or Iranian rule, the transition to Muslim rule was eased.

ABBASID AND UMAYYAD CALIPHATES

With the death of 'Ali, and the end of the era of the *Rashidun*, the Muslim world entered a period of expansionist, hereditary empires. The first of these was the Umayyad dynasty (661–750 CE), established by Mu'awiyah and based in Damascus (Map 4.3). The Umayyad territory continued to expand. By the first half of the eighth century, Muslim armies had entered southern Spain, crossing North Africa. To the east, the caliphate included Iran and as far as modern-day Pakistan.

With such a vast empire to rule, internal conflict is unsurprising. Though the Umayyads now controlled a territory populated by peoples of many ethnicities and backgrounds, those of Arab descent were given pre-eminence and made up the ruling elite. The mistreatment

Box 4.2

SHIISM: 'THE OTHER ISLAM'

Michael Christopher Low

While most Western descriptions of the Islamic and Arab worlds tend to focus their attention almost exclusively on Sunni Islam, Shiism is often ignored or described as a kind of aberration in the course of Islamic history. This is perhaps to be expected, given that the vast majority of the world's 1.3 billion Muslims are Sunnis. Conversely, Shias number from 130 million to 195 million or 10–15 percent of the total number of Muslims worldwide. However, as Vali Nasr points out in *The Shia Revival: How Conflicts within Islam Will Shape the Future* (2006), across a wide swath of the Islamic world's core territory, from Lebanon to Pakistan, the Sunni and Shia populations are roughly equal. Moreover, Nasr also reminds us that in and around the 'economically and geostrategically sensitive rim of the Persian Gulf, Shias constitute 80 percent of the population'. Indeed, with Iran pursuing nuclear technology and possibly nuclear weapons, Hezbollah's recent military success against Israel, and the emergence of Shias as the dominant sectarian force in the post-Saddam Hussein Iraq, Nasr and many others have prophesied the emergence of a crescent of Shia domination and political influence stretching across Lebanon, Syria, Iraq, Iran, and even over the Arab Shia populations of the Gulf states. Such estimates have sent American intelligence officials, think-tanks and universities scrambling for a deeper understanding of this previously overshadowed 'other Islam'.

The rift between Shias and their Sunni counterparts is of course the most basic and important division in the history of Islam. This schism dates back to the earliest days of Islam and the succession crisis that followed the Prophet Muhammad's death in 632 CE, when Abu Bakr, the Prophet's close friend and father-in-law, was elected as his successor, or *khalīfah* (caliph). This election was carried out according to Arab tribal customs in which a council of elders would endeavor to reach a consensus (*ijmā'*) as to who was the most senior and respected member of the community. According to Sunni thought, the Prophet's successor need not have any divine qualities. Rather, he would merely need

to be an exemplary Muslim capable of handling the community's religious and political affairs. However, a small circle of the Prophet's companions, the *Shī'at 'Alī* (literally, 'partisans of 'Alī'), believed that 'Alī ibn Abi Tlib, the Prophet's cousin and son-in-law, was more qualified to lead the young Muslim community. The early Shias claimed that the Prophet had chosen 'Alī as his successor and had made his wishes clear while preaching to a congregation at Ghadīr al-Khumm (an oasis between Mecca and Medina) during his return journey from the famous 'Farewell Pilgrimage'. It was there that the Prophet is said to have taken 'Alī by the hand and proclaimed that 'whoever recognizes me as his master (*mawlā*) will recognize 'Alī as his master'. Thus, for Shias, the *shahāda* (or declaration of faith) is 'There is no god but God and Muhammad is his Prophet, and 'Alī is the executor of God's will'.

Despite these claims, the Sunni consensus prevailed, and the partisans of 'Alī, and even 'Alī himself, accepted the caliphate of Abu Bakr. Abu Bakr was succeeded by Umar ibn al-Khattab, by 'Uthman ibn Affan and finally by 'Alī. Sunnis refer to these first four caliphs, whose successive reigns stretched from 632 to 661, as the Rightly Guided (or *Rashidun*) caliphs. All of these men had been among the close companions of the Prophet. For Sunnis, this era is seen as a golden age, an era when the bond between political and spiritual legitimacy remained intact and the Muslim community remained true to the values of the Prophet's message. However, Shias believe that, even though 'Alī was eventually elected as the fourth caliph, the initial usurpation of his right to rule by Abu Bakr, Umar and 'Uthman was a grave mistake.

Shias believe that, just as the Prophet had guided the earliest Muslims, subsequent generations would also need the help of holy or divinely inspired persons in order to ensure that Islamic society is conducted as God intended. Shias believe that only 'Alī and his descendants possessed these necessary qualities. These descendants are believed to bear the light of Muhammad (or *nūr-i Muhammad*) and are considered

Box 4.2

SHIISM: 'THE OTHER ISLAM'—CONT'D

as his trustees or inheritors (*wāsi*). Thus, these descendants, collectively known as *imāms* (not to be confused with the ordinary clerics who lead prayers at the mosque), are believed to understand the most esoteric inner truths of the faith. As a result of these beliefs, Shias argue that only those who have the blood of the *Ahl al-Bayt* (the Prophet's family) running through their veins are fit to lead the Islamic community.

In 661, 'Alī was assassinated after a turbulent caliphal reign, which included both a rebellion led by Aisha, Abu Bakr's daughter and the Prophet's wife, and a civil war sparked by Mu'awiyah, the governor of Damascus and cousin of 'Uthman. After 'Alī's death, Mu'awiyah assumed the caliphate and founded the Umayyad dynasty (661–750). While Sunnis accepted Mu'awiyah, despite his lack of religious authority, Shias rejected Umayyad rule, under which the caliphate was effectively transformed into a monarchy and religious and political legitimacy were separated. Shia dissent eventually came to a head at the battle of Karbala (in present-day Iraq) in 680, when the forces of the second Umayyad caliph, Yazid, slaughtered 'Alī's son Husayn and seventy two of his family members and companions. Husayn's refusal to recognize the legitimacy of Umayyad rule was shared by the people of 'Alī's capital, Kufa (also in Iraq, near Najaf), many of whom were liberated slaves and Persian prisoners of war who resented the distinctly Arab character of Umayyad rule.

Following the martyrdom of Husayn at Karbala, Kufan resistors were never again able to mount a direct threat to Umayyad rule. However, Husayn's martyrdom transformed Shiism into a form of moral and spiritual resistance, which eventually spawned its own theology and spiritual ethos. Husayn became the Shia standard-bearer and a symbol for courage in the face of tyranny, but more importantly his martyrdom helped imbue Shia devotional practices with a passion altogether different from that of their Sunni counterparts. As a result, Karbala became the holiest shrine of Shiism, and the annual rites of mourning Husayn's martyrdom, known as *Ashura'* (the tenth day of the month of Muharram), became the most important religious ceremony of the Shia religious calendar.

While Shias have never enjoyed a majority status in the Islamic world, they have enjoyed favorable conditions under the Buyyids in Baghdad and Iran (945–1055), during which time major collections of Shia *hadith* were compiled and Shia legal thought began to take shape. Scholars of the Fātimid, Mongol, Safavid and Qajar periods also made major contributions to the development of Shia literature, philosophy and theology.

Today there are three main branches of Shiism: the Zaydis, the Ismā'ilis and the Ithna 'ashariyyah. The Zaydis (followers of Zayd ibn 'Alii ibn al-Husayn) are located in Yemen, Iraq and parts of Africa. The Ismā'ilis (Seveners) take their name from the seventh *imam*. They flourished during the Fatimid period in Egypt (909–1171) and represent an esoteric interpretation of Shiism. Finally, the Ithna 'ashariyyah (Twelvers) are most numerous among the three Shia branches. They believe in twelve *imams*, beginning with 'Alī and ending with the *Mahdi* or *Imam al-Muntazar* (the expected or awaited one), who is believed to be in a state of occultation and is expected to return at the end of time as the messianic *imam* responsible for restoring justice and equality on earth. During the Safavid period (1501–1732), Twelver Shiism became the state religion of Persia. Even today, Twelver Shiism is the official religion of modern Iran. Moreover, Twelver theology was the foundation upon which Ayatollah Ruhollah Khomeini formed his political ideology and around which the government of the Islamic Republic of Iran was built in the wake of the Islamic Revolution in 1979.

Momen, M. (1985) *An Introduction to Shi'i Islam: The History and Doctrines of Twelver Shi'ism*. New Haven, Conn./London: Yale University Press.

Nasr, V. (2006) *The Shia Revival: How Conflicts within Islam Will Shape the Future*. New York/London: W. W. Norton.

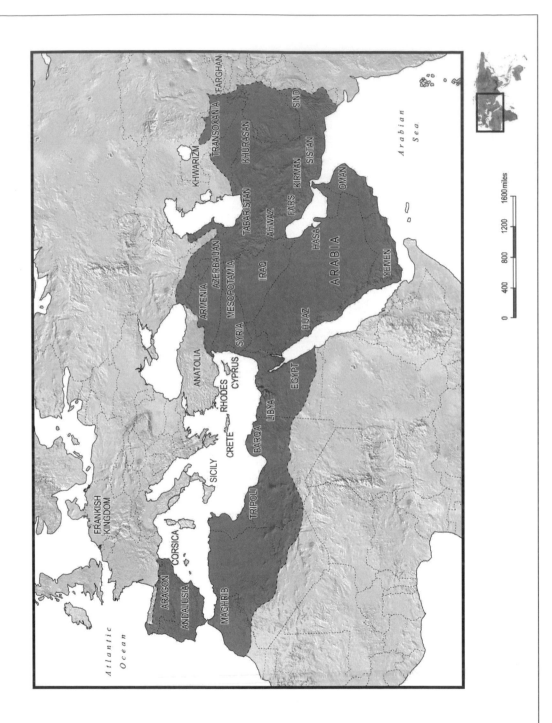

Map 4.3 The Umayyad Empire

Box 4.3

IBN BATTUTA: THE MUSLIM MARCO POLO OR THE GREATEST TRAVELER IN WORLD HISTORY?

Michael Christopher Low

In both Europe and the United States, Marco Polo (1254–1329) has typically been regarded as the pre-modern world's greatest traveler. Even in the minds of young school children, the mere utterance of his name has become synonymous with exploration and adventure. Such acclaim is undoubtedly an expression of the immense influence that travel literature has wielded in shaping the West's conception of its place in world history. However, Polo's enduring fame may also be a lingering expression of the Eurocentric worldview generated by Europe's recent past of colonial domination throughout the globe. As a result of its colonial expansion from the sixteenth to the twentieth centuries, the West gradually came to presume its superiority over other civilizations and has accordingly regarded itself as the prime mover of world history. Thus, the history of Western civilization has often been presented as an acceptable representation of world history in general, leaving important figures from other civilizations virtually ignored.

Perhaps no case illustrates this point more vividly than the life of Abu 'Abd Allah Muhammad ibn 'Abd Allah al-Lawati al-Tanji Ibn Battuta (1304–68/9). Among travelers of the pre-modern era who left a written record of their exploits, including Polo, Ibn Battuta is unrivaled for distance traveled and sights seen. The account of his travels across vast stretches of Africa and Eurasia, from 1325 to 1354, is among the most valuable records of the medieval world. His *Rihla* (book of travels) reveals both the extent and the cosmopolitan nature of the Islamic civilization that lay at the heart of the dense networks of cross-cultural exchange linking nearly all parts of the Eastern Hemisphere during the fourteenth century.

Born in Tangier, Morocco, during the time of the Marinid dynasty, Ibn Battuta was reared in a family renowned for its legal scholarship. He received training in law, literature and religious sciences – an education befitting an Arab gentleman and member of the *ulama*, the Muslim learned class. In 1324, Ibn Battuta left his native Morocco to perform the *hajj*, the pilgrimage to Mecca. While he appears to have intended only to make the pilgrimage and study Islamic law in Cairo or one of the other centers of Islamic jurisprudence, instead he embarked upon a twenty-nine-year odyssey, covering some 120,000 kilometers across parts of North and West Africa, Arabia and East Africa, Central Asia, India, Southeast Asia, and even as far as China.

Ibn Battuta's motives for travel were multi-faceted. First and foremost, he traveled as a pilgrim. He performed the *hajj* six or seven times during his lifetime. As with many other scholars and merchants from throughout the Islamic world, Mecca became a hub for Ibn Battuta's journeys. As Ibn Battuta's *Rihla* illustrates, pilgrimage provided not only the impetus for travel but also access to a network of personal and professional contacts that would allow further exploration of the Islamic world. Second, he traveled in order to advance his training in Islamic law, attending lectures in Damascus and Mecca. While Mecca is without rival as the religious epicenter of the Islamic world, the *hajj* also fostered the emergence of cosmopolitan gateway cities, such as Baghdad, Cairo and Damascus, along the pilgrimage routes. As a result, pilgrimage often entailed lengthy sojourns in these cities, making them contact zones for cross-cultural exchanges of goods and ideas between the Islamic heartland and its frontiers. Third, he traveled as a Sufi devotee, exploring the more mystical aspects of Islam. As a result, his travels are punctuated by frequent visits to living scholar-saints as well as to the tombs of deceased ones from which he sought to benefit from the divine blessings associated with them. Fourth, he traveled in search of employment. Displaying the piety, dress, manners and educational background shared by the *ulama* class, wherever he traveled Ibn

Box 4.3

IBN BATTUTA: THE MUSLIM MARCO POLO OR THE GREATEST TRAVELER IN WORLD HISTORY?—CONT'D

Battuta was granted access to the homes and palaces of the rich and powerful. In Delhi, he was handsomely rewarded for his service as both a judge and the administrator of a royal mausoleum in the employ of the Turkic Muslims who ruled the Delhi Sultanate at the time. He even served as a judge for a short time in the Maldive Islands.

Upon returning to Morocco, Ibn Battuta is reported to have served as judge in an as yet unspecified Moroccan town. While he is traditionally thought to have been buried in his native Tangier, other evidence suggests that his remains may lie in Anfa, a port town buried beneath modern Casablanca. What is certain about Ibn Battuta's later years is that he spent some time in Fez, where he wrote an account of his adventures in collaboration with a young scholar, Muhammad Ibn Juzayy (1321–56/8). Their collaboration resulted in the *Rihla*, formally titled 'A Gift to the Observers Concerning the Curiosities of the Cities and the Marvels Encountered in Travels'. Ibn Battuta's *Rihla* is among the best-known examples of an influential genre of Arabic travel writing that flourished in North Africa and Muslim Spain between the twelfth and fifteenth centuries. Though normally centered on the pilgrimage to Mecca, such accounts also provided readers with rich depictions of the various peoples, places and pious institutions of the Islamic world.

Ibn Battuta's *Rihla* circulated in manuscript form among the educated elite of North Africa during the fourteenth century and in West Africa, Egypt and beyond in subsequent centuries. Following the French occupation of Algeria, several copies of the *Rihla* were discovered by French scholars, which led to the publication of the Arabic text and a French translation between 1853 and 1858. Since then, the *Rihla* has been translated into numerous languages. Moreover, Ibn Battuta has become widely known and written about in the West.

The *Rihla* is of immense historical value, documenting observations on almost every conceivable aspect of both Muslim and non-Muslim societies throughout Afro-Eurasia, including topics as diverse as education, politics, trade, geography, religion, gender relations and slavery. In addition to factual descriptions, its author reveals much of his personal attitudes and opinions in colorful anecdotes ranging from talk of disease and piracy to blizzards and banditry. We are even privy to details about his twenty-three marriages and the estimated seventy children he fathered.

The *Rihla* also provides a record of the relative political calm that prevailed over much of North Africa and Eurasia during the mid-fourteenth century, an age before European exploration and expansion. This was a world dominated by the Mongols. When Ibn Battuta began his journey, four great Mongol states, three of which were Muslim, ruled over most of Eurasia. At the same time, the Mamluks in Egypt, the Delhi Sultanate in North India, and the empire of Mali in West Africa – all Muslim states – dominated much of the rest of the known world. The dominance of the Mongols and Islamic civilization in North Africa and Eurasia also points to the fact that during the fourteenth century Europe was little more than a cultural backwater. This also sheds light on a key difference between the journeys of Ibn Battuta and Marco Polo. Whereas Marco Polo was a 'stranger in a strange land', visiting lands well beyond the borders of his own civilization, places where Europeans had never been and were virtually unknown by local inhabitants, Ibn Battuta's journey took place almost exclusively within a culturally integrated Islamic world, where Islamic rule and customs reigned supreme. Thus, while Marco Polo's journey to China is often heralded as the precursor of the age of European exploration and imperial expansion, as Ibn Battuta's account illustrates, these events were far from a foregone conclusion in a world dominated by Islamic civilization.

of non-Arab subjects led to uprisings. At the same time the empire faced significant external military challenges from the Byzantines, Turkic peoples to the east and India.

Weakened by internal and external conflict, the Umayyads were overthrown by the Abbasids in 750 CE. Though nearly all of the ruling family was killed, a prince, Abd ar-Rahman, escaped and founded a new Umayyad dynasty in Muslim Spain. There, in Andalusia, a magnificent culture flowered well beyond the end of the Umayyads in Spain until 1031 CE.

Under the Abbasids (AD 750–1258), the capital shifted from Damascus to Baghdad (Map 4.4). The Abbasids focused not on the further expansion of the empire's territory but on its internal development.

Box 4.4

AL-ANDALUS: A MUSLIM HERITAGE IN EUROPE

For eight centuries, southern Spain was under Muslim rule, leaving a rich cultural legacy. At its greatest extent, Muslim-controlled territory on the Iberian peninsula, known as al-Andalus, covered much of Spain, Portugal and parts of southern France. The Muslims on the Iberian peninsula were commonly called Moors by Europeans.

Muslim rule was first established in Iberia in 711 CE by representatives of the Umayyad caliphate, based in Damascus. This first Muslim empire expanded rapidly; after sweeping across North Africa, it sought to expand into southern Europe. The caliphate in Damascus found it difficult to control its governor in distant Iberia. By 740 CE an independent ruler had taken control. Yet, through an odd twist of fate, the Umayyads would regain control of al-Andalus.

In 750, the Baghdad-based Abbasid Empire overthrew the Umayyad caliphate. The last surviving member of the royal family, Abd ar-Rahman I, made his way to al-Andalus. There, in 756, he overthrew the local leader and declared himself emir of Cordoba. At Cordoba, he and his successors created a rival caliphate and built a civilization based on learning, science and tolerance unequalled by any in Europe.

During its Golden Age (*circa* 912–1031 CE) Cordoba, with a population of 500,000, was a leading cultural center, designed to rival the famed 'House of Wisdom' in Baghdad. Scholars in fields such as mathematics, astronomy and medicine, writing in Arabic, then the international language of science, made significant advances. Poets, musicians, historians and even scholars from Christian Europe all came to Cordoba seeking its intellectual opportunities. It was here that the works of Greek philosophers such as Averroes (Ibn Rushd) and Avicenna (Ibn Sina) were translated, commented on, and eventually transmitted to Christian Europe, laying the foundation for the Renaissance.

While Europe was struggling through a period of economic and intellectual poverty, known as the 'Dark Ages', al-Andalus was prosperous; Cordoba came to be known as 'the ornament of the world'. Menocal (2002: 32) describes what travelers to the city would have seen:

> First the astounding wealth of the caliph himself and of his capital, then the 900 baths and tens of thousands of shops, then the hundreds or perhaps thousands of mosques, then the running water from aqueducts, and the paved and well-lit streets.

The caliph's library, one of seventy in the city, reportedly held 400,000 books. At the time the largest library in Christian Europe probably held only 400. The Muslims also created a vast educational system of universities and teaching hospitals. The rich architectural heritage created under Muslim rule is still evident in southern Spain today. The Alhambra, a vast fortress, looks down on the city of Granada. In Cordoba, the Mezquita, once the second-largest mosque in the world, is now a Roman Catholic cathedral.

Box 4.4

AL-ANDALUS: A MUSLIM HERITAGE IN EUROPE—CONT'D

Perhaps the most notable feature of al-Andalus was its religious tolerance. Andalusian society included Christians, Muslims of various ethnic origins, and Jews. Mozarabs were Christians who, while retaining their religious observances, adopted many aspects of Arab culture and language. As *dhimmis,* or 'people of the book', Christians and Jews had a protected minority status guaranteeing them certain rights and privileges. Though the extent of religious tolerance in Andalusia remains a subject of debate among scholars, Andalusia had a flourishing Jewish community. While Jews faced growing persecution in Christian Europe, many Jews joined the Jewish community in Andalusia where they played an active role in commercial, scholarly and political life.

Military conflict between Muslim al-Andalus and Christians to the north was nearly constant during the centuries of Muslim rule. Slowly, the Christians, waging the Reconquista, regained control over the entire peninsula. The Muslim presence finally ended in 1492 after the conquering of Granada by Catholic rulers Ferninand and Isabella, perhaps best known for sponsoring Christopher Columbus' voyage that discovered the New World.

Lunde, P. (2004) 'Science in Al Andalus'. *Saudi Aramco World*, 55: 20–7.
http://www.saudiaramcoworld.com/issue/200407/science.in.al-andalus-.compilation.htm.

Menocal, M. (2002) *The Ornament of the World: How Muslims, Jews and Christians Created a Culture of Tolerance in Medieval Spain*. Boston, Mass.: Little, Brown.

They developed administrative, bureaucratic, legal and commercial systems to manage the empire's great wealth and large population more effectively and efficiently.

Their 500-year rule was characterized by political stability and economic growth. This allowed the creation of a high Islamic civilization, noted for its intellectual and scientific contributions and urban-based cosmopolitan life. Even the wars waged by Christian forces did little to undermine prosperity.

A key factor in the Abbasid success was their embrace of non-Arab cultural elements within their empire, and recognition of the equality of all Muslims. In Baghdad, they came in contact with Persian administrative practices, adapting them for their own use. The palace library, known as the 'House of Wisdom', welcomed scholars persecuted by other empires. Their intellectual advancements in medicine, philosophy, mathematics and literature created an unprecedented period of high intellectual and cultural development, often known as the Golden Age of Islam. This knowledge, accumulated at a time when Europe was experiencing the 'Dark Ages', would later spark the European Renaissance.

Under the Abbasids some authority was devolved to local leaders as some territories became independent principalities. Most significantly, the Mamluks, a military caste originally composed of slave soldiers who had served the Umayyad caliph as well as the Abbasid, established independent control over Egypt in 1250. Similarly, power over other territories in North Africa was ceded to local rulers.

INFLUENCE FROM THE STEPPES: THE MONGOL AND TURKIC INVASIONS

At the same time, influences from the east were exerting greater influence in the traditional Arab/Islamic heartland. In 1055 the Seljuks seized control of the caliphate in Baghdad, and exercised administrative and military leadership. The Seljuks, though of Turkic origin, were Persian-speaking and had established control over

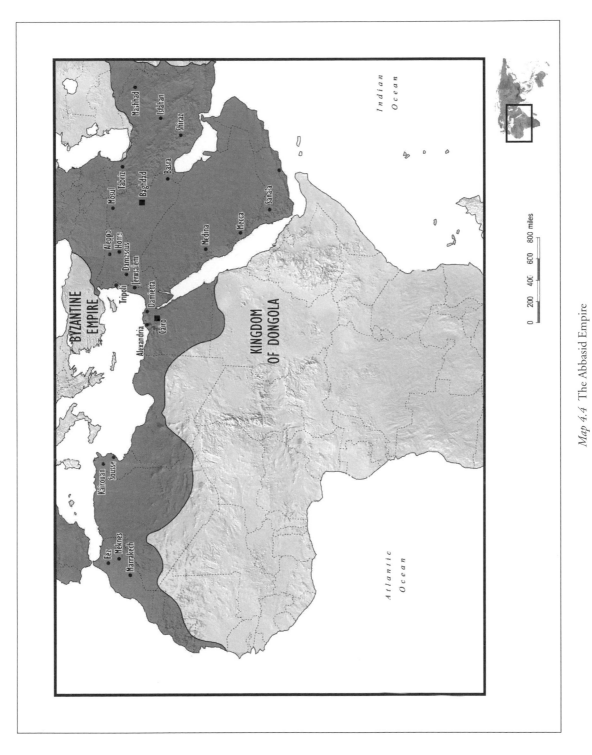

Map 4.4 The Abbasid Empire

BYZANTINE EMPIRE

KINGDOM OF DONGOLA

Indian Ocean

Atlantic Ocean

Mashhad
Isfahan
Shiraz
Mosul
Tabriz
Baghdad
Basra
Samara
Aleppo
Homs
Damascus
Jerusalem
Tripoli
Damietta
Mecca
Medina
Cairo
Alexandria
Kairouan
Sousse
Fez
Meknes
Marrakech

0   200   400   600   800 miles

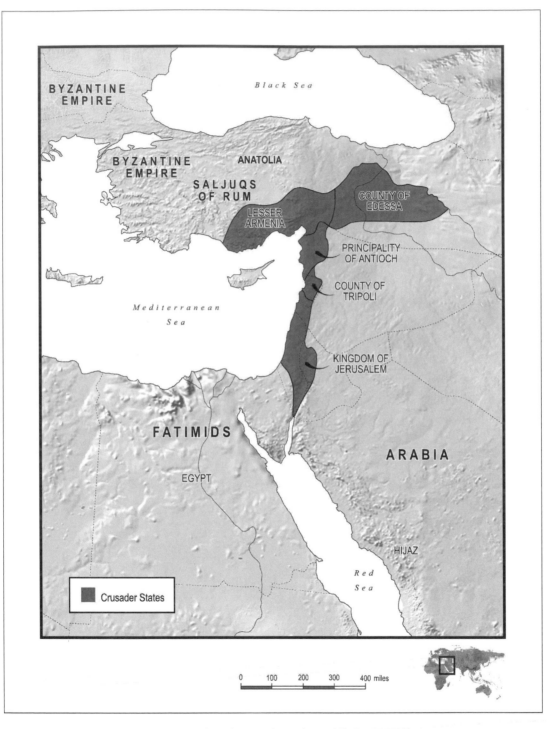

Map 4.5 The crusades in the Middle East

Box 4.5

AN ARAB PERSPECTIVE ON THE CRUSADES

The Crusades were a series of military campaigns carried out by various Christian armies against Muslim empires in the Middle East between 1095 and 1291. The Crusades focused particularly on Jerusalem and the surrounding 'Holy Land'.

The Byzantine Christian Empire first lost control over Jerusalem in AD 614 when the Persia-based Sassanid Empire expanded into the area. With the coming of Islam later in the century, Islam became the dominant political and social force. For the next 300 years, however, Muslim rule did not disrupt the arrival of Christian pilgrims in Jerusalem, and Christian communities continued to live in the holy city.

A number of factors contributed to the launching of the Crusades in the eleventh century. The growing success of Muslim military campaigns against the weakening Byzantine Empire in the east was a growing concern for the Christian religious and political leadership in Western Europe. Europe was also experiencing a wave of religious zeal, under which soldiers of the Church, including those who fought in the Reconquista of Spain, received indulgences, or remission for their sins. News of the destruction of Jerusalem's Church of the Holy Sepulchre, the site of Jesus' crucifixion, by the Fatimid caliph Al-Hakim in 1099 was received with horror by Christian Europe. This destruction underscored the need to liberate the Holy Land.

The First Crusade, sanctioned by the Roman Catholic pope, had been launched in 1095 following a plea from the Byzantine Empire. By all accounts the arrival of armed Westerners, or 'Franks' or 'Franjs' as they were known by the Muslims, came as quite a surprise. To the Muslims, the invaders were barbarians, and the Crusades were not seen as a threat by the Seljuk Turks and their successors.

In 1099 the Franks succeeded in capturing Jerusalem and reclaiming it for Christianity.

Arab historians recorded the events (Maalouf 1984: xiv):

> Two days later, when the killing stopped, not a single Muslim was left alive within the city walls.

Some had taken advantage of the chaos to slip away, escaping through gates battered down by the attackers. Thousands of other lay in pools of blood on the doorsteps of their homes or alongside the mosques.

The fate of the Jews of Jerusalem was no less atrocious. ... Re-enacting an immemorial rite, the entire community gathered in the main synagogue to pray. The Franj barricaded all the exits and stacked all the bundles of wood they cold find in a ring around the building. The temple was then put to the torch. Those who managed to escape were massacred in the neighbouring alleyways. The rest were burned alive. ...

Even the destruction of Jerusalem did not elicit a call to war against the Franks by the ruling Muslim empire, the Seljuk Turks. For the next two hundred years Muslim armies fought Christian invaders as new waves of 'soldiers of the Church' arrived. The Crusaders managed to establish control over some territory in the Levant, created Crusader mini-states and built fortifications in the European style. In 1187, Saladin recaptured Jerusalem. The unsuccessful Third Crusade (1189–92), led by Richard I of England attempted to reclaim it. Though the Christians managed to control Jerusalem for ten years in the mid-thirteenth century, it was back under Muslim control by 1243. With the failure of the Ninth Crusade (1271–2) and the fall of the Crusader states of Antioch, Tripoli and Acre, the religion-driven military expeditions ended.

Though the Crusades have a very central role in the collective Christian consciousness, their historical impact on the Muslim world was minor. Military threats from the east were always of far greater concern. The Crusader presence was short-lived, sporadic and geographically limited.

Maalouf, A. (1984) *The Crusades through Arab Eyes*. New York: Schocken Books.

the territory in Persia and much of Central Asia. The Abbasid caliphate was reunited and re-energized under Seljuk administration, which brought new administrative practices and a merging with Persian language and culture. The Seljuks' success was short-lived, however; by 1157 the empire was fragmenting, and strong centralized authority had given way to control of territory ruled by Seljuk princes and other dynasties. It was during this period of waning imperial control that the Christian leaders in Europe sent the Crusaders to re-establish control over Jerusalem. Their impact, however, was short-lived and paled in comparison to that of the Mongols.

The formal end of the Abbasids came at the hands of Mongol warriors from the steppes of central Asia who moved west, wreaking havoc in their path of destruction. In 1258, Hulagu Khan, son of Genghis Khan, seized Baghdad, captured and killed the Abbasid caliph, and ended the city's 500-year rule as the center of the Muslim world. The Mongols destroyed the great library; legend tells how the waters of the Tigris ran black with the ink from books flung into it. Mongol armies continued to hold territories in the Middle East through the fourteenth century, most notably under the armies of Timur Lang (known in English as Tamerlane). The Mongols invaded Iran, raided India, annexed Iraq, overran Syria and Anatolia, and mounted attacks on the Ottomans. After Tamerlane's death in 1405 the Mongol empire fragmented.

The Mongols' march westward was checked by the Mamluks. Once a slave military caste under the Ayyubids, who ruled Egypt between 1169 and 1250, the Mamluks overthrew the Ayyubids in 1250. The Mamluks defeated the Mongols, and established control over Syria and Armenia as well as over Egypt. The Mamluks also expelled the Crusaders and were the center for Sunni political and religious authority. At a time when much of the region had devolved to weaker, more local power structures, the Mamluks established the longest-lived Muslim state in the period between the end of the Abbasid rule and the rise of the Ottomans, who would take control of Mamluk territory in 1517 (Lapidus 2002).

The recovery from the Mongol devastation gave rise to the creation and consolidation of new empires – the Ottoman in the west and the Safavid in the east.

THE SAFAVIDS AND THE OTTOMANS

In the late thirteenth century, a member of the Safavid family, thought to be of Turkish or Kurdish origin, founded a Sunni Sufi religious brotherhood in Azerbaijan (northwestern Iran). The brotherhood expanded its influence into Anatolia and Syria, and successfully conquered the Christians in the Caucasus. In 1494 a 7-year-old boy, Ismail, succeeded his brother as head of the Sufi order. In a few short years he dramatically expanded Safavid control over territory and proclaimed himself king. Shortly thereafter he extended his control over eastern Anatolia and parts of Iraq, including Baghdad. His advances in eastern Anatolia were suppressed by the Ottomans, but the Ottomans were never able to lower their guard on their eastern flank.

At some point during Ismail's reign – the exact date is unclear – the Safavids adopted Shia (Twelver) Islam as the state religion. The Sunni Sufi brotherhoods were dissolved; anyone who refused to accept Shiism was killed. State-sponsored Shiism under the Safavids provided the environment for the growth of Shia legal thought and the creation of Shia religious practices which remain so important today.

The creation of dynasties led by the minority Shia in the midst of a region dominated by the far more numerous Sunni guaranteed the survival of Shiism and created a legacy for Shia-led states such as Iran in the modern world. Earlier, in Egypt, the Fatimids had established a Shia-led dynasty, but it failed to establish Shiism as a permanent presence there. For much of the second millennium, the Muslim world was largely divided between the Shia Safavids, in what is modern-day Iran, and the Sunni Ottoman Empire (Maps 4.6 and 4.7). The Safavid Empire lasted for over three hundred years, until the mid-eighteenth century, when it fell to anarchy. Its rival, the Ottoman Empire, survived even longer.

Further to the east, a Muslim Mughal Empire ruled most of India between the sixteenth and the eighteenth centuries. Though a detailed discussion of this empire is outside the scope of this text, the legacy of this empire is important for understanding the religious heterogeneity of the Indian subcontinent (Map 4.8).

Box 4.6

SHIA HOLY SITES IN IRAQ: KARBALA AND NAJAF

Michael Christopher Low

While many Americans and Westerners have become familiar with the names Karbala and Najaf as a result of the years of news coverage related to America's occupation of Iraq, most are still ignorant of the historical and spiritual importance of these two southern Iraqi towns. Indeed, some may only associate these places with frightening images of young American soldiers facing off against the 'fanatical' Shia militiamen of Muqtada al-Sadr's Mahdi Army. As a result, the golden domes of Shia Islam's holiest shrines have been reduced to nothing more than symbols of sectarian violence, insurgency and terrorism. Such views are extremely dangerous, however, because they ignore the intense spiritual influence that connects these towns with the hearts and minds of Iraqis, Iranians and Shias more generally.

While the *hajj* to the holy sites in Mecca and Medina is still an obligation for Shia Muslims, a *ziyārah* (pilgrimage other than the *hajj*) to Karbala and Najaf is considered almost if not equally as meritorious. In the wake of Saddam Hussein's ouster at the hands of American forces, Shias are once again free to mourn openly Imam Husayn's martyrdom, visit the sites associated with these events, and make pilgrimages to his tomb. While such expressions of piety by the Shia had been banned by Saddam Hussein's Sunni-dominated government, in many ways the center of gravity in the post-Saddam era has shifted to southern Iraq and the Shia majority. This has meant an increase in pilgrimage traffic both within Iraq and, more importantly, from Iran, as well as the re-emergence of Karbala and Najaf as pre-eminent centers of Shia scholarship and religio-political leadership.

Karbala is the site of Imam Husayn's martyrdom in 680. The shrine, around which the city has grown, is considered the holiest shrine of Shia Islam. The shrine was first constructed during the Buyyid period in 979. Today, there is also a domed shrine over the tomb of Husayn's half brother, 'Abbās. However, these shrines

have been destroyed several times by Sunni rulers, who like Saddam Hussein viewed these shrines as the epicenter of Shia resistance and millenarian hopes. The most famous of these Sunni demolitions occurred in 1801 at the hands of the Wahhabis of present-day Saudi Arabia. In the face of Sunni and other forms of oppression, Shia leaders, most notably Ayatollah Khomeini, have used Karbala as a religio-political symbol of human suffering and resistance to tyranny. The shrines have also served as a physical space of refuge for those fleeing political persecution at the hands of tyrannical Iraqi and Iranian regimes. From a spiritual perspective, Karbala also serves as a place of refuge for the aged and the dying, who await death there in the belief that the city is one of the gates of paradise promised to the faithful in the Qur'an.

Najaf is the site of Imam 'Alī's tomb, though the actual place of his burial is unknown. 'Alī was assassinated in Kufa. According to Shia tradition, it was his wish that his body be placed upon the back of a camel and the place where the camel kneeled was to become the site of his burial. Najaf, just four miles from Kufa, is reportedly that site. The city of Najaf is thought to have been founded by the Caliph Hārūn al-Rashīd in 791. While Kufa retained its role as the pre-eminent center of Shiism until the fifteenth century, it was eventually overtaken by Najaf. Like Karbala, the construction of tombs flourished under Buyyid supervision. As the number of pilgrims visiting the tombs grew, hospitals, schools, libraries and Sufi lodges were established around the shrine complex. As a result, Najaf became the epicenter of Shia theology and learning. However, it was eventually overtaken by the seminaries of Qom in Iran in the late nineteenth century. Some argue that this trend was reversed with the rise of Ayatollah Khomeini, who spent several years in exile in Najaf, and the Iraqi Ayatollah Muhammad Bāqir al-Sadr. Moreover, in the post-Saddam era, Najaf seems poised for a period of revitalization.

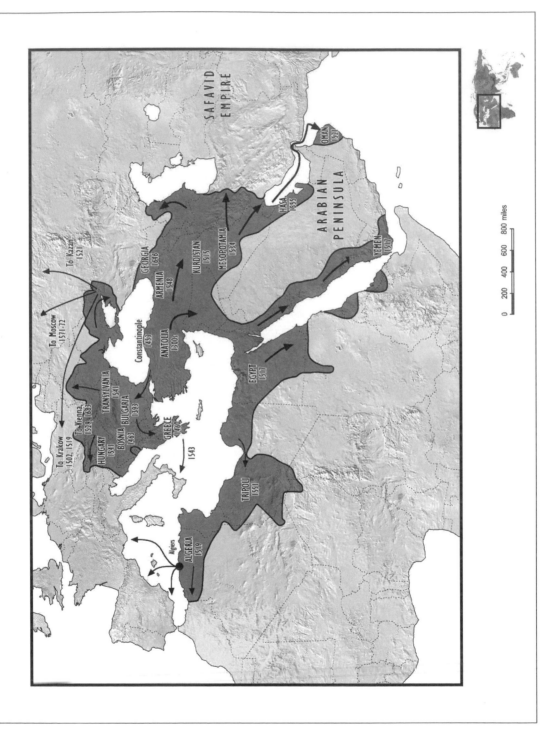

Map 4.6 The Ottoman Empire

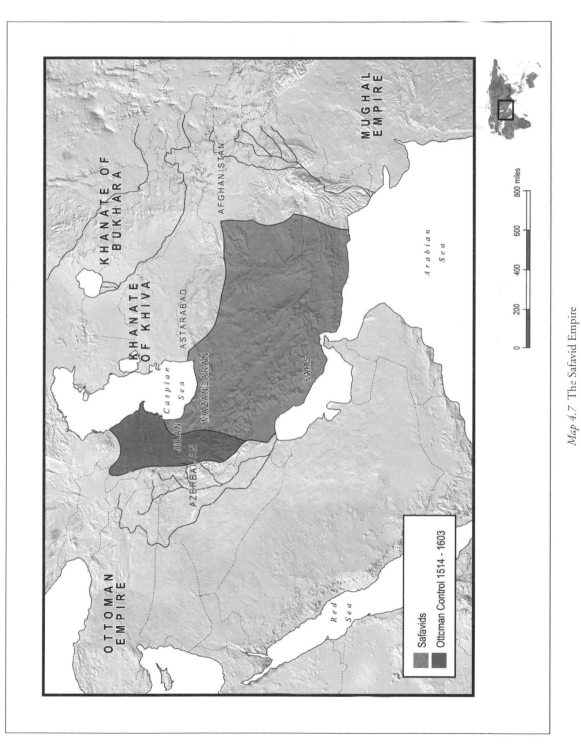

Map 4.7 The Safavid Empire

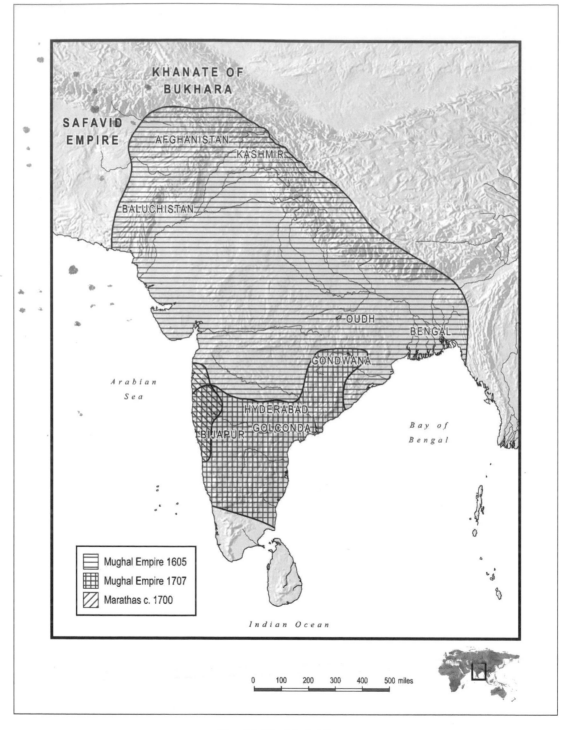

Map 4.0 The Mughal Empire

Box 4.7

THE TAJ MAHAL AND THE MUGHAL EMPIRE

Michael Christopher Low

In 1631, Mumtaz Mahal, the Mughal emperor Shah Jahan's favorite wife, greatly celebrated as an extraordinary beauty of her time, died during childbirth. Mughal chroniclers report that Shah Jahan was inconsolably racked with grief. As a symbol of his love and devotion, Shah Jahan commissioned the construction of a magnificent mausoleum for his deceased wife. While construction of the mausoleum began in 1632, the project was not completed until 1648.

For this project, Shah Jahan procured a virtual army of artisans from India, Persia and Central Asia. This synthesis of design styles blended and expanded upon previous Indian, Persian and Central Asian motifs in the creation of a distinctly Mughal or Indo-Persian architecture. This specific combination of influences reflects the legacy of the Mughal Empire's Mongol and Timurid ancestors. In particular, the tomb of Timur (or *Gūr-i Amīr*) in Samarkand may be seen as the initial template upon which Mughal monuments like Humayun's tomb and Shah Jahan's Jama Masjid (both in Delhi) were conceived. Each of these structures feature similar edifices crowned by bulbous domes. However, unlike these earlier examples of monumental Mughal architecture, which featured the use of red sandstone, Shah Jahan promoted the use of white marble lavishly inlaid with semi-precious stones in calligraphic and floral designs. Like other Mughal tombs, the grounds of the Taj Mahal complex also feature a *chahār bāgh* design (a Persian-style garden, divided into four parts), meant to evoke images of Paradise as described in the mystical Persian poetry favored by the Mughal court.

In many ways, the legendary yet tragic story of the Taj Mahal serves as a useful metaphor for the reign of Shah Jahan and the decline of the Mughal Empire more generally. Though Shah Jahan is generally credited with having expanded and consolidated the empire bequeathed to him by his ancestors and having presided over a period greatly admired as the golden age of Mughal art and architecture rivaling and arguably surpassing similar accomplishments by the Ottoman and Safavid empires, his reign was also marred by excessive financial expenditure and the bloody succession struggle which ensued when he became seriously ill in 1657. After defeating his three brothers in 1658, Shah Jahan's son, Aurangzeb, had his father imprisoned in the Red Fort at Agra. There, in a cell overlooking the Yamuna river and his beloved Taj Mahal, Shah Jahan would languish until his death in 1666. Meanwhile, Aurangzeb reversed the Mughal Empire's previous policies of religious tolerance, which had long helped to reconcile Muslim rule with India's cultural diversity. Aurangzeb's reign of religious orthodoxy and constant warfare laid the foundation for the Mughal Empire's eighteenth-century decline and destruction at the hands of smaller successor states and the British East India Company.

THE OTTOMANS

The Ottoman Empire, the last of the Muslim empires, left a dramatic imprint on the modern Middle East. Spanning over 600 years (1299–1922), the Ottomans traced their roots in the scattered Turkic peoples who lived on the fringes of the Byzantine Empire in the aftermath of the Mongol invasion. Following the fall of the Seljuk sultanate, the Mongols created smaller Turkish principalities – *beyliks* – headed by a *bey* ('chief') who swore allegiance to the Mongols. In 1299 one of these *beys*, Osman, declared independence from the Mongols while consolidating territory of surrounding feuding *beyliks*. Osman also enjoyed a series of military successes against the Byzantines, which attracted additional followers.

The Ottoman Empire is named for its founder, Osman.

Within a century the Ottoman state had expanded into the eastern Mediterranean and the Balkans. In 1453 it finally succeeded in capturing Constantinople, the symbol of Christendom in the east. The Ottomans then launched military campaigns deep into Europe, conquering Belgrade in 1523. The unsuccessful attempt to take Vienna, under the leadership of Suleyman ('The Magnificent'), shook Europe to its core. The Ottomans established control over Egypt, much of North Africa as well as Mesopotamia. At its greatest extent, in the sixteenth and seventeenth centuries, the empire spanned three continents. The empire contained nearly all Arab lands as well as some European and Persian territories. Ottoman success was a product of both strong leadership and military superiority. The Ottoman army was a professional military, rather than a conscripted force, that put gunpowder to its fullest use in mobile artillery units, earning its nickname as the 'Gunpowder Empire'. The navy was able to dominate the Mediterranean. Meanwhile, life in the empire flourished; Istanbul (formerly Constantinople), with a population of 700,000 in the seventeenth century, was larger than any city in Europe.

To maintain such a large empire the Ottomans developed a flexible administrative system, which undoubtedly contributed to the empire's longevity (Cleveland 2004). Administrative practices accommodated local customs and practices, which reduced the alienation of the subject populations. One such practice was the *millet* system whereby minority religious and ethnic communities were given significant local autonomy. Each *millet* was led by a national leader from that community, who reported to the sultanate. In exchange for loyalty to the empire, *millets* were allowed to follow their own laws and collect and distribute taxes.

The empire also applied uniform legal and administrative practices. Islamic law (*sharia*) was the legal code throughout the empire, applied by an administrative and court system. A professional civil service ran a huge and complex bureaucracy that oversaw the empire's affairs.

At the top of society was the sultan-caliph who ruled as an absolute monarch. Succession was hereditary, though not automatically to the eldest son. All of the sultan's sons were trained to assume rule, creating a situation in which brothers killed each other in order to assume the throne, though this practice had died out by the seventeenth century.

Ottoman society was highly stratified, but oddly dependent on the service of slaves at the highest levels of the military and civil service. The Ottomans ran a system for conscripting young men, the *devshirme* ('collecting'), instituted in the fourteenth century. Under this system, adolescent male children, often from European provinces, were taken to the capital and converted to Islam. They provided service to the empire at all levels, including the highest. Slaves were able to marry, and some were able to amass great personal wealth, though they were beholden to the sultan. For this reason, Christian families, and even poorer Muslim ones, sometimes sought to have their children enter the *devshirme*.

The *janissary*, the Ottoman army's professional standing infantry corps, was also composed of conscripts. This infantry was kept ready and well equipped at all times, housed in barracks and not allowed to marry. They were the most effective military unit in Europe.

Despite the size and strength of their empire, Ottoman power was checked by Safavids on their eastern border. The border between the two powers was not stable, but moved back and forth in the area of what is today modern Iraq. The result was to create a zone of substantial cultural heterogeneity, with the mixing of Sunni and Shia populations. The competition between the Sunni Ottomans and the Shia Safavids institutionalized a religious rivalry, the legacy of which exists today.

SUMMARY OF MAIN POINTS

- In ancient times, vast empires controlled the Middle East. Their intellectual contributions and practices left an imprint that influenced later development.
- The coming of Islam overturned the existing social order in the region and created a strong,

QUESTIONS FOR DISCUSSION

1 What facets of society in the pre-Islamic Middle East contributed to the successful spread of Islam?
2 In what way did Islam develop as both a political and a religious force?
3 How is the historical experience of the Shia community of significance today?
4 What factors contributed to the development of a Muslim 'Golden Age'? What is the significance of this period today?
5 How did the Safavid Empire lay a foundation for the creation of the modern state of Iran?
6 In what ways did the Ottoman Empire leave a lasting imprint on the Middle East?

SUGGESTIONS FOR FURTHER READING

Cleveland, W. (2004) *A History of the Modern Middle East*, 3rd edn. Boulder, Colo.: Westview Press. A comprehensive and authoritative history of the Middle East since the rise of Islam.

Cook, M. (2000) *The Koran: A Short Introduction*. Oxford: Oxford University Press. A concise and readable introduction.

Esposito, J. I. (2005) *Islam: The Straight Path*. Oxford: Oxford University Press. An introduction to Islam, including its historical development in the region.

Frye, R. (1975) *The Golden Age of Persia: The Arabs in the East*. New York: Barnes & Noble. The classic account of cultural transmission between Persia and the Arab world during the age of the Islamic empires.

Hourani, A. (1991) *A History of the Arab Peoples*. Cambridge, Mass.: Harvard University Press. An older, but classic, history of the region.

Imber, C. (2002) *The Ottoman Empire, 1300–1650: The Structure of Power*. New York: Palgrave. Examines change and transformation within the Ottoman Empire; note particularly the Tanzimat period.

Lapidus, I. (2002) *A History of Islamic Societies*. Cambridge: Cambridge University Press. Extensive history of the origin and spread of Islam across the globe and the civilizations linked to this expansion.

Maalouf, A. (1984) *The Crusades through Arab Eyes*. New York: Schocken Books. Using Arab sources, documents the activities of the Crusaders in the Middle East.

May, T. (2007) *The Mongol Art of War*, Barnsley: Pen and Sword Books. Analyzes the strategies and techniques that allowed the Mongols, known for their ferocity as warriors, to create an expansive empire.

Menocal, M. (2002) *The Ornament of the World: How Muslims, Jews and Christians Created a Culture of Tolerance in Medieval Spain*. Boston, Mass.: Little, Brown. Recounts the lost 'golden age' in southern Spain during the medieval period.

Moojan, M. (1985) *An Introduction to Shi'i Islam*. New Haven, Conn.: Yale University Press. An extensive history of Shiite Islam, from its origins to the present day.

5

THE MAKING OF THE MODERN MIDDLE EAST

The origins of the modern Middle East lay not only in the aftermath of the Ottoman Empire, whose territories were carved up and placed under European control, but in the growth of new ideas that emerged prior to World War I. Particularly important was the idea of nationalism and a desire for independence among local inhabitants in the region. At the same time European interests in the Middle East, economic and political, deepened. Indeed, though the Ottoman Empire spanned over 500 years, by the seventeenth century it was a decidedly different empire, in its form and function, from the one led by Suleyman that had challenged European control of Vienna.

THE TRANSFORMATION OF THE OTTOMAN EMPIRE

The 'decline' of the Ottoman Empire, once an accepted premise by scholars, is now a disputed issue. Instead, the reasons for Ottoman loss of dominance vis-à-vis Europe, and the internal challenges this created, must be understood. In the seventeenth century, the Ottoman Empire's territorial expansion was halted by growing European military strength. The Ottomans lost control of Hungary through conflict with the Hapsburgs and lost Black Sea territories to the Russians. At the same time, they had to guard their eastern flank against Safavid expansion.

The discovery of the New World profoundly changed the global economy and system of trade, to the detriment of the Ottomans. New sea-based trade routes lessened the significance of the overland routes under Ottoman control. The discovery of vast amounts of silver in the New World also created inflationary pressures, reducing the value of the imperial treasury. Moreover, an industrializing and expansionist Europe established colonies overseas to secure sources of raw materials and markets for their finished products. In this way Europe accumulated vast amounts of capital. Meanwhile, demand for goods manufactured by the Ottomans declined, and revenues shrank. The Ottoman Empire also became a supplier of raw materials to Europe, and a market for its products. The empire took numerous loans from European institutions and became deeply indebted, rendering it unable to support key institutions, including the military.

To counter its loss of competitiveness, the empire entered into a series of reforms and modernization policies beginning in the mid-nineteenth century. The reforms, known as the *Tanzimat* ('reorganization'), were intended both to modernize and to Westernize the empire. The establishment of Ottoman embassies in London, Paris, Berlin and Vienna under Sultan Selim III (1789–1806), though short-lived, enabled the transmission of European ideas to the Ottoman elite that would shape the country's future. Reforms included modernization of the military, overhaul of the banking system, the creation of universities, and the incorporation of French law into the empire's legal code. In addition, factories were built to replace production by craftsmen. The result of these reforms was to create 'institutional dualism', in which traditional institutions continued to exist alongside new, modern ones (Cleveland 2004). For example, Islamic schools co-existed alongside those with 'modern', Western-based curricula. This dualism broadened an already existing divide between the poor, who had little access to any institutions, and elite populations. The dualism also reinforced clashes within the upper class over the desired shape and form of Ottoman society, either as one influenced heavily by institutions and practices based heavily on religion and tradition, or as one based on modernization heavily influenced by emulation of Western practices.

Perhaps the most significant outcome of the reforms was the introduction of a constitution in 1876, under Sultan Abdul Hamid II, which introduced an elected chamber of deputies and a senate, appointed by the sultan. Despite creating institutions to expand participation in governance, the constitution did little to limit the powers of the sultan. By 1878, Abdul Hamid II had disbanded the chamber of deputies and ruled without limit.

During his harsh reign, the empire brutally attacked Armenian Christians seeking an independent state within Ottoman territory and crushed an uprising against the Ottomans on the island of Crete, prompting Greece to declare war. With Western intervention, Crete gained its autonomy. The empire also lost control of the Balkans. By the end of Abdul Hamid II's thirty-year reign, the Ottoman territories were much less diverse. The concept of 'Ottomanism', and the embrace of all religions within the empire, was replaced with pan-Islam, and the idea of the empire as guardian of Islam.

However, the European-inspired idea of parliamentary limits on the monarchy was not forgotten, and Abdul Hamid II's actions helped fuel a growing dissident movement among the new middle-class elite.

These dissenters, known collectively as the Young Turks, promoted the principles of secular society and constitutionalism. Often, they themselves held government positions, from which they challenged traditional Ottoman rule. They were active in a secret political movement, led by students in the military, called the Committee of Union and Progress that succeeded in restoring the constitution in 1908 and would be pivotal in the creation of modern Turkey after World War I.

This period also witnessed an overall decentralization of power within the empire as power was ceded to local authorities. Under Muhammad Ali (1769–1849), then governor of the Ottoman province, Egypt launched an extensive modernization program. Ali's ultimate goal was to achieve independence from the Ottomans and establish his own dynasty. Extensive military and commercial reforms were designed to modernize Egypt's economic, military, educational and administrative systems. Higher education was modeled after European standards; new institutions were created for the study of medicine, engineering and the sciences. From the graduates of these institutions a cadre of civil servants took over administration of the state, using Arabic rather than Ottoman Turkish. Close commercial and trade ties were formed with European states, while European military technology, training methods and practices were adopted. Egypt developed an industrial sector, producing items ranging from guns to textiles while developing commercial agriculture based on cotton cultivation. Muhammad Ali also removed his greatest rival for power, the Mamluks, massacring them after a banquet at his citadel. Muhammad Ali revolted against the Ottomans, and after armed conflict gained recognition as the hereditary ruler of Egypt – another territorial loss for the empire.

His successor, Ismail Pasha (1863–9), continued Egypt's modernization program, though many of his schemes sank the country deep into debt. Ismail Pasha was deeply enamored of Western culture and institutions. He remade Cairo, draining marshland near the Nile to create new districts laid out in European form. A grand boulevard was cut from the historic Islamic city to connect this new district. Here, European-style villas were created, along with parks lit by 500 gas lights.

Streets were laid out in a radial pattern, mimicking Hausmann's plans for Paris, and an opera house built. Ismail Pasha is famously quoted as saying 'My country is no longer in Africa ... it is now in Europe!' (Vatikiotis 1991: 73).

EUROPEAN PENETRATION OF THE MIDDLE EAST

By the seventeenth century, the European commercial and political presence had increased significantly in the Middle East. They had forced the Ottomans to sign a series of agreements, known as the Capitulations, exempting Europeans from Ottoman taxes and granting them preferential tariff rates. To fund their modernization plans, the Ottomans borrowed extensively from Europe. Over a twenty-year period beginning in 1854, they borrowed approximately 180 million English pounds (Owen and Pamuk 1999). By 1876 the empire was failing to make payments, and lost its financial independence when an external board of creditors was created to assure repayment of European debt.

Though brief, France's occupation of Egypt (1798–1801), touched off by the Napoleonic expedition to Egypt, heralded a new era of European political and military control. Few parts of the Middle East were unaffected by European political rivalry. Having already established control over much of India by the 1860s, Britain sought to secure the routes to this jewel of their empire. With Aden (1839) under its control, Britain sought alliances along the Persian Gulf, signing treaties with Bahrain (1880), Muscat (1891), the Trucial Coast (1892) and Kuwait (1899). In 1882, Britain occupied Egypt, in an effort to safeguard the Suez Canal and thwart French ambitions to reclaim control of the country.

France established an empire in North Africa, establishing control first over Algiers (1830), Tunisia (1881) and Morocco (1912). Italy belatedly entered the colonial fray, acquiring the Ottoman province of Tripoli in 1911. Though the end of World War I marks the imposition of a formal system of European control, under the League of Nations mandate system, European control was already well established in the region. Indeed, the Ottoman Empire was itself deeply embroiled in a growing European rivalry which pitted Britain and France against Germany. Ottoman involvement in this rivalry ultimately brought about its downfall.

WORLD WAR I AND THE END OF THE OTTOMAN EMPIRE

World War I erupted in Europe in June 1914 following the Austrian invasion of Serbia in response to the assassination of Archduke Ferdinand in Sarajevo. This invasion activated a system of military alliances between the European countries, so that by August most of Europe had entered the war.

The Ottomans had a secret alliance with the Germans, as a means to counter Russian interests in Ottoman territories, and entered the war on the side of the Central Powers, composed of Austria-Hungary, Germany and Italy. They fought against the Alliance of the Triple Entente composed of Britain, France and Russia and referred to as the Allies.

The Middle East was an epicenter of military activity during World War I. The Ottomans fought the Russians on their eastern flank. Meanwhile, the Allies attempted to seize Istanbul. The ensuing battle at Gallipoli exacted heavy casualties among the Allies, who were eventually forced to withdraw. At Gallipoli a young Ottoman colonel, Mustafa Kemal, displayed strong military leadership; later his leadership would define modern Turkey. The Allies were more successful in Mesopotamia, conquering Baghdad and seizing southern Iraq in order to defend Iranian oil fields and protect the passages to India.

On their western flank, Ottoman forces attacked the British based in Egypt and Palestine, and attempted to seize the strategically important Suez Canal. The British war effort was aided by local Arab guerrilla forces who sought the opportunity to throw off Turkish rule. Led by the legendary T. E. Lawrence and Feisal, the son of Sharif Hussein of Mecca, the informal forces of the Arab Revolt proved effective against the sultan's armies. The Arab irregular forces disrupted the Ottoman supply lines, rendering the railroad unusable and seizing the key port of Aqaba. In October 1918, they captured Damascus.

The involvement of Arab forces was the result of an alliance between the British and Sharif Hussein bin Ali, the emir of Mecca and guardian of the holy cities

Box 5.1

T. E. LAWRENCE AND THE ARAB REVOLT

Perhaps no figure in modern Middle Eastern history is more legendary than Thomas Edward Lawrence (1888–1935), known as 'Lawrence of Arabia'. An Arabic-speaker who often dressed in robes, Lawrence was a passionate advocate for Arab independence.

As a university student, Lawrence spent much time in the Middle East and worked on numerous archaeological sites after graduation. With the outbreak of World War I, Lawrence enlisted and was posted to British Military Intelligence in Cairo, Egypt.

With his linguistic skills, and his experience in the region, Lawrence was assigned to make contact with Arab nationalists and gain their assistance in fighting the Ottoman Turks. Lawrence worked closely with Emir Feisal (later king of Iraq), the son of Sharif Hussein of Mecca to coordinate Arab military attacks. These attacks, known as the Arab Revolt, significantly undermined the Ottoman ability to advance on British forces and hold territory.

The Arab forces kept a large number of Ottoman troops tied down in Medina, to keep them from fighting the British in Palestine. They also seized the strategic port of Aqaba, opening a supply line for deeper British advanced into Syria. Finally, Arab forces repeatedly attacked the Hejaz railway, a key communications and supply channel for Ottoman forces.

Following the war, Lawrence became a strong advocate for Arab self-determination and for fulfillment of the promises made to them during wartime. With Feisal, he appeared at the Paris Peace Conference in 1919 to promote this cause. He was frustrated and bitterly disappointed with the conference's outcome, which established the League of Nations mandates.

Lawrence continued his military career in the Royal Air Force, but used a new name as a highly popular documentary about his role in the Arab Revolt raised his public profile. He also devoted himself to writing. His book *The Seven Pillars of Wisdom* is a rich and detailed account of the Arab Revolt and his role in it.

Lawrence's tragic death, at the age of 46, contributed to the legend surrounding him. His death occurred as he swerved his motorcycle to avoid hitting two young cyclists.

of Mecca and Medina. This position was a key post within the Ottoman Empire; from it Hussein, a direct descendant of the Prophet Muhammad, was able to build a large network of tribal alliances. In exchange for his support against the Ottomans, Hussein sought the creation of an independent Arab state composed of the Arabian peninsula, Greater Syria (Lebanon and Palestine) and the provinces of Iraq. In a series of ten letters the British High Commissioner in Egypt, Sir Henry McMahon, while excluding the territories of Syria and Iraq, agreed that 'Great Britain is prepared to recognize and uphold the independence of the Arabs in all the regions lying within the frontiers proposed by the Sharif of Mecca' (Cleveland 2004: 160).

Though the Arabs anticipated the creation of an independent Arab state following Ottoman defeat, this goal was in direct conflict with a secret agreement between the British and the French, signed in 1916, to divide Ottoman territories between them. Under the Sykes–Picot Agreement, Britain would control a zone in the southern portion of Mesopotamia (Iraq) and an area stretching from Gaza to Kirkuk. The French area of control included the Syrian coast and interior, and portions of southeastern Turkey and northern Iraq. Palestine was to be under international administration (Map 5.1). The document became public in 1917, following the Bolshevik revolution in Russia, to the embarrassment of the British and the French.

The defeat of the Central Powers resulted in the Ottoman Empire's unconditional surrender, on October 31, 1918, ending over 400 years of continuous rule by the sultanate.

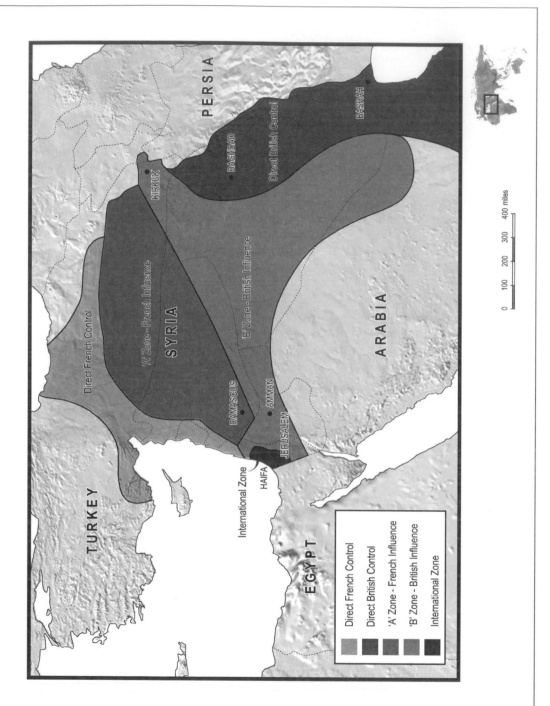

Map 5.1 The Sykes–Picot Agreement

DRAWING THE NEW MAP OF THE MIDDLE EAST

The new borders of the Middle East were drawn largely in Paris, where world leaders, including US president Woodrow Wilson, British prime minister David Lloyd George and French foreign minister Georges Clemenceau, met to divide the territories of the defeated German, Austria-Hungarian and Ottoman empires. The Paris Peace Conference of 1919, held at Versailles, was a massive undertaking meant to resolve competing claims on the territories that belonged to the defeated. Deliberations lasted six months; and, though World War II would cause further border modifications, the postwar settlement left a lasting imprint. This is particularly true in the Middle East, where vast Ottoman territories were divided, laying the foundation for the modern state system.

EMERGING NATIONALISM

Both Britain and France held pre-existing interests in the former Ottoman territories, as indicated in the Sykes–Picot Agreement. The French had longstanding connections to Syria and the Levantine coast, with its Maronite population. Britain sought to turn oil-rich Mesopotamia into a single state, including the key cities of Baghdad, Basra and Mosul. Britain also sought Palestine, which was to be a homeland for the Jewish people. In 1917, British foreign secretary Arthur Balfour had written to Lord Walter Rothschild, a leader of Britain's Jewish community, informing him of

---

Box 5.2

THE LEAGUE OF NATIONS MANDATE SYSTEM

The League of Nations was established in the aftermath of World War I, in part to set up a framework through which conflicts could be resolved through a system of collective security and negotiation rather than by warfare.

The mandates system was designed for the administration of the territories held by the Ottoman Empire and Imperial Germany prior to their defeat in the war. The mandates were administered by some of the Great Powers, namely Britain and France, involved in the war. As the mandatory power was required to answer to the League of Nations, and submit reports on the mandate territory's progress, the mandates were not officially colonies, though in many ways they functioned as such.

All of the mandates in the Middle East were Class A Mandates. These territories were 'provisionally recognized as independent nations' and were expected to reach independence with the advice and assistance of the mandatory power. The United Kingdom was given the mandates for Iraq, Palestine and Transjordan; France had control over Lebanon and Syria. In truth the preparations made for independence, both political and economic, often tended to favor the mandatory power rather than lay the framework for true self-sufficiency at independence.

Class B Mandates were concerned with former German territories in sub-Saharan Africa, such as Tanganyika and Kamerun. These territories were considered much less ready for independence and needed substantial development and control. For the Class C Mandates, which included Southwest Africa and islands in the South Pacific, there was no real prospect of independence.

In 1945 the League of Nations, which had failed to prevent another world war, was supplanted by the newly formed United Nations. The remaining mandates became UN Trust Territories. In the Middle East only the British Palestine mandate remained; UN attempts to find a solution based on separate Jewish and Arab states failed. In 1948 the British pulled out, and Jews in Palestine declared the creation of Israel. This led to the first war between Israel and the Arabs.

Box 5.3

ISAIAH BOWMAN: AMERICAN GEOGRAPHERS AT VERSAILLES

The American entry into World War I, which tipped the balance in the conflict, leading to the Allied victory, assured the US a place in the postwar settlement process. Even before the end of the war, Woodrow Wilson led the negotiations with Germany. But it was the ideas in Wilson's Fourteen Points that came to influence the work of the peace-makers, trying to create a permanent and lasting peace. Included in Wilson's Fourteen Points were the idea of territorial nationalism and the readjustment of the boundaries of European states and protection of various nationalities in the former Ottoman Turkey. In essence, Wilson's plan sought to eliminate future conflict by resolving competing ethnic-based territorial claims.

Determining these claims, and accurately locating them on the ground, was a monumental task. To begin, Wilson assembled a team of America's top geographers. The group was known first as 'The Inquiry' and later, at the Paris Peace Conference, as the 'American Committee to Negotiate Peace'. The group collected extensive amounts of geographical data, attempting to create political units based on scientific principles rather than on warfare. The American Geographical Society archive holds over 530 maps related to the Paris Peace Conference, many of which were produced by the Inquiry.

Difference, particularly between ethnic groups, was thought to be at the root of political instability. Cartographic techniques such as thematic mapping were used to map differences in language, religion and ethnic affiliation. A major question was to which political unit did each group of people belong. In doing so, the work of the Inquiry divided populations into categories based on the concept of 'race'. Race, however, was perceived as a socio-cultural concept, and the Inquiry sought to make a racial map of Europe and Turkey, showing national boundaries as well as 'mixed' and 'doubtful' zones. In this manner the peace-makers made adjustments to Europe's territory.

This level of scientific inquiry only applied to the territories of Europe and parts of Turkey, where the characteristics and desires of the population were given great consideration. In the former Ottoman territories of the Middle East, whose fate was determined largely at the San Remo Conference in 1920, the ethnic composition of the inhabitants and their history were not taken into consideration in creating the League of Nations mandates.

Wilson's team was headed by geographer Isaiah Bowman, who held the title of chief territorial advisor to the president. Bowman (1878–1950) was director of the American Geographical Society for twenty years and served as editor of the *Journal of Geography* and associate editor of the *Geographical Review*. The author of over sixteen books, largely on issues in political geography, he served as the president of Johns Hopkins University for thirteen years.

Crampton, J. (2006) 'The cartographic calculation of space: race mapping and the Balkans at the Paris Peace Conference of 1919'. *Social and Cultural Geography*, 7: 731–52.

Britain's support for a Jewish 'national home' in Palestine. The Balfour Declaration further stipulated that it be 'clearly understood that nothing shall be done which may prejudice the civil and religious rights of existing non-Jewish communities in Palestine'. This position was, of course, in direct conflict with the promises made to Sharif Hussein.

In determining the post-Ottoman borders and installing a system of external control by European governments, the peace-makers at Versailles often failed to acknowledge the wishes and desires of the local population (MacMillan 2001). This position was contrary to that established in President Wilson's famous 'Fourteen Points' speech of 1918 that laid out the principles for creating lasting peace in Europe. In this speech he called for an independent and sovereign state to exist in the Turkish part of the former Ottoman empire, and 'the other nationalities which are now under Turkish rule should be assured an undoubted security of life and an absolutely unmolested opportunity of autonomous development'. Many in the Middle East, including Arabs, Kurds and Armenians, interpreted Wilson's words as a guarantee of their right to self-determination. However, their nationalist aspirations remained largely unfulfilled. The disposition of Ottoman territory, though discussed in Paris, was not completed until 1920 at the Conference of San Remo and embodied in the Treaty of Sèvres (Map 5.2).

The Armenians were Christians who had lived under the rule of various empires, including the Byzantines, Persians and Ottomans, following the demise of an independent Armenian state in 1375. A large Armenian population existed inside the Ottoman Empire; they had previously been subject to attacks by both the sultanate, who saw Armenian nationalism as a threat to the empire, and Kurds, who viewed Armenian nationalism as a threat to their own nationalist aspirations. The Western world reacted in horror and sympathy to the massacre of Armenians carried out in 1915–16. Despite rhetorical support for the plight of the Armenians, and vast campaigns in Europe and the US to collect funds for Armenian refugees, the peace-makers at Versailles did not back the idea of an independent Armenia to be created from the ashes of the Ottoman Empire. Following Ottoman defeat, Armenia declared independence in 1918; and, though the Treaty of Sèvres, which ultimately disposed of Ottoman territory, provided for an independent Armenia, no steps were taken to ensure its survival. Without a protector to save it from reoccupation by the newly independent Turkey, Armenia was absorbed by the Soviet Union in 1922.

The nationalist aspirations of the Kurds, who sought an independent Kurdistan, were similarly dashed. It is clear that the peace-makers knew little about the Kurds, whose identity is based largely on a shared ethnic identification and Kurdish linguistic bond. Kurds are predominantly Sunni Muslim, but can also be Shia or Christian. Though Britain initially supported the idea of Kurdistan, as a means to provide a buffer state to protect Mesopotamia and its oil, the Kurds rebelled against the idea of a Kurdistan under British protection. In the end, though an autonomous Kurdistan did appear on the maps of the Treaty of Sèvres, the rise of a strong republic of Turkey, under the leadership of Kemal Ataturk (Mustafa Kemal), meant the end to Kurdish nationalist dreams.

Despite Wilson's lofty language in the Fourteen Points speech, Arabs were little represented at the postwar settlement talks. By all accounts, Feisal's reception in Paris was chilly, with Balfour stating (MacMillan 2001: 380): 'I am quite unable to see why Heaven or any other Power should object to our telling the Moslem what he ought to think.' No Arabs, including Palestinian Arabs, were present at San Remo. In essence, the Arabs were expected to do as they were told.

Though Sharif Hussein's son, Feisal, accompanied by T. E. Lawrence, journeyed to the Paris conference to speak for Arab independence and for fulfillment of the promises the Arabs felt were made by McMahon, it did little to ensure Arab self-determination. In Paris, they found little support from the British and great resistance by the French. By 1918, Feisal, in anticipation of the peace settlement, had already begun to establish an independent state in Syria, a great threat to French interests. With Palestine held by the British, and Syria by the French, Hussein's wartime support was rewarded by the creation of Transjordan, an autonomous area inside the British Palestine mandate. His eldest son, Abdullah, was placed on the throne. The British did not abandon Feisal; in 1921 they made him king of the newly created Iraq.

A new entity, Transjordan, was created under British rule, included within the British mandate of Palestine. The British mandate included the area of historic Palestine, including Jerusalem, though its boundaries had never been precisely determined, and areas previously belonging to the Ottoman province of Syria. The Transjordan, the precursor to modern Jordan, was also included in this mandate. The British placed Sharif Hussein of Mecca, their ally during World War I, on Transjordan's throne.

The vast Ottoman territories were reduced to a small portion of the Anatolian peninsula around the city of

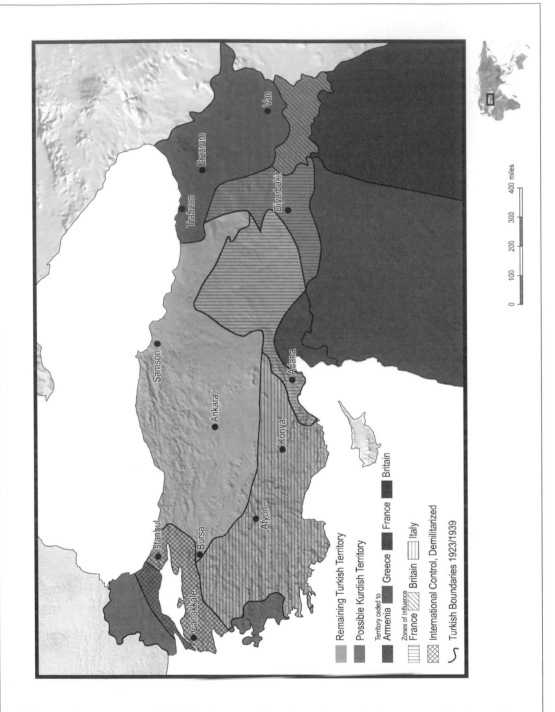

Map 5.2 The Treaty of Sèvres

Box 5.4

THE ARMENIAN GENOCIDE

Between 1915 and 1917 approximately 1 million of Turkey's Christian Armenians were killed or deported. They died from starvation, exhaustion on forced marches, bludgeoning and rape. At the time, no word existed in the English language to describe killings on such a scale, and the apparent attempt to eliminate an entire people.

Ottoman Turkey entered World War I on the side of Germany, fighting against Russia, Britain and France. The 'Young Turk' government of the Ottoman Empire feared its Armenian population, numbering approximately 2 million, would betray Turkey. The Armenian Christian population had existed in the area for 3000 years, and under the Ottoman *millet* system was a protected minority (*dhimmis*). Though Russia encouraged the Armenians to revolt, and a few did, the vast majority remained loyal.

The genocide of the Armenians was led by the government, and was an intentional act to rid Turkey of its 'Armenian problem' and not an unexpected outcome of fighting associated with the war. The government ordered the deportation of Armenians, closed their schools and desecrated its churches. In Constantinople, and in cities throughout Turkey, leading Armenian citizens and intellectuals were executed.

The events were covered up, and denied by Turkey and her ally Germany. However, as word leaked out, the international community did nothing to stop the killing. The US ambassador in Turkey, State Department officials, returning missionaries and even former president Theodore Roosevelt urged President Woodrow Wilson to take action. Wilson failed to denounce the 'race murder' as the US had not yet entered the war and he sought to preserve American neutrality. Through the American Near East Relief Committee, the US did provide $110 million in humanitarian aid to the survivors.

Though Britain, France and Russia (though not the United States) wanted to see the perpetrators of the genocide tried by an international tribunal, this tribunal never took place. Military tribunals in Turkey convicted two senior Ottoman officials for their involvement in the killings; they were sentenced to hard labor and death by hanging. Others, who had escaped from Turkey, were sentenced *in absentia*.

Over two decades later, the crime of systematic elimination of a people was given a name: genocide. It is derived from the Greek *geno*, meaning race or tribe, and the Latin *cide*, meaning killing. It was coined by Raphael Lemkin, who survived the Holocaust and sought to find a name that could capture the scale of these crimes. The Armenian genocide is often recognized as the first true genocide, though the Turkish government does not describe the events as genocide. The subject of the Armenian genocide remains contested in Turkey.

Power, S. (2002) *A Problem from Hell: America and the Age of Genocide*. New York: Basic Books.

Ankara. Italy and Greece controlled the southern and southeastern portion of the peninsula, including the coasts. Constantinople (now Istanbul), an international zone, was occupied by Allied troops. The settlement was designed to ensure that the Ottoman Empire never again rose to rival Europe, or threatened European interests in the Middle East. The Ottoman parliament was disbanded, the CUP of Young Turks fled, and the Allies took control of Ottoman finances. Though the sultan continued to rule officially, all decisions were made in cooperation with the Allies.

THE CREATION OF MODERN TURKEY

The settlement imposed by the Treaty of Sèvres fed a Turkish nationalist movement that had its roots in the reform period. The occupation of the Ottoman heartland, and of Istanbul in particular, by foreign troops inspired a strong reaction from the local Turkish population. Even before the treaty was concluded, resistance movements formed that would challenge the implementation of the Treaty of Sèvres. Under the leadership of Mustafa Kemal, a fledgling national resistance was formed whose main goal was to achieve Turkish sovereignty over areas with a Turkish majority. By 1920, they had formed a government in Ankara, with Mustafa Kemal as president, to represent the Turkish people. A national assembly, composed of local representatives and members of the parliament previously disbanded, was formed and quickly adopted a constitution.

Under the leadership of Mustafa Kemal, Turkish military strength grew, and easily dislodged Greek forces in southern Turkey in 1922. With Kemal's troops threatening to engage the British in Istanbul, the two parties agreed to renegotiate the terms of the Treaty of Sèvres. In the renegotiations, Turkish representatives pushed for adoption of the principles in the National Pact, which stated the right of full Turkish sovereignty over the remaining portions of the empire with a Turkish majority. The final treaty, the Treaty of Lausanne, largely adhered to this principle and restored Turkish control over the entire Anatolian peninsula, including Istanbul. On November 1, 1922 the sultanate was abolished, and the Republic of Turkey was created the following year. Mustafa Kemal (Ataturk) was its first president.

EGYPTIAN NATIONALISM

The British occupied Egypt in 1882 in order to protect the Suez Canal, prevent French involvement in the region, and rein in an economic crisis that had forced foreign monitoring of Egypt's economy. The arrival of British troops also quelled a nationalist revolt, led by an Army colonel, Ahmed Urabi, and other officers. Urabi sought to establish a popularly elected legislature that would control Egypt's budget and the heavy taxation on the poor needed to maintain the khedive's high spending levels and debt payments. British troops, after defeating the nationalist troops, restored the khedive to power.

Britain's subsequent occupation had a profound effect on the Egyptian economy and political system, increasing its dependence on Britain and thereby spurring the growth of Egyptian nationalism. Though Egypt technically remained an Ottoman province, and was not formally a British protectorate, Britain assumed control of its internal and external affairs. The power of the khedive paled in comparison with that of the British consul general, Lord Cromer, who oversaw a vast network of British civil servants and administrators who served as – highly paid – advisors in Egyptian government ministries. Britain controlled the budget and the decision-making.

This fueled tension with the well-educated Egyptian elites, who had benefited from the educational reforms during previous modernization and wished to administer their own country. Britain's involvement in the Sudan further enraged nationalists.

An economic crisis, as a result of a global recession, badly hurt exports of cotton, which had become Egypt's dominant crop under British policy. Farm incomes plummeted, creating unrest in the countryside. At the same time, nationalists voiced their opposition in the press. The wounding of the wife of a village prayer leader in the rural area of Dinshaway in June 1906 by five British officers on a pigeon-shooting outing touched off local protests. In the ensuing trial by British authorities, meant to dissuade others from protesting, thirty-two peasants were convicted of premeditated murder (and four executed). The Dinshaway incident further inflamed nationalists, of both Islamic and secular ideologies.

The hardships borne by the Egyptian population during World War I, when 100,000 British troops were stationed in Egypt, further stirred nationalist sentiments. Following the war, Egypt officially became a British protectorate, increasing British control. In 1919 riots erupted throughout the country following the British expulsion of popular nationalist leader Saad Zaghlul. In 1922, Britain, unable to reestablish control over Egypt, unilaterally granted it independence. Though Egypt then established a parliament and elected Saad Zaghlul as its first prime minister, the monarchy continued to exert ultimate authority and maintained a close relationship with the British. Full realization of nationalist goals would not happen until 1952 when a revolution led by military officers overthrew the monarchy.

Box 5.5

ATATURK: THE FATHER OF MODERN TURKEY

The characteristics and structure of modern Turkey were profoundly influenced by Mustafa Kemal (1881–1938), also known as Ataturk.

A successful military officer, Kemal served Ottoman Turkey in the battle of Gallipoli in 1915. Though the Allies eventually prevailed, the battle was a formative event in the development of modern Turkish nationalism. After the war, Kemal led the nationalist movement and the series of military conflicts against Greece, the United States and the French, who sought to implement the provisions of the Treaty of Sèvres. Kemal ignored the treaty, whose provisions included an autonomous state for the Armenians, and led the creation of a new, modern Turkey.

As Turkey's first president, Kemal sought to break ties with the Ottoman past. He moved the capital from Istanbul (Constantinople) to Ankara. Turkey became a republic, ending over 500 years of hereditary rule by sultans. A National Assembly was elected by all males aged 18 or older. Women received full political rights, including the right to vote and to serve in parliament, in 1934 – well before women in many European countries. The president was elected by the national assembly from amongst their membership.

Secularism was chief among the principles of the new state. Ataturk closed the religious schools, eliminated the Ministry of Religious Endowments, and instituted a legal code based on Swiss and other European law, rather than on *sharia*. Islam, followed by the vast majority of Turks, was seen as a personal belief system, separate from the state. To this end, he abolished the caliphate, by which the Ottomans had claimed leadership of the Muslim world. Polygamy, acceptable under Islam, was outlawed, and the Sufi religious orders were driven out. Sunday replaced Friday as the day of rest. Kemal also took steps to reduce the power of the religious leadership.

His efforts to modernize Turkey's economy were only partially successful. He attempted industrialization through state-led capitalism, targeting specifically the textile and steel industries. The decision, in 1928, to replace the Arabic alphabet with the Latin to write Turkish is credited with raising national literacy levels to over 90 percent, one of the highest in the region. Today, this combination of secularism, high educational attainment and an open economy has made Turkey an economic leader in the region.

Kemal was criticized for the rapid pace of his reforms and the loss of traditional Turkish culture to one based on modernity and European influences. The reforms were also seen as bringing greater benefit to urban elites than to the peasantry. Moreover, there was little tolerance for opposition to his plan.

In 1935, Turkey's National Assembly bestowed upon him the title 'Father of the Turks', or Ataturk. He died in November 1938 at the age of 57. The true test of the system he put in place was the smooth transition to his successor, a strong supporter of Kemalist ideology, Ismet Inonu. Kemal remains a major symbol of Turkish nationalism; his portrait can be found in government offices and private businesses throughout Turkey.

THE IRANIAN CONSTITUTIONAL REVOLUTION

The constitutional revolution in Iran marks both the first of the constitutional and parliamentary revolutions that swept through the Middle East in the pre-World War I era and the end of the Qajar hereditary dynasty that had succeeded the Safavids and ruled Persia since 1781.

From the late nineteenth century, Russian expansion in central Asia and British hegemony over India had pressed Iran on both sides. By 1907 the British and the Russians had signed an agreement dividing the country into spheres of influence between them. Both Russia and the British sought to control the country's oil resources and strategic ports. Lavish spending by the monarch, Shah Muzzafir al-Din (1898–1906), had led to Iran's economic dependence on both Britain and Russia; the central government could function only with the aid of foreign loans. To repay these loans Britain had forced a series of highly unpopular concessions on the monarchy. One of the earliest gave the British a monopoly on the production, domestic sale and export of tobacco in 1891. Highly unpopular, the concessions heightened nationalist sentiments, which were led by the religious leaders (*ulama*). Widespread protests forced the shah to repeal the concessions the following year. The repeal of the concessions illustrates a common tendency in Iranian politics: that of the religious leaders to enforce the populist will.

By the turn of the century a diverse group of merchants, religious leaders and intellectuals constituted a growing nationalist movement. The granting of an oil concession to the British, known as the D'Arcy concession, further angered the nationalists. The terms of the concession gave the British control of Iranian oil reserves for sixty years, with Iran receiving only 16 percent of the net profits. Widespread protests erupted in 1905, focused on limiting the powers of a highly unpopular monarch. Protests ended in 1906, following the shah's agreement to convene a constitutional assembly (*Majlis*).

The *Majlis* created an elected legislature and reduced the power of the shah, especially over financial issues. The status of Islam was secured by the *Majlis*, which reaffirmed Twelver Shiism as the official state religion and the *sharia* as the basis for law. By 1908 the country was caught up in a civil war between those who backed the monarchy, and sought to restore its power, and the constitutionalists. Britain and Russia both entered Iran to protect their economic interests. Though the parliament continued to function, it did so under the watchful eye of foreign powers.

The interwar period saw a short-lived return of the monarchy, when Reza Pahlavi, the minister of war, led troops into Tehran in 1921, forcing the government to resign. The Qajar shah named him prime minister and sought exile in Europe. In 1926 a puppet *Majlis* crowned Reza Pahlavi the new Shah of Persia. With this, the Qajar dynasty ended, and the Pahlavi dynasty was established.

Reza Shah embarked on an extensive modernization and Westernization program. The country's name was changed from Persia to Iran, to evoke images of the nation's past. Nearly all institutions, including the military and educational systems, were modernized in European tradition. The shah sought to emulate the secularization of European society, banning Iranian dress, the all-concealing *chador* worn by women, and the veil. The wearing of hats and European dress became compulsory.

Reza Shah also reduced the power of the religious leaders, in part by creating a new legal system based on French law, which required judges to hold degrees from European-style institutions rather than from Islamic schools. He also seized much land belonging to the religious endowment system.

Reza Shah's rule was highly authoritarian; criticism was suppressed through the use of harsh punishments and the secret police. The press was controlled, and Reza Shah accumulated vast wealth and greatly expanded his land holdings.

World War II saw another round of European intervention in Iran. Despite Reza Shah's attempts to keep it neutral, both Britain and the Soviet Union feared he would support the Germans. Both Britain and the USSR invaded in 1941, forcing Reza Shah to abdicate his throne. His son, Mohammad Reza Pahlavi, took the throne.

MOVING TOWARD INDEPENDENCE

The dawn of the twentieth century brought great change to the Middle East. By mid-century the old empires were gone and new borders drawn. European control was formalized through League of Nations (subsequently United Nations) mandates. The countries of the region were increasingly characterized by 'institutional dualism', by which European institutions were created alongside traditional, such as European courts alongside Islamic ones.

The penetration of European institutions into society at the hands of rulers who sought to emulate Europe, or who had become deeply indebted to the European powers, helped foster a growing sense of nationalism. By the end of World War II, it was becoming more difficult for Europe to exert control over their colonies. In a few short years most of the countries in the region would reach independence within a new world order defined by the rising strength of the United States and the Soviet Union.

Box 5.6

THE RISE (AND FALL) OF ARAB NATIONALISM

While nationalist movements developed in the individual countries of the region, such as Egypt and Syria, a form of nationalism with a broader mandate, to unite all Arabs, also grew. The Arab nationalists sought to increase the strength of the Arab countries through uniting them in solidarity against their major foe, the imperialist powers and Israel. They argued that imperialism had artificially divided the Arabs, a single people, into many states. Through political unity, and the creation of a single Arab state, the Arab world would be reinvigorated and recharged. The loss of the 1948 war with Israel could be attributed to the division of the Arabs into many states.

Many of the intellectual ideas behind Arab nationalism can be traced to the writings of Michel Aflaq, a Syrian and co-founder of the Ba'ath party. The Ba'ath party is a secular nationalist organization, founded in Syria in 1947. It had branches in many countries, including Iraq; however, after an internal disagreement, the Iraqi Ba'ath party split from the Syrian in 1963. According to Aflaq, the Arab fatherland was an indivisible economic and political unit.

But no one did more to advance the cause of Arab nationalism than Egyptian president Gamal Abdel Nasser, who served as the self-proclaimed leader of the Arab world in the 1950s and 1960s. A charismatic leader, Nasser's anti-imperialist rhetoric against both the US and the USSR, and his anti-Israel statements, made him enormously popular in Egypt and throughout the Arab world. On the international stage he was active in the Non-aligned Movement, along with Nehru of India and Tito of Yugoslavia. The NAM is an anti-imperialist, anti-colonialist and anti-Zionist organization of states. In 1956 he nationalized the Suez Canal, further bolstering his anti-imperialist credentials. He was strongly committed to the idea of a single Arab state (led by Egypt, of course); and, in 1958, Egypt and Syria joined to form the United Arab Republic. The union was short-lived, lasting for only three years.

In 1967, Nasser led the Arab states in an war against Israel (see Chapter 6). The war, which caused further territorial losses to Israel, was a disastrous defeat for the Arabs. In its aftermath, Nasser attempted to resign. Millions of Egyptians poured into the streets to demand his return to office.

Though Nasser remained in office, Arab nationalism, which peaked in the 1950s, began to wane. A number of factors contributed to its decline. The Arab defeat in 1967, which underscored the permanence of a strong Israel in the region, and demonstrated the weakness of the Arab militaries, dealt a huge psychological blow.

A further reason was the dismantling of European control over the region, removing imperialism as Arab nationalism's major rallying cry. By the 1960s, much of the Arab world was independent; even Algeria had managed to shake off French control, though at a great price.

Without imperialism to provide a common enemy, internal cohesion among the Arab states, which had always been problematic, worsened. Nasser, reeling from his defeat, began verbally to attack other Arab governments, reducing his stature as leader of the Arab world Increasingly the Arab states began to focus on their own internal needs, such as rapid population

Box 5.6

THE RISE (AND FALL) OF ARAB NATIONALISM—CONT'D

growth and economic stagnation, rather than on the unrealized dream of Arab nationalism.

As Arab nationalism, grounded in secular thought, had been unable to deliver on its promises, new ideologies gained ground. Islamist thought began to grow in popularity as it offered a different, religion-based, path for raising the conditions faced by the population in these newly independent countries. Islamists lashed out at the explicitly secular nationalist governments. Saddam Hussein in Iraq carried the

mantle of Arab nationalism in the latter part of the twentieth century. His execution can perhaps been seen as the 'last gasp' of Arab nationalism.

Dawisha, A. (2003) *Arab Nationalism in the Twentieth Century: From Triumph to Despair*. Princeton, NJ: Princeton University Press.

Kaplan, R. (2007) 'Arab nationalism's last gasp', *The Los Angeles Times* (Opinion), January 7.

SUMMARY OF MAIN POINTS

- By the sixteenth century the Ottoman Empire was losing its global position to new competition from Europe and the New World.
- To combat this loss of competitiveness, the Ottoman Empire instituted a series of modernizing reforms.
- These reforms increased European control over the MENA in the eighteenth and nineteenth centuries which grew as European countries competed with each other to control the region.
- The post-World War II settlement created the modern system of states in the MENA and placed most of them under direct European control.
- During this time, nationalist ideas emerged and grew, laying the foundation for independence movements.
- Modern Turkey was created out of the remains of the Ottoman Empire and under the leadership of Ataturk established a strong secular republic.
- In Iran, the Pahlavi dynasty was established, while Russia and Britain each sought to control the country

QUESTIONS FOR DISCUSSION

1   What factors contributed to a decline in Ottoman power in relation to that of Europe?
2   How did the reforms in the Ottoman Empire and Egypt contribute to a rise in nationalism?
3   Give an example of institutional dualism. How does this dualism still survive in modern Middle Eastern countries today?
4   How did the postwar settlement create challenges for states in the Middle East today?
5   How has the influence of Ataturk shaped modern Turkey? In what ways does Turkey differ from other countries in the Middle East?

SUGGESTIONS FOR FURTHER READING

Cleveland, W. (2004) *A History of the Modern Middle East*, 3rd edn. Boulder, Colo.: Westview Press. A comprehensive and authoritative history of the Middle East since the rise of Islam.

Fisk, R. (2005) *The Great War for Civilisation: The Conquest of the Middle East*. New York: Vintage Books. This sweeping account of the region's modern history, augmented by the author's personal accounts, adds a much-needed dimension beyond what history books can provide. The author is an award-winning journalist with thirty years' experience in the region.

Fromkin, D. (1989) *A Peace to End All Peace: Creating the Modern Middle East, 1914–1922*. New York: Holt. The classic and highly detailed account of the demise of the Ottoman Empire. Fromkin does an excellent job of demonstrating how the postwar settlements contributed to instability in the region.

Hodgson, M. (1974) *The Venture of Islam*. Vol. 3, *The Gunpowder Empires and Modern Times*. Chicago, Ill.: University of Chicago Press. Historian Hodgson coined the term 'gunpowder empires' to explain the rise of empires, beginning with China, based on advances in weaponry. In this book he explores the links between state formation and gunpowder in the Middle East.

Keddi, N. (2006) *Modern Iran: Roots and Results of a Revolution*. New Haven, Conn.: Yale University Press. Traces the roots of the Iranian revolution and its ideology through to the present. Essential reading for understanding modern Iran.

MacMillan, M. (2001) *Paris 1919: Six Months That Changed the World*. New York: Random House. A highly detailed account of the peace conference at Versailles following the end of World War I. See especially chapters 26–9 that cover the end of the Ottoman Empire, the creation of new Arab states and the roots of modern Turkey.

Myntti, C. (2003) *Paris along the Nile: Architecture from the Belle Epoque*. New York: American University in Cairo Press. Packed with photographs, this volume documents the historic, and threatened, architecture of 'European' Cairo.

Owen, R. and Pamuk, S. (1999) *A History of Middle East Economies in the Twentieth Century*. Cambridge, Mass.: Harvard University Press. See especially Chapter 2 for a discussion of Egypt's economic dependency.

Palmer, A. (1993) *The Decline and Fall of the Ottoman Empire*. London: John Murray. Extensive examination of the decline of the empire and possible explanations.

Tyldesley, J. (2005) *Egypt: How a Lost Civilization Was Rediscovered*. Berkeley, Calif.: University of California Press. A light-hearted look at the archaeological frenzy touched off by the Napoleonic expedition to Egypt.

Vatikiotis, P. J. (1991) *The History of Modern Egypt: From Muhammad Ali to Mubarak*, 4th edn. Baltimore, Md: Johns Hopkins University Press. Set against the backdrop of growing nationalism and European penetration, this volume provides insight into the critical decades before Egyptian independence.

Zurcher, E. (2004) *Turkey: A Modern History*. London: I.B. Tauris. Traces the development of the Republic of Turkey, the implementation of Ataturk's reforms and current challenges.

6

THE EMERGENCE OF INDEPENDENT STATES AND GEOPOLITICS

This chapter examines the region's 'place in the world', focusing on regional tensions created at independence, the role of foreign-power intervention, the significance of oil politics and the regional strategic balance. Often the desires of external powers, in particular the United States and the Soviet Union who each attempted to exert control over the region during the Cold War, conflicted with those of local leaders who sought to navigate an independent path in their search for a post-colonial identity. Religious revolution in Iran, the growing significance of oil resources, and the end of the Soviet Union created a radically different regional strategic balance, which resulted in an expanded role for the US, as hegemonic power, in the region. The heightened level of American involvement in the Middle East has been marked by two wars with Iraq within a fifteen-year period (Map 6.1).

POST-WORLD WAR II INDEPENDENCE

The majority of the states in the region achieved independence shortly after World War II; independence was often the result of long, protracted nationalist struggle (Table 6.1). This struggle was perhaps most violent in the French-controlled Maghreb. The French had deeply integrated colonies such as Algeria, Tunisia

and Morocco into French commercial and political life. Under direct French rule, unlike the indirect rule method preferred by the British, Algeria was considered another French province and the local population harshly assimilated. The population was subjected to 'modernization' policies designed to turn them into appropriate French subjects (though they were denied French citizenship unless they converted from Islam). Algeria achieved independence only after a lengthy war against France, lasting from 1954 to 1962. Morocco and Tunisia, which both had very active armed resistance movements, became independent in 1956. During World War II, France relinquished her Syrian mandate, which included Syria and Lebanon. This move was prompted by fear that Nazi Germany could take over control of these territories.

With the creation of a British-backed monarchy, Iraq had become independent in 1932; however, Britain retained military bases in the country and exercised considerable political influence. The monarchy was short-lived and was toppled by a military coup in 1958. Following a period of instability, the Ba'ath party gained control in 1963, paving the way for Saddam Hussein's eventual rise.

In 1946, Britain's mandate over Transjordan ended; and Jordan, which had enjoyed semi-autonomy

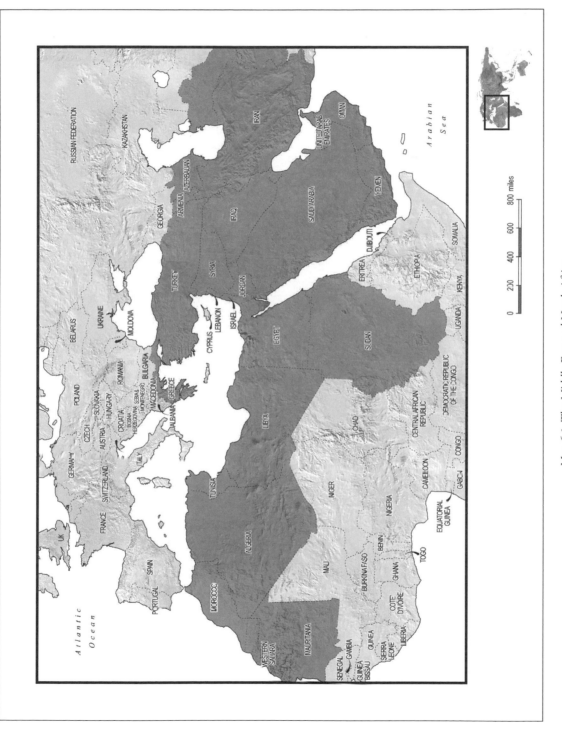

Map 6.1 The Middle East and North Africa

Table 6.1 MENA independence dates

Algeria	1962
Bahrain	1971
Egypt	1952[1]
Iran	not applicable
Iraq	1932
Israel	1948
Jordan	1946
Kuwait	1961
Lebanon	1943
Libya	1943
Morocco	1956
Oman	1970[2]
Qatar	1970[3]
Saudi Arabia	1932[4]
Sudan	1956
Syria	1946
Tunisia	1956
Turkey	1923
UAE	1971[5]
Yemen	1967[6]

Source: CIA World Factbook, www.cia.gov

[1] Egypt achieved nominal independence from Britain in 1922. Britain continued to exert control in its affairs and over the monarchy.

[2] Oman, Qatar, Kuwait and the UAE were never formally colonized, but had treaties with Britain that provided political, military and economic advice.

[3] ibid.

[4] Saudi Arabia was never colonized; the Kingdom of Saudi Arabia was created in 1932.

[5] Ras al-Khaimaih joined the UAE in 1972.

[6] Britain maintained a protectorate around Aden in South Yemen until 1967. In 1990 North and South Yemen unified.

since 1921 under King Abdullah's leadership, became an independent country. Though Egypt had been officially granted independence by Britain, the monarch, backed by the British, continued to dominate political life. He was overthrown by a military coup, led by military officers, including Gamal Abdel Nasser, who became president in 1954.

Independence came much later to the countries of the Gulf, where Britain had concluded agreements with the local leaders granting Britain a role in their military affairs and external relations. British control of Oman and the Trucial Coast states continued until the 1970s. In 1971 the United Arab Emirates was formed by the creation of a federation of emirates: Abu Dhabi, Dubai, Ajman, Fujairah, Sharjah, Umm al-Quwain and, shortly thereafter, Ras al-Khaimah.

THE BRITISH WITHDRAWAL FROM PALESTINE

The end of the British Mandate in Palestine, and the creation of the modern state of Israel, laid the foundation for intra-regional conflict which spawned three wars and continues to this day (Map 6.2). (A more complete discussion of the Israeli–Palestinian conflict, and attempts to resolve it, is located in Chapter 9.)

A small Jewish population had long existed in Palestine; in the early 1880s its size was estimated at 5000. The vast majority of Palestine's population, estimated

---

Box 6.1

SADDAM HUSSEIN: NATIONALIST, DICTATOR, FUGITIVE

Saddam Hussein Abd al-Majid al-Tikriti (1937–2006), generally referred to as Saddam, has been the center of US political and media interest for the past two decades. Between his rise as the authoritarian ruler of Iraq and his execution by the US-installed Iraqi interim government, he was a dominant player in the region's politics.

Saddam was born near the town of Tikrit, Iraq, a member of the Sunni minority. He was raised by

his uncle, a nationalist who fought against the British, who continued to control Iraq through the monarchy they created at the end of World War I. Saddam joined the Ba'ath party. The Ba'ath party in Iraq was founded during the wave of Arab nationalism and pan-Arabism which swept through the region after World War II. Like other nationalist parties, it was secular, and sought to throw off colonial rule. In 1963, army officers

Box 6.1

SADDAM HUSSEIN: NATIONALIST, DICTATOR, FUGITIVE—CONT'D

overthrew King Feisal II, placing General Abdul Karim Qassim in control. The Ba'athists opposed the Qassim government, which imprisoned much of its leadership – including Saddam, then party secretary. After escaping from jail in 1967, Saddam helped lead the coup that placed the Ba'athists in control. By 1969, Saddam was second in power only to the new president, Ahmad Hassan al-Bakr.

Over the next decade, Saddam consolidated his power, promoting Ba'ath unity but also creating multiple security forces to address any threats from within the party. He exercised influence over the economy, and nationalized Iraq's oil industry in 1972. With its oil wealth, Iraq created a society much envied throughout the region. Education was both free and compulsory; a system of universities was created; its free healthcare system was the most modern in the region. Iraq had a large and well-educated middle class; Baghdad was a center of cultural life in the 1970s and 1980s. Industrialization drew more people to the cities while agrarian reform programs improved the economic situation in the countryside.

In 1979, Saddam seized power from the ill al-Bakr. The process exemplified his often brutal methods for suppressing dissent. Following his assumption of the leadership, he accused sixty-eight leaders of the Ba'ath party of disloyalty at a party meeting and had them removed one by one. All were placed on trial; twenty-two were executed.

During the 1980s, Saddam focused on further consolidating his control on Iraqi society. He created a Stalinesque cult of personality, covering the country with his portraits and statues to his accomplishments; meanwhile there was no possibility of dissent. Like Nasser, Saddam was a staunch secularist; he reduced the power of the clergy and abolished the *sharia* courts. (After the war with Kuwait, he began to portray himself as a devout Muslim, despite being known for heavy drinking and debauchery, and added 'God is Great'

to the Iraqi flag.) Saddam kept a tight grip on Iraq's majority population, the Shia, especially after the 1979 Iranian revolution. The Kurds also fared poorly; they were forcibly relocated and subjected to an 'arabization' program. During the war with Iran he used chemical weapons against the Kurdish population, killing over 5000 in Halabja on March 16, 1988.

During the 1980s there was close cooperation between the US and Saddam; both were concerned about the possible spread of Islamic extremism from Iran. A visit by Donald Rumsfeld in 1984, acting as envoy between President Reagan and Saddam, paved the way for the restoration of full diplomatic relations with Iraq. A CIA liaison team in Baghdad provided intelligence on Iran to Saddam. Iraq was able to purchase military helicopters from the US and received American funds funneled through third parties.

Following Iraq's invasion of Kuwait in 1990, the US joined Britain and the Soviet Union in calling for Iraqi withdrawal. The United States eventually led the UN-backed coalition that fought Iraq. The US also called for Iraq's Shia and Kurdish populations to rise up and overthrow Saddam. When the rebellions did take place, however, the US provided no assistance. After the war the US patrolled the no-fly zones over Iraq and executed occasional military strikes. Accusations of weapons violations, and the mistaken belief in links between Iraq and al-Qaeda, ultimately led to the US invasion of Iraq in 2003.

When US troops occupied Baghdad, in April 2003, they were unable to find Saddam. He was captured that December near Tikrit. Saddam was charged with 'crimes against humanity', and found guilty in November 2006. He was hanged on December 30, 2006 and buried in Tikrit.

Cockburn, A. and Cockburn, P. (1999) *Out of the Ashes: The Resurrection of Saddam Hussein.* New York: Harper Perennial.

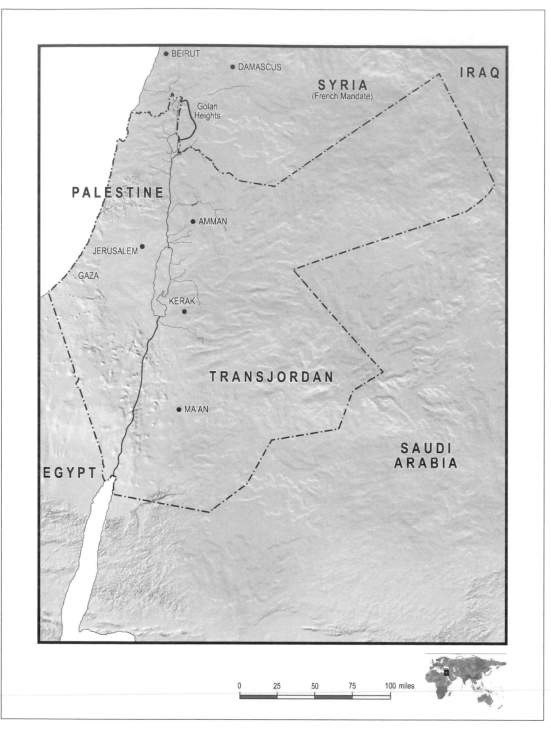

Map 6.2 The British Mandate in Palestine

between 250,000 and 300,000, were Sunni Muslims. A further 25,000–30,000 Arab Christians also lived in the area (Tessler 1994: 20). With the rise of the Zionist movement, Jews, many fleeing from the rising anti-Semitism in Eastern Europe and Russia, began to emigrate to Palestine. The first of these immigration waves, known as *aliya*, took place between 1881 and 1900, bringing 25,000 Zionists into the mandate territory. The Balfour Declaration of 1917, the appointment of a pro-Zionist British civilian high commissioner in Palestine, and the rise of Nazi Germany encouraged

further migration. Before the end of World War II, five *aliyas* had taken place; the fifth (1932–9) alone brought 200,000 legal immigrants (Kamrava 2005: 76). By the end of 1939, the Jewish community in Palestine numbered approximately 445,000, making up about 30 percent of the mandate's total population (Tessler 1994: 208).

The Zionists' goal was the creation of a national home, which in the age of nationalism and self-determination meant a state. This goal, of creating an independent Jewish state in Palestine, conflicted with

---

Box 6.2

ZIONISM AND THE ESTABLISHMENT OF ISRAEL

Between 66 and 73 CE, Jews living in Palestine revolted against their Roman rulers. The Romans crushed the revolt, destroying King Herod's tomb, and massacred or enslaved much of the Jewish population. Those who could fled, and joined the diaspora of Jews living outside Palestine. Since that dispersion of the Jews, the idea of return of the Jewish community to historic Palestine has been an important part of Jewish religious thought. In the nineteenth century, the idea of return became incorporated into the political ideology of Zionism. The movement's name comes from Zion, a hill in Jerusalem.

Political Zionism was created against a backdrop of growing persecution and discrimination against the Jews, particularly in Eastern Europe and in Russia. At the same time nationalist thought, and the belief in self-determination for each nation, was gaining ground internationally. In Russia, where a virulent anti-Semitism included government-backed pogroms, political Zionism formed in the early 1880s and led to the first *aliya*, or migration of Jews to Palestine, then part of the Ottoman Empire. These early immigrants, with few financial resources, created agricultural settlements.

At this point Zionism was not a unified movement. Numerous organizations were created throughout Europe that shared broadly Zionist goals. The growth of

a more defined movement was spurred by publication of a pamphlet that argued that Jews would never be treated as equals in Europe and they must seek the establishment of their own state. The Dreyfus Affair, in which a French Jewish soldier was wrongfully accused of treason, further encouraged Jews to doubt their future in Europe.

Under the leadership of Theodor Herzl (1860–1904), the Zionist movement began to solidify. He laid a foundation for a theory of political Zionism in his book *The Jewish State* (1896). In 1897 the first Zionist Congress met; its goal was to secure a home in Palestine for the Jewish people. Other locations had been proposed as the possible homeland, including Cyprus, the Sinai peninsula and Uganda, but Palestine was the most favored.

With the breakup of the Ottoman Empire at the end of World War I, Palestine became a British mandate. Britain adopted a pro-Zionist policy. In part this was an attempt to forge an alliance with the US and a response to heavy lobbying by the Zionist spokesman in London, Chaim Weizmann (1874–1952). British commitment to the idea of a Jewish state in Palestine had been secured before the end of World War I in the Balfour Declaration of 1917.

the British attempts to balance the interests of both the Arab and the Jewish inhabitants. In 1939, Britain, alarmed by the rapid rate of growth of the Jewish population, issued the MacDonald White Paper. The paper restricted the level of Jewish immigration to Palestine to 75,000 persons a year for five years and placed restrictions on purchase of land by Jews. The paper also called for the establishment of an independent Palestine to be governed by Arabs and Jews. The conditions of the White Paper were rejected by the League of Nations, which oversaw the mandate, but enforced by Britain. At times ships loaded with Jewish immigrants, fleeing the Holocaust, were turned away.

Under the British Mandate the Jews in Palestine established many institutions with governmental functions, including the Jewish Agency, which served as the official representative of the Jewish community, and the Jewish National Fund, which purchased land in Palestine for Jewish settlers. The Jewish Agency also created a military force, the Haganah. As tension between the Jewish leadership and British officials increased, other military groups, the Irgun Zvai Leumi (Irgun) and the Stern Gang (formally Fighters for the Freedom of Israel) were formed. These military forces conducted operations against both the British and the Arab Palestinians. One of the most deadly was an attack by the Irgun on July 22, 1946 that killed ninety-one, including twenty-eight British, inside Jerusalem's famed King David Hotel.

In the interwar period the Arab Palestinian population had fewer resources, in terms of both finances and external political support, and political leadership of the Palestinian community was less centralized than that of the Jewish. After the fall of the Ottoman Empire, Arab leaders, generally in urban areas, began to assume leadership of the community. These urban notables often led governmental and religious institutions under Ottoman control and collectively made up the leading families of the area. With the onset of large-scale Jewish settlement, the Palestinians began to create institutions to represent Arab Palestinian interests in the mandate more fully. The Palestinian Arab Congress, made up of local branches of Muslim and Christian associations, first met in 1919. The organization's goal was to oppose Zionism and seek Arab independence. The authority of the Congress was undermined both by Britain's refusal to recognize its leadership of the community and by discord among its membership. In 1924 the Congress broadened its membership and created a body called the Arab Executive, which represented the Palestinian community until 1934.

Perhaps the most influential leader among the Arab Palestinians was Hajj Amin al-Husseini (1895–1974), appointed the mufti of Jerusalem by the British. As mufti, or the highest Islamic scholar, he was responsible for handling Islamic affairs in the mandate. Amin was both a nationalist and an anti-Zionist, and as leader of the Palestinian resistance encouraged the Palestinian Arabs to revolt while also working closely with the British authorities.

During the interwar period, conflict between the Arab Palestinians, Jewish immigrants and the British grew as they asserted their nationalist claims. Arab militant groups formed, and riots often broke out, culminating in the Arab Revolt of 1936–9. Led by Hajj Amin, it began as a strike against rapidly growing Jewish immigration and land purchases but escalated into attacks on Jewish neighborhoods and conflict with British troops protecting them.

In the midst of the revolt a British Royal Commission of Inquiry, headed by Lord Earl Peel, was sent out to determine the revolt's cause and make recommendations for the future of Palestine. In July 1937 the Peel Commission, as it became known, recommended partitioning of the mandate into Arab and Jewish states, with Jerusalem remaining an international territory. The plan was rejected by the Palestinian Arabs, who were largely to receive land that was unfertile, and received a mixed reaction from the Jews. The revolt continued through 1939. By its end over 5000 Palestinians, 400 Jews and 200 British had been killed (Hourani 1991).

Deliberation over the future of the mandate was interrupted by World War II, in which the Middle East became a major theater of combat. In the deserts of North Africa, American, British and French troops fought German and Italian troops in combat dominated by tank warfare. Finally, in October 1947, an exhausted Britain announced its intention to withdraw from Palestine if no agreement was reached on future governance by Arabs and Jews within six months.

On November 29, 1947, the UN adopted UN General Assembly Resolution 181 which called for the creation of two states in Palestine, one Arab and one Jewish, with Bethlehem and Jerusalem under international administration. The Jews quickly accepted. The Arabs rejected the proposal (Map 6.3). Kamrava (2005: 79) sums up the reason for this:

> Although at the time Jews made up only about 33 percent of the inhabitants of Palestine and owned between 6 and 7 percent of the land, the plan awarded the Jewish state 55 percent of historic Palestine, most of it fertile. The area under Jewish control was also to include some 45 percent of the Palestinian population. The proposed Arab state, however was given only 45 percent of the total land in dispute, much of it not fit for agriculture and was to include a negligible Jewish minority.

On December 8, 1947, Britain recommended to the United Nations, which had replaced the League of Nations, that the Palestine Mandate terminate on May 15, 1948 and independent Jewish and Palestinian states be established two weeks later (Map 6.4). The following January, Britain announced that predominantly Jewish or Palestinian areas would be gradually handed over to whichever group had a majority. In advance of this date, Jewish troops expanded their control over more territory; many Arab Palestinians were forced from their villages or fled from the militarily superior Jewish troops.

On May 14, 1948, the state of Israel was declared, and the United States, under President Harry Truman, was one of the first to recognize the new country.

THE FIRST ISRAELI–ARAB WAR (1948)

The declaration of Israeli independence touched off the first of the Arab–Israeli wars. Troops from Egypt, Transjordan, Syria, Lebanon and Iraq, as well as volunteers from other Arab countries, invaded Israel. Israeli forces, led by future prime minister David Ben Gurion, though outnumbered, were better trained and perhaps more highly motivated than the Arab troops. With the exception of Transjordan's Arab Legion, which had been trained and equipped by the British, the Arabs were poorly supplied. The war ended with a series of armistices between the warring countries in 1949.

The 1948 war was a disaster for the Palestinians and the Arab states. By the end of the war Israel was able to field over 100,000 troops, against Arab forces of 55,000. During the war, Israel gained much territory; its new state boundaries contained 78 percent of the Palestine Mandate, 50 percent more than they would have been allotted under the UN partition plan. The 1948 war created a massive Palestinian refugee problem, a major issue that continues to thwart resolution of the conflict today. In 1949 only 160,000 Palestinians remained inside Israel; approximately 700,000 had been forced out or had fled to surrounding areas. Many of those who left were fleeing an advancing Israeli army, and assumed their evacuation would be temporary. In December 1948 the United Nations passed UN General Assembly Resolution 194, which included provisions for the return of the refugees:

> Resolves that the refugees wishing to return to their homes and live at peace with their neighbors should be permitted to do so at the earliest practicable date, and that compensation should be paid for the property of those choosing not to return and for loss of or damage to property which, under principles of international law or in equity, should be made good by the Governments or authorities responsible.

Fulfilling this 'right of return' has been a problematic issue in attempts to resolve the conflict.

THE COLD WAR AND THE MIDDLE EAST

During the Cold War that followed World War II, the Middle East was a primary arena of competition between the United States and the Union of Soviet Socialist Republics as each superpower sought regional alliances. This superpower competition benefited from the political vacuum left by the departure of the colonial powers. The US, wary of Soviet expansionism and the potential for communism to spread throughout

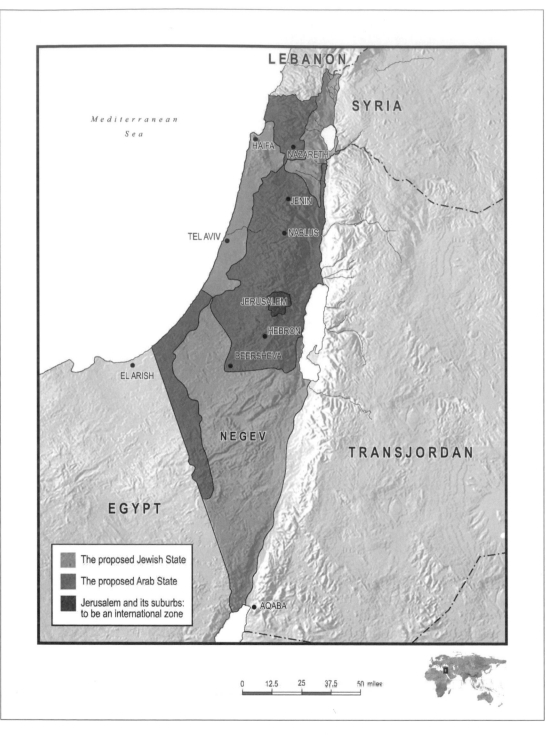

Map 6.3 The UN Partition Plan for Palestine

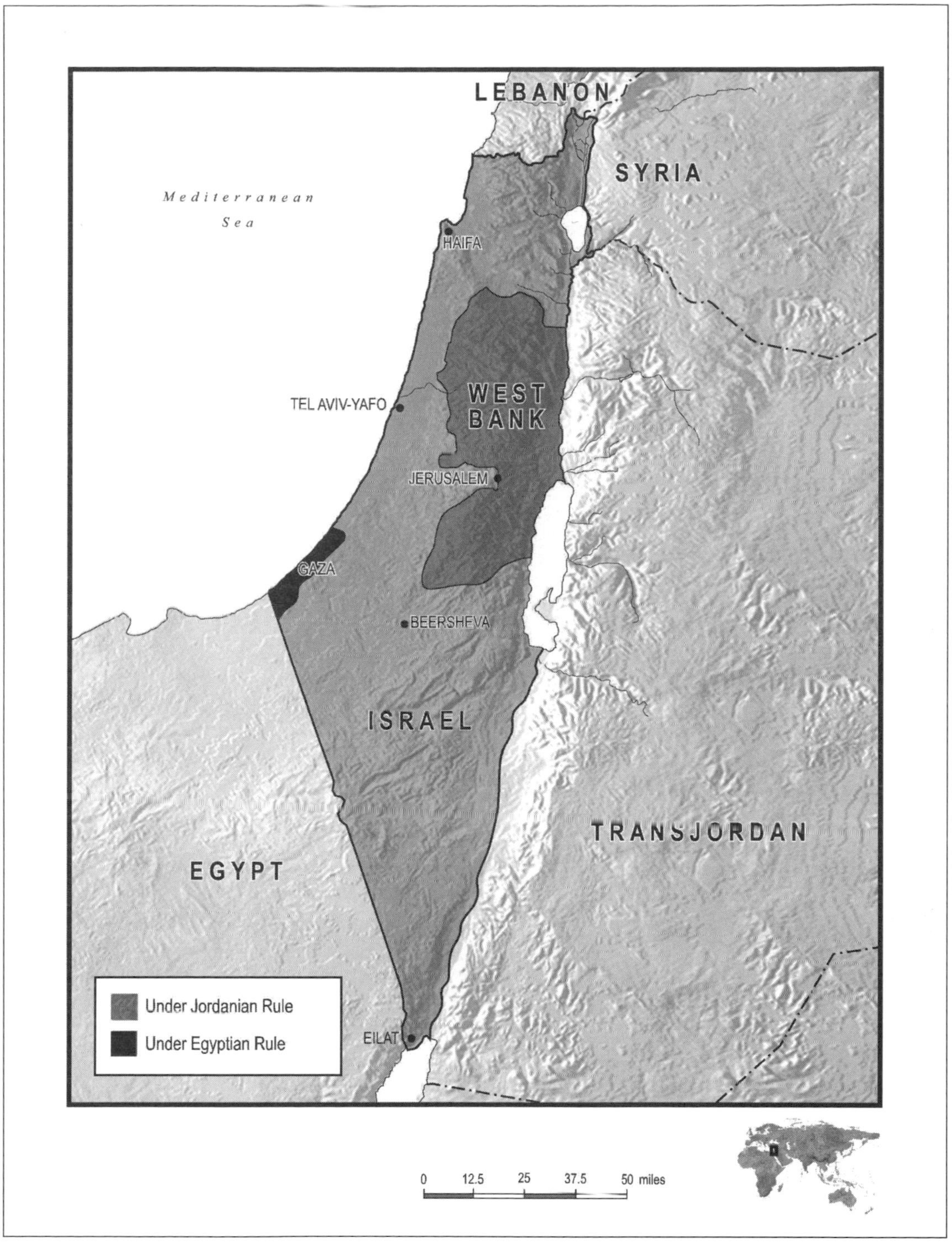

Map 6.4 Israel's border after 1948

the region, adopted policies to contain Soviet influence. The Truman Doctrine (1947) provided for large amounts of US foreign aid to Greece and Turkey lest they enter the Soviet orbit. Eventually, the US provided economic aid and military assistance to many countries in the region in an effort to influence their foreign policy. Considerable assistance was provided under the Eisenhower Doctrine (1957) that provided military aid to countries fighting communism. Jordan, for example, was receiving $50 million a year by the 1960s (Cleveland 2004: 333). Lebanon and Egypt also received significant amounts of aid, though the US relationship with Egypt was often difficult.

Throughout the Cold War the US built a system of military alliances designed to prevent Soviet control. Both Turkey and Greece became members of the North Atlantic Treaty Organization (NATO). The United States orchestrated the Baghdad Pact (1955), a mutual protection agreement which included Britain, Pakistan, Iran and Iraq, though Iraq left the organization in 1959. In the case of Iran, a key member of the US anti-Soviet alliance, the US supported a coup removing a nationalist prime minister and keeping the pro-US monarch on the throne.

NASSER: EGYPT DURING THE COLD WAR

The Arab states did not willingly accept superpower control; the actions of Egypt, under the leadership of

---

Box 6.3

THE MOSSADEQ COUP: US INTERVENTION IN IRAN

In the 1950s, the ardent nationalism of Iranian prime minister Mohammed Mossadeq brought him into conflict with the Iranian monarchy, and with its supporters, the United Kingdom and the United States.

A longstanding member of parliament, Mossadeq was an Iranian nationalist who deeply opposed foreign intervention in the country, and particularly British control over Iran's oil resources. He was a focal point for anti-imperialist sentiment and highly popular with the Iranian public. Shortly after he was appointed prime minister in 1952, Mossadeq nationalized Iran's oil resources, canceling the concessions granted to the Anglo-Iranian Oil Company (today British Petroleum). In response, Britain blockaded Iran, allowing no oil to be exported. In 1952 he cut relations with Britain. Though Iran lost over $100 million a year in oil revenues, and its economy suffered, Mossadeq remained popular with the people, if not with the monarch and his political opponents.

The nationalization brought Mossadeq into increasing conflict with the monarchy; at the same time his relations with other factions in parliament deteriorated.

In 1953, facing mounting criticism, he dissolved parliament and attempted to force the shah to leave Iran. In response, the shah dismissed him from his position as prime minister on August 16, 1953. When Mossadeq resisted, the military removed him, installing a more manageable prime minister, Fazlollah Zahedi, in office. Zahedi later negotiated new oil agreements with Britain.

The overthrow of Mossadeq was planned, supported and funded by the United States and the United Kingdom. The British hoped to install a new government that would again allow Britain control over oil; Zahedi later negotiated new oil agreements with Britain. The US was convinced to participate, believing, erroneously, that Mossadeq had communist leadings. US involvement was crucial as British diplomats had been expelled in 1952. The US ran a field office in Iran, which exerted pressure on the shah and hired demonstrators to turn out in support of the coup.

US involvement in the Mossadeq coup resulted in intense anti-American sentiment. The events of the coup, as proof of US imperialism, figured prominently in the 1979 Iranian revolution.

Gamal Abdel Nasser, exemplified the Arab states' drive to establish a distinct identity. Nasser called for unity among all Arabs, regardless of country, as a means to resist external control. As a secular movement, pan-Arabism was strongly anti-colonial and opposed to the existence of Israel. Two expressions of Nasser's pan-Arab policies were the creation of the United Arab Republic and military intervention in Yemen. The United Arab Republic, the first step in creating the pan-Arab nation, was formed by the union of Egypt and Syria in 1958. It was short-lived, however, with Syria pulling out in 1961 in reaction to Egyptian dominance of the relationship and a coup in Syria. In 1962, Nasser sent troops to Yemen to support the newly formed Yemen Arab Republic (North Yemen), which had overthrown the hereditary imam. Egyptian troops fought royalists until 1967. In these ways, Nasser sought to establish himself as the de facto leader of the Arab world and its spokesman to the outside world.

Nasser also advocated an ideology labeled 'Arab socialism' that sought to modernize and industrialize Arab society and overcome the economic effects of colonialism. Arab socialism included secularism and the elimination of economic inequalities through the nationalization of land and factories. Nasser also helped create the Non-aligned Movement, a bloc of lesser-developed countries (known then as the Third World), including India and Yugoslavia, which refused to be in alliance with any of the superpowers.

In 1956, Cold War politics and Arab socialism culminated in the Suez Crisis. In response to Nasser's purchase of tanks from Czechoslovakia and diplomatic overtures to China, the US and Britain withdrew their offer to fund the construction of the Aswan High Dam, badly needed to control the Nile's floodwaters and produce electricity. On July 26, 1956, Egypt nationalized the Suez Canal, still partially owned by British banks. On October 29, 1956, Israel invaded the Sinai peninsula. Though security of the canal was the justification, the real motive was to end Egyptian support for Palestinian militant attacks on Israel and its leadership of an economic embargo against them. British and French military forces supported Israel's invasion and provided aerial bombardment of Cairo. Though a military victory for the British and French, it developed into a political crisis when the US demanded a halt to the invasion and threatened to use fiscal policy

to undermine Britain's economy. Under pressure, British and French troops withdrew at the end of 1956; Israeli troops withdrew from Sinai in March 1957. Nasser was able to claim the nationalization as a victory and gain significant prestige in the region for standing up to the Western powers and Israel.

THE 1967 WAR

The Cold War period was one of rising tension within the region, especially between Israel and the Arab states. In 1967 a series of events led to renewed warfare between Israel and the Arab states. Since the 1950s, Palestinian military organizations had been attacking Israel from bases inside Jordan. Israel retaliated with attacks inside Jordan. In May 1967 the USSR issued intelligence reports, later found to be false, that showed Israel preparing for large-scale military action against Syria, a major supporter of Palestinian militants. At the same time, Nasser, to distract attention from domestic issues and to bolster his claim to pan-Arab leadership, amplified his anti-Israeli rhetoric and actions. He also requested the withdrawal of United Nations troops that had been stationed in Sinai since the 1956 Suez Crisis and closed the strait of Tiran in the Red Sea to Israeli ships. He signed a military agreement with Jordan and Syria. However, given that many Egyptian troops were in Yemen, it was unlikely that he intended to force a military confrontation at the time. Overall, however, his actions gave the impression of an impending attack on Israel.

On June 5, Israel attacked Egypt. Within hours the Egyptian air force was destroyed; most planes never got off the ground. Syria and Jordan entered the war believing Nasser's claims of strong advances against the Israeli army. Israel, able to establish air superiority over its foes, quickly occupied the Sinai, Jerusalem, the Golan Heights and the West Bank, then under Jordanian control. The war was very brief; a ceasefire was signed with Egypt on June 9 and with Syria on June 11.

The 1967 war, also know as the Six-day War or the June War, was a devastating defeat for the Arabs, and for Nasser in particular. The Egyptian military lost 12,000 troops. The war firmly established Israel's military dominance in the region. More importantly, the 1967 war marks the beginning of Israel's occupation of Jerusalem, with its Muslim and Christian holy places, the Gaza Strip, the West Bank and Sinai (Map 6.5). The war intensified the refugee crisis in the Middle East as 300,000 refugees fled from the West Bank into Jordan and 80,000 Syrians fled from the Golan Heights. Israel became responsible for administering territories containing 1.5 million Palestinians. For the Arabs, the war was a humiliating defeat.

The United Nations passed Security Council Resolution 242, which called for the withdrawal of Israeli armed forces from territories occupied in the recent conflict and an end to the state of belligerency between all parties.

THE 1973 ARAB–ISRAELI WAR

The Arabs' humiliating defeat in 1967 led directly to the 1973 war. Here, again, Egypt – now under the leadership of Anwar Sadat, a close confidant of Nasser – played a pivotal role. Sadat sought a military victory over Israel in large part to restore Arab dignity and Egypt's position as leader of the Arab world. In 1969, Sadat began a war of attrition against Israeli forces that continued to occupy the Suez Canal in the aftermath of the 1967 war. The war of attrition lasted until 1970, ending only after an Israeli bombardment of Cairo's suburbs. On October 6, 1973, during the Muslim holy month of Ramadan and the Jewish holiday of Yom Kippur, Egypt and Syria launched a surprise attack on Israel, entering both Sinai and the Golan Heights. Initially, the Arab assault was highly successful. In Sinai, Egyptian troops breached Israeli defenses on the eastern side of the Suez Canal. However, following a massive US airlift of military supplies to Israel, including jet fighters and tanks, Israeli forces gained the advantage. Within a week Syrian troops were pushed out of the Golan Heights and Syria's port cities were heavily damaged. In Sinai, the Egyptian third army was entrapped, without food or water, by Israeli troops. The United States, with the aid of US Secretary of State Henry Kissinger, mediated an end to the conflict, keeping Israel from destroying the trapped army. The war ended on October 26, 1973.

Though the October War failed to alter the territorial status quo between Israel and the Arab states, the Arabs' early success in the conflict allowed Sadat to reclaim dignity for the Arabs. The conflict also shattered the myth of Israeli invincibility as its success was due largely to US intervention. Finally, the 1973 war laid the foundation for the Camp David Peace Accords.

RISING IMPORTANCE OF OIL

The October War demonstrated the growing ability of Arab oil producers to control the world's oil supply and have a direct impact on the West. Shortly after the start of the October War, members of the Organization of the Petroleum Exporting Countries (OPEC), as well as Egypt and Syria, stopped shipments of petroleum to countries that backed Israel during war, including the United States, the Netherlands and Japan. The reduction of the world oil supply, as a result of the Arab oil embargo, led to enormous price increases and gasoline shortages in the US.

> By 1972 annual US consumption of foreign oil had skyrocketed to 811 million barrels, nearly one-third of which came from the Middle East. During the first nine months of 1973 the United States imported 413 million barrels, nearly 10 percent of its total oil consumption, from the Persian Gulf and North Africa.
>
> (Little 2002: 65)

The embargo exacerbated an economic recession in the US and contributed to a global recession the following year. The embargo underscored the US's growing dependence on Middle Eastern oil – a situation that would worsen despite short-time implementation of conservation efforts. At the time of the embargo, 30 percent of the US oil supply was from foreign sources; by 2005, 60 percent was from foreign sources. Of the 11 million barrels per day (mpd) imported into the US in 2005, 3 million came from the Middle East. Securing access to Middle Eastern oil has long been a major aspect of US foreign policy. The alliance with Saudi Arabia dating back to the historic meeting in 1945 between US President Franklin Delano Roosevelt and King Abdelaziz

Map 6.5 The Middle East after the 1967 war

Box 6.4

THE CAMP DAVID ACCORDS: PEACE IN THE MIDDLE EAST

The Camp David Accords were signed on September 17, 1978, and laid the foundation for the peace treaty between Israel and Egypt the following year. The treaty was the first peace agreement between Israel and an Arab country after the 1973 war. The accords were the result of conflict resolution efforts by the Carter administration, culminating in secret negotiations at Camp David. The accords were signed by Egyptian president Anwar Sadat and Israeli prime minister Menachem Begin.

The first step toward this peace took place in November 1977 when Egyptian president Anwar Sadat became the first Arab leader to visit Israel – a visit that took place after secret meetings, unbeknownst even to the Americans, between the two countries. Sadat was motivated in part by a desire to seek help from the US for Egyptian economic growth and by a belief that an agreement between Israel and Egypt would spur resolution of the Israeli–Palestinian conflict.

Under the peace treaty, normal diplomatic relations were established between the two countries. Israel agreed to withdraw from Sinai, which it had acquired in the 1973 war, and evacuated the 4500 Israelis living there. Israel was guaranteed freedom of passage through the Suez Canal and other waterways.

The US provided both Israel and Egypt with a 'peace dividend' amounting to billions of dollars in annual aid, which continues to this day. In general, Israel receives about $3 billion in grants and subsidies each year, Egypt receives about $1 billion. Both countries have been able to acquire large amounts of US military hardware.

Sadat was much criticized in the Arab world for signing a 'separate peace' with Israel, rather than holding out for a 'comprehensive peace' that would include settlement of the Palestinian situation. Indeed, the treaty led directly to the assassination of Sadat by a member of the Islamist group Egyptian Jihad, which opposed the treaty and normalization of relations with Israel.

The peace between Egypt and Israel has been described as a 'cold' peace, meaning that it exists only as an agreement between the two governments, not the peoples. There is little direct contact between Israeli and Egyptian society, and even government relations are strained during times of heightened conflict between Israel and the Palestinians.

The Egyptian–Israeli peace, having broken the taboo on Arab relations with Israel, led to the signing of the 1994 peace treaty between Israel and Jordan. Here, too, a political leader paid the price for peace. In 1995, Israeli prime minister Yitzhak Rabin, who not only brokered the agreement with Jordan but was also instrumental in bringing about the Oslo Accords, an agreement between Israel and the Palestinians, was assassinated by a right-wing Israeli radical who did not support the Oslo Accords. The assassination took place at a peace rally.

---

established the 'enduring relationship' between the US and Saudi Arabia.

THE IRANIAN REVOLUTION

Soon after, the Iranian revolution sent shockwaves through the region and the world. For the US, the revolution, which ended the Pahlavi monarchy and created an Islamic republic, meant the loss of a major Cold War ally. Moreover, it dramatically illustrated the potential for an Islamic identity to trump secular Arab nationalism.

Two factors, growing public discontentment and the political rise of the clergy, led by Ayatollah Khomeini, led to the revolution. Mounting dislike of the monarchy resulted from a variety of issues. Reza Shah's policies were avidly pro-Western, at a time when dislike of the US, due to its support of Israel, was mounting.

Though by 1977 his relationship with the US, under the Carter administration, was growing strained owing to his human rights record, many in Iran considered him to be a puppet of the United States. He also imposed Westernization policies on a population that was still very religious and in many ways traditional.

Despite huge oil revenues, the Iranian economy was in crisis. Inflation was soaring, shortages were common, and the black market was rampant. Inequality between the rich and the poor widened. Amid severe unemployment, the shah brought in large numbers of foreign workers to operate technical equipment, creating further anger.

The monarchy grew increasingly out of touch with the population and led a very extravagant lifestyle, far removed from that of the religious masses. The celebration to mark the 2500th anniversary of the founding of the Persian Empire, held at the ancient city of Persepolis, drew widespread criticism. The festivities, to which only foreign dignitaries were invited, cost $40 million by official estimates, but the real cost may have been three times as high. Two hundred chefs, flown in from Paris, prepared food for the guests.

Reza Shah tolerated no dissent, and used the much dreaded secret police, SAVAK, to suppress his critics. Keddi (2006: 237) describes his 'growing megalomanic self-confidence' in the years leading up to the revolution. Incidents such as the use of live ammunition to disrupt demonstrations further increased his unpopularity and lost him the support of the most Western-oriented sector of Iranian society, the liberal middle class. The shah's relations with the ulema were particularly hostile as he sought to reduce the role of Islam in Iranian society through actions such as changing the legal code and even the calendar, adopting one that marked the ascension to the throne of Persian king Cyrus the Great.

At the same time, an opposition movement based within the clerics increased the religious leaders' influence. The clerics joined forces with liberals in the middle class, nationalists, women and students to form a broad-based movement supporting the overthrow of the monarchy. The ideology of Ayatollah Khomeini, which departed from the traditional Shia idea of non-involvement in political life while awaiting the return of the mahdi, and called for active engagement in politics,

grew increasingly popular. Khomeini had been an early opponent of the shah, and was forced into exile in 1964 for denouncing him. He spent much of his exile in Najaf, Iraq, a holy Shia city, until Saddam Hussein forced him to leave in 1978. He then took up residence in France.

The first public demonstrations took place in 1978, in Qom, the historical center of Islamic scholarship in Iran, following publication of negative comments about Khomeini in the official press. The army responded, and several students were killed. The deaths prompted additional protests at the forty-day period marking their death; over a hundred demonstrators were killed in Tabriz. Protests spread to include attacks on symbols of the monarchy, such as banks, cinemas and government offices. The arrest of leading clerics prompted more protests; martial law was declared; and, in December 1979, 2 million people marched in Tehran demanding the removal of the shah and the return of Khomeini from exile. On January 16, 1979, the shah, who was dying from cancer, and the empress fled. Upon his return Khomeini was greeted by several million followers. On April 1, 1979, the Iranian population overwhelmingly approved a referendum creating the Islamic Republic of Iran. The shah had a difficult time finding refuge in exile, and traveled to Morocco, Mexico and the Bahamas. His supporters in the US finally convinced the Carter administration to allow him entry on medical grounds. He died on July 27, 1980, after seeking medical treatment in the US.

IRAQ AND THE GULF WARS

The creation of an Islamic republic in Iran disrupted the regional strategic balance, distressing Iran's neighbors, who feared revolution inside their own borders, as well as the US. With the revolution, the historical rivalry between Iraq (formerly Mesopotamia) and Iran (formerly Persia) culminated in open warfare, and led indirectly to three regional wars.

Soon after the revolution, Khomeini urged Iraq's majority Shia population, many of whom had familial ties to Iran, to overthrow Saddam Hussein. Simmering border disputes, over the Shatt al-Arab waterway and the Iranian province of Khuzestan, were additional explanations for Hussein's attack on Iran in 1980.

Though he anticipated a quick victory, the war would last a long eight years and exact a heavy toll in human losses and financial terms. The Iranian military proved stronger than Iraq had anticipated and were able to field thousands of zealous volunteers who attacked Iraqi troops in human waves (Map 6.6).

The US was at first neutral in the war, and attempted primarily to stop the attacks by both combatants on non-combatant oil tankers in the Gulf. Eventually, the US provided significant support to Iraq, including arms, helicopters and computers. The US, as well as other countries, provided Iraq with the knowledge to create chemical and biological weapons. Chemical weapons, particularly gas, were used by Iraq both against Iranians and against Iraqi Kurds in Halabja during the war. Hussein received financial support from Kuwait, Saudi Arabia and the United Arab Emirates.

In the course of the war, nearly a million more people were injured. A great number of prisoners of war were taken. The war was an overwhelming defeat for Iraq. The Iraqi economy was devastated, and huge debts were owed to Saudi Arabia, Kuwait and the United Arab Emirates.

THE IRAQI INVASION OF KUWAIT

The loss to Iran laid the foundation for the Iraqi invasion of Kuwait, launching the Second Gulf War. This time Iraq fought a much weaker opponent. On August 2, 1990, nearly 100,000 Iraqi troops crossed the border with Kuwait, occupying the tiny country with little opposition. Hussein claimed Kuwait as its nineteenth province, producing a military victory for a demoralized Iraq. The occupation in effect canceled Iraq's substantial war debt to Kuwait.

By most accounts it seems that Saddam miscalculated the response to the invasion by the United States and the international community. The US saw the invasion as a direct threat to its strategic interests, which included, first and foremost, securing oil from the Gulf and protecting Saudi Arabia. Of less significance was the principle of maintaining Kuwaiti sovereignty. Initial attempts by the US to force an Iraqi withdrawal through diplomatic pressure failed, in part because Hussein

anticipated that the US, still reeling from the memory of Vietnam, would not use substantial military action. Instead the US put together a coalition of states, over thirty members strong, to fight Iraq. The coalition included the United Kingdom, France, and most of the Arab countries of the Middle East.

Indeed, the US was concerned about the strength of the Iraqi army, which numbered over 1 million, many of them with battle experience from the Iran–Iraq War. Military action on the part of the coalition was supported by a UN resolution that demanded the withdrawal of Iraqi troops from Kuwait by January 15, 1991. On January 17, 1991, after the deadline set by the UN resolution, the coalition launched a massive air attack on the Iraqi forces, deploying over 1000 bombing runs a day. The coalition quickly knocked out Iraqi defenses and destroyed the Iraqi air force. The war was particularly notable for the use of precision-guided missiles, which allowed very accurate targeting and afforded television viewers an intimate view of the destruction. Iraq launched SCUD missiles against coalition troops based in Saudi Arabia and against Israeli civilians, though the crude missiles exacted comparatively little damage. The US deployed Patriot anti-missile batteries to Israel to protect it while keeping Israel from entering the war.

On February 22, the US gave Iraq twenty-four hours to begin withdrawing its forces from Kuwait. Shortly thereafter the coalition launched a major ground offensive inside Iraq, and Iraqi forces began to retreat from the border with Kuwait. Iraqi forces proved to be very weak, suffering from battle fatigue and undersupply. At times large numbers surrendered without firing a shot. Coalition troops advanced to within 150 miles of Baghdad, but did not enter the city. Only a hundred hours after it had started, the ground war ended, and the coalition declared Kuwait liberated.

The 1991 Gulf War established the United States as the dominant power in the region and marked the end of Cold War competition for the region. The US, and its allies, adopted a policy of 'containing' Iraq. No-fly zones were established in northern and southern Iraq monitored by the US and the UK, to protect the Kurds and the Shia respectively from attack by Hussein.

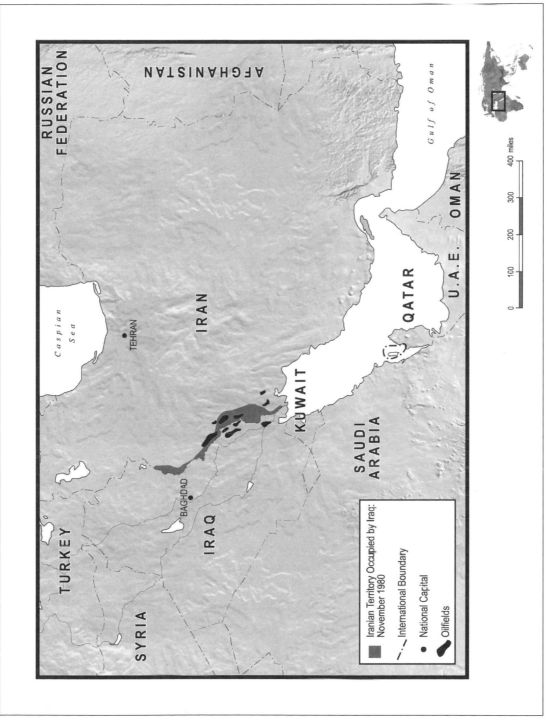

Map 6.6 The Iraqi–Iranian border

Both economic sanctions and weapons inspections were imposed on Iraq by the UN. The impact of the sanctions on the civilian population was quite severe, and generated much international opposition to continuation of the sanctions.

Weapons inspection became an increasingly contentious issue between Iraq and the United States. Iraq would often refuse to comply with the inspections seeking weapons of mass destruction. In 1997, Iraq expelled the UNSCOM (UN Special Commission) inspectors, contending that the inspection team collected information for US intelligence agencies. Iraq's failure to comply with weapons inspections became a key justification for the US invasion of Iraq in 2003.

THE US INVASION OF IRAQ

Why, then, did the US decide to remove Saddam Hussein from power over four years after he expelled the weapons inspectors? The decision to effect a regime change in Iraq is the result of a variety of factors and motivations, which came together in 2002.

Under the Clinton administration, US policy began to shift from one of containment, which had had little impact on Saddam's regime, to one focused on creating regime change. The Iraq Liberation Act of 1998 provided assistance, including military training, to groups inside Iraq that sought to overthrow Saddam. Kurdish groups and Shia groups were both funded. The US continued military action against Iraq, including bombing attacks. When the Bush administration came into office in 2000 it took a more active stance on Iraqi regime change.

The events of September 11, 2001 can be considered both a cause of and justification for the US invasion of Iraq. After 9/11 the Bush administration sought a means to both retaliate for 9/11 and demonstrate US military strength to militant Islamists who might attack the US in the future. The NATO-sponsored attack on the Taliban in Afghanistan had met this goal to a certain extent, but Osama Bin Laden remained at large and the al-Qaeda network clearly was not broken. The occupation of Iraq was linked to a new US policy that allowed pre-emptive action against potential terrorists and the states that harbored them. However, there was little credible evidence linking Hussein, long a secularist who adopted Islamic rhetoric only for political gain, to al-Qaeda.

The influence of a group of neo-conservative thinkers, both in the administration and close to it, played a very significant role in the decision to go to war. Among this group, the idea of removing Hussein existed prior to 9/11, but the terrorist attack provided an easy justification. Among the primary goals of regime change in Iraq was to increase Israeli security by installing a pro-US government in Iraq.

Box 6.5

THE 'NEO-CONS' AND US IRAQ POLICY

The switch to an aggressive policy of regime change in Iraq, using direct US military force, instead of enabling internal dissident groups, can largely be attributed to the efforts of a small but influential group of people inside the Bush administration.

Known as the neo-conservatives or 'neo-cons', they advocated an ideologically driven course of action that pushed the US toward overthrow of Saddam, even while other groups inside the government, including many career State Department officials and members of intelligence agencies, cautioned against such action. Politically the neo-cons tended to be affiliated with the Republican Party and were influential during the administrations of Ronald Reagan and George H. W. Bush. In the American political spectrum, 'liberals' and 'neo-cons' would occupy opposite ends.

Key members of the neo-cons included Paul Wolfowitz, then Deputy Secretary of Defense, Douglas Feith, Under-secretary for Policy, and Donald Rumsfeld, Secretary of Defense. The neo-cons were able to exert so much influence on policy because they

Box 6.5

THE 'NEO-CONS' AND US IRAQ POLICY—CONT'D

were closely affiliated with Vice-president Dick Cheney's office. In addition to Cheney, prominent neo-cons included his chief of staff, Lewis 'Scooter' Libby, and Elliot Abrams, then National Security Council Senior Director for Middle East and North African Affairs. Though he did not hold office, William Kristol, the editor of the conservative periodical *The Weekly Standard* and founder of the Project for the New American Century, was instrumental in supporting the neo-con agenda in the Middle East. Generally the neo-cons advocate an activist US foreign policy and the use of military power to achieve US interests. They advocate a unilateralist stance and are wary of organizations such as the United Nations. They strongly support the spread of democracy, through military means if necessary. US policy in the Middle East should be based on a strong US and Israeli military presence. By the mid-1990s the neo-cons were advocating the removal of Saddam Hussein both to promote Israeli security and to gain access to Iraq's oil resources. Opponents of the neo-cons argue that they are willing to put Israel's strategic interests ahead of those of the United States. Further neo-con goals in removing Saddam included achieving a 'win' in the war on terror and creating a democratic government that would support US interests in the region.

The neo-cons have been criticized for allowing ideology to blind them to the realities of overthrowing Saddam and occupying Iraq. They relied heavily on dubious intelligence, much of it supplied by Iraqi National Congress opposition leader Ahmed Chalabi who provided unsubstantiated 'first-hand' accounts of Iraq's weapons of mass destruction and downplayed the possibility of violence between the Sunni and the Shia. The neo-cons set up their own intelligence agency, bypassing the CIA and the NSA, inside the Defense Department, dubbed the 'Office of Special Plans', to collect their intelligence information.

By the end of 2007, the neo-con influence in the Bush administration had waned considerably. Libby was found guilty of obstruction of justice for his actions relating to the investigation of the 'Plame Affair' in which the identity of an undercover CIA agent was disclosed. Wolfowitz left the administration and became president of the World Bank in 2005. In May 2007 he was forced to resign after an investigation involving a promotion he had arranged for his girlfriend. In December 2006, Rumsfeld, who had come under increasing criticism, including by other neo-cons, for his handling of the war, resigned. Douglas Feith resigned in 2005.

And yet the neo-cons still remain a significant force in American politics. Indeed, as of late 2007, Elliot Abrams held the position of Deputy National Security Advisor with a portfolio for advancing democracy abroad. Some neo-cons support a US-led war with Iran.

Hersch, S. M. (2003) '"Selective Intelligence". Donald Rumsfeld has his own special sources: Are they reliable?, *The New Yorker*, May 12.

http://www.newamericancentury.org/, website of the Project of the New American Century, contains numerous neo-con-authored articles on Iraq and the Middle East.

Still another motivation for the Iraq war was the administration's plan to promote democracy in the region. The removal of Hussein and the installation of a more democratic, pro-US regime was expected to set off a 'democratic tsunami' across the region, resulting in more democratic governments and pro-US sentiment. The democratization policy (discussed in more detail in Chapter 10) was seen as hypocritical by many in the region as the US continued strongly to support Saudi Arabia and Egypt, both with poor records of civil society participation in government. Finally, securing more direct access to oil supplies, reducing US dependence on supplies from Saudi Arabia, was another prime motivation.

Initially, the US tried to achieve its goal of regime change by working with the international community. On September 12, 2002, it presented its case for invasion to the UN Security Council. Key US allies, namely France and Germany, rejected the idea, calling instead for continued diplomacy. As a compromise the UNSC passed UN Resolution 1441 that initiated new weapons inspections and called for 'severe consequences' should Iraq fail to comply. The resolution did not authorize invasion as a potential consequence. Domestically, the US Congress authorized the use of force against Iraq in October 2002. Through the winter the US continued efforts to gain UN backing for an invasion. In February 2003, Secretary of State Colin Powell provided the UN General Assembly with the administration's evidence of Iraq's weapons of mass destruction program and al-Qaeda links. Again, the UN failed to pass a resolution authorizing the use of force; the move was blocked by Canada, France, Germany and Russia.

On March 17, 2003, President Bush issued an ultimatum to Saddam Hussein, requiring that he and his two sons leave Iraq within forty-eight hours. The ultimatum was refused, and on March 20, 2003, the US launched a military action known as Operation Iraqi Freedom. Shortly after the deadline passed, bombs were dropped on Baghdad and coalition troops crossed the border from Kuwait into Iraq. The bulk of the force were troops from the US (120,000) and the UK (45,000). Around the world large anti-war protests were held, though much of the US population supported the war.

The planned invasion, entering Iraq from both the north and the south, was hampered by Turkey's refusal to allow the US to utilize its airspace. However, the 'shock and awe' campaign, which combined an aerial bombardment with ground-force assault, was highly effective. Within three weeks the Iraqi government had collapsed, and Hussein and high-ranking Ba'athists went into hiding. On April 9, 2003, the coalition occupied Baghdad. In May 2003, speaking aboard USS *Abraham Lincoln*, which boasted a banner emblazoned 'Mission Accomplished', President Bush declared the end to major combat in Iraq, At that point, total US casualties were 140.

Providing security, reconstructing Iraq and fostering a democratic Iraqi government have proved to be far greater challenges than anticipated. During the war, much of the infrastructure needed to function normally was destroyed by looting; and there were criticisms that too few troops were deployed for the invasion. Insurgents, from all of Iraq's major ethnic divisions as well as foreigners, have filled the political vacuum left by the removal of Saddam. Five years after the US invasion, Iraq has descended into civil war; and neighboring countries are swamped with refugees. The disintegration of Iraq has increased Iranian influence in the region.

Box 6.6

KEY REGIONAL ORGANIZATIONS

A few key regional organizations play a role in regulating the region's political and economic life.

The Arab League

This is the oldest regional organization in the region. It was formed in 1945, with an initial membership of seven, to coordinate among the Arab states and advance their status. As the 'Arab' League it excludes Iran and Turkey, but includes Djibouti and Comoros, which also have close ties to sub-Saharan Africa. Today the Arab League contains twenty-two members. It generally meets during an annual summit.

Box 6.6

KEY REGIONAL ORGANIZATIONS—CONT'D

The focus of the Arab League's activities is primarily on political relations between the states and attempts, at times, to coordinate aspects of a foreign policy. Major policy initiatives have included the Arab boycott of Israel, beginning in 1945, and creation of the Arab Peace Initiative for resolving the Israeli–Palestinian conflict in 2002. Overall, however, there is little political and economic integration across the region. At times the work of the League has been hampered by internal conflict, making it difficult to agree on an agenda, much less achieve agreement on resolutions.

The Arab League's activities are closely associated with Arab nationalism. Its headquarters are in Cairo. Egypt has often dominated the affairs of the Arab League; five of its six secretary-generals, including the current one, have been Egyptian. In 1979 the League suspended Egypt's membership following President Anwar Sadat's visit to Jerusalem and the peace agreement with Israel. The League's headquarters were moved to Tunisia. Egypt was reinstated in 1989, and the headquarters returned to Cairo.

Organization of the Islamic Conference

All the members of the Arab League are also members of the Organization of the Islamic Conference (OIC). With fifty-seven members, the OIC is a much larger body, composed of predominantly Muslim states in the Middle East, East Asia, Central Asia and Africa. It was formed in 1969; its parliament is headquartered in Tehran. The OIC holds a summit each year; foreign ministers of OIC members meet yearly.

The OIC focuses on topics of concern to the Islamic states. These include resolution of the Israeli–Palestinian conflict, the Israeli–Arab conflict and the status of Muslim holy places in Jerusalem.

The Gulf Cooperation Council

The Gulf Cooperation Council (GCC) is composed of Bahrain, Kuwait, Oman, Qatar, Saudi Arabia and the United Arab Emirates. The GCC was formed in 1981 in response to the outbreak of war between Iraq and Iran, neither of which is a member of the GCC. Preventing external intervention in the gulf region is a primary goal of the GCC. The GCC also addresses economic and social issues. The GCC attempts to standardize trade policies and regulations amongst its members and increase economic integration.

The GCC is headquartered in Riyadh, Saudi Arabia. The presidency of the GCC rotates annually amongst the members.

The Organization of Petroleum Exporting Countries

The oil-exporting countries of the Middle East are also members of OPEC. OPEC was created at the Baghdad Conference in 1960 by Iran, Iraq, Kuwait, Saudi Arabia and Venezuela. Today, its membership includes: Libya, Algeria, Qatar, the United Arab Emirates, Indonesia, Angola and Nigeria. It is headquartered in Vienna, Austria.

The stated goals of OPEC include providing stability in world oil prices and protecting the interests of the producing nations – goals that can sometimes be at odds with each other. In 1973, OPEC demonstrated its ability to control the world oil market, and influence the global economy, when it enacted an oil embargo during the 1973 Arab–Israeli war. Though the OPEC nations control two-thirds of the world's known oil reserves and produce 41.7 percent (2005) of global production, the rise of export from new producers such as Mexico and Russia may be diminishing OPEC's influence. Within OPEC, Saudi Arabia is by far the leading producer.

SUMMARY OF MAIN POINTS

- The post World War II era is characterized by the fruition of nationalist movements and the birth of independent states.
- The struggle for self-determination between Jews and Palestinians led to the creation of Israel and resulted in a large number of Palestinian refugees.
- Three regional wars between Israel and the Arab states in 1948, 1967 and 1973 have dominated politics in the region.
- The Middle East 'peace process' is an attempt to resolve issues resulting from these wars.
- A revolution established a theocracy in Iran and fears that other countries would follow the same path.
- The US is the most dominant external power in the region.
- Post-Saddam Iraq is the greatest source of instability in the region.

QUESTIONS FOR DISCUSSION

1 In what ways did the actions of colonial powers contribute to the diversity of state structures in the Middle East following independence?

2 Why did efforts to strike a compromise between the Palestinian right to self-determination and the Jewish desire for a national home fail prior to 1948?

3 What resources (political, economic, military) did each group, the Palestinians and the Jews, have available to pursue their goal of independent statehood?

4 Why was the 1967 war such a devastating loss for the Arab states? What was the impact on Israel?

5 In what ways did the Cold War impact on the US choice of allies in the region?

6 What was the significance of the Iranian revolution?

7 How has US policy toward Iraq changed in the last twenty-five years?

SUGGESTIONS FOR FURTHER READING

Cockburn, A. and Cockburn, P. (1999) *Out of the Ashes: The Resurrection of Saddam Hussein.* New York: Harper Perennial. A biographical overview of Saddam Hussein and description of the regime he created, to the end of the 1991 Gulf War.

Halliday, F. (2005) *The Middle East in International Relations: Power, Politics and Ideology.* Cambridge: Cambridge University Press. See particularly chapters 3 and 4 that discuss formation of the modern states and the Cold War period.

Hinnebusch, R. (2003) *The International Politics of the Middle East.* Manchester: Manchester University Press. See particularly Chapter 2, 'Core and periphery: the international system and the Middle East', for an understanding of how external factors such as the Cold War and increasing oil dependency impacted on the Middle East.

International Crisis Group (2006b) 'The next Iraq war? Sectarianism and civil conflict'. *Middle East Report*, No. 52, February 27. Examines the increasing sectarian violence in Iraq: http://www.crisisgroup.org/home/index.cfm?id=3980&l=1.

Kamrava, M. (2005) *The Modern Middle East: A Political History since the First World War.* Berkeley, Calif.: University of California Press. A comprehensive overview of the region's modern history. See especially chapters 3 and 4 and the discussion of Palestinian nationalism and Zionism.

Keddi, N. (2006) *Modern Iran: Roots and Results of a Revolution.* New Haven, Conn.: Yale University Press. Traces the roots of the Iranian revolution and its ideology through to the present. Essential reading for understanding modern Iran.

Kimmerling, B. and Migdal, J. (2003) *The Palestinian People: A History.* Cambridge, Mass.: Harvard University Press. The first four chapters of this extensive history of the Palestinian people trace the roots of Palestinian identity and creation of a Palestinian nationalist movement.

Little, D. (2002) *American Orientalism: The United States and the Middle East since 1945*. Chapel Hill, NC: University of North Carolina Press. See especially Chapter 2 on the US and Middle East oil.

Moore, C. H. (1970) *Politics in North Africa: Algeria, Morocco and Tunisia*. Boston, Mass.: Little, Brown. Describes the rise of nationalism in North Africa and the end of the colonial era.

Oren, M. (2007) *Power, Faith and Fantasy: America in the Middle East: 1776 to the Present*. New York: W. W. Norton. In particular see chapters 27 and 28 that detail how support for Israel became a central part of US foreign policy.

Sachar, H. (1996) *A History of Israel: From the Rise of Zionism to Our Time*, 2nd edn. New York: Alfred Knopf.

A comprehensive account of the formation of Israel; see especially sections on the rise of political Zionism.

Tessler, M. (1994). *A History of the Israeli–Palestinian Conflict*. Bloomington, Ind.: University of Indiana Press. A highly detailed, well-researched and balanced history of the Israeli–Palestinian conflict up to the signing of the Oslo Accords in 1993.

Yergin, D. (1991) *The Prize: The Epic Quest for Oil, Money and Power*. New York: Simon & Schuster. A sweeping, and fascinating, account of the discovery of oil in the Middle East and its impact on the region and the world.

http://www.yale.edu/lawweb/avalon/. A website, run by the Yale Law School, containing key historical documents.

7

CONTEMPORARY ISLAMIST THOUGHT

To most in the West, the attacks on the United States by the Islamist militant group al-Qaeda on September 11, 2001 were an enormous shock. Not since the Japanese attack on Pearl Harbor had an enemy mounted an attack on US soil. But this enemy was very different: it fought not in the name of a sovereign state that had declared war on the United States, but in the name of (a particular interpretation of) Islam. The fighters, members of no national army, claimed to fight for Muslims worldwide.

As new and shocking as the attacks were, the idea of fighting to restore 'true' Islamist values is not new. Indeed, the ideology of al-Qaeda, its beliefs and principles, are rooted in Islamist intellectual tradition, but represent a modern departure and implementation. Al Qaedism, the ideology of al-Qaeda, is an amalgam – and, some argue, a corruption – of ideas found in Wahabbism and the ideas of Islamist thinkers such as Sayyid Qutb. So, if militant Islamist thought was not 'invented' by Osama Bin Laden, what are its origins? What are the major questions addressed by Islamist thinkers? What are the central ideas that shape Islamist thought today?

Contemporary Islamist thought has its roots in the eighteenth and nineteenth centuries. Like Arab nationalism, Islamist thought was in many ways a response to external control by European states. Islamist thinkers argued that the suffering of the Muslim community was a result of their abandonment of Islam through the adoption of Western legal codes, education and other practices. Many Islamist thinkers preached a return to traditional values and 'pure' Islam as a means of improving the quality of life and resisting foreign domination.

THE DEVELOPMENT OF WAHHABISM IN ARABIA

Wahhabism, the Sunni interpretation of Islam, followed in Saudi Arabia, and less rigorously in Qatar, has its origins in the writings of Muhammad ibn 'Abd al-Wahhab (1703–92). Concerned with what he perceived as the moral decay of society in Arabia at the time, ibn 'Abd al-Wahhab sought a return to a more 'pure' or fundamental form of Islam. In fact, Wahhabis refer to each other as *muwāhiddūn*, meaning Unitarians; the term Wahhabi is largely used by Westerners.

Ibn 'Abd al-Wahhab rejected all forms of innovation (*bid'ah*) in the practice of Islam, such as the celebration of the Prophet's birthday, the veneration of saints, and the wearing of charms. Also considered deviant are practices associated with Shiism, such as praying at the tombs of martyrs, saints or prophets, and the mystical practices of Sufis. In practical terms this means the rejection of any religious practices within Islam that came after the first

Box 7.1

KEY CONCEPTS IN ISLAMIST THOUGHT

Michael Christopher Low

Ijtihād: an Islamic legal concept, meaning independent reasoning or interpretation as opposed to *taqlīd* (blind imitation of traditional thought and practice). This process is to be utilized when the Qur'an and the Hadīth are silent or inexplicit on a particular topic. Only those equipped with a thorough knowledge of the Arabic language, Islamic theology and philosophy (*kalām*), revealed texts, and legal theory (*usūl al-fiqh*) are considered as worthy *mujtahidūn* (interpreters). *Mujtahidūn* are to rely upon *qiyas* (analogic reasoning), which provides a method of deducing laws related to matters not explicitly discussed in either the Qur'an or the Hadīth without relying on unsystematic personal opinions. Moreover, no interpretation may contradict the Qur'an, nor may it be used in cases where *ijma'* (consensus) has already been reached. As a result of the voluminous rulings created by Islamic jurists from the four major law schools of Islam (Hanafi, Shafi'i, Maliki and Hanbali), by roughly 1300 CE, the *bāb al-ijtihād* (gate of interpretation) was considered to be closed. However, in the nineteenth and twentieth centuries, Islamist reformers have sought to bypass the accumulated corpus of legal texts and reopen this gate in order to reinterpret Islamic law to reflect the changing circumstances facing modern Muslims.

Islāh: reforms, aimed at the revival (*ihyā'*) and renewal (*tajdīd*) of the Muslim community based on a return to the first principles of the Qur'an and the Hadīth. The term is typically used to describe reformist movements from the eighteenth century to the present. Modern calls for reform have generally been driven by a perception of backwardness and stagnation in the Muslim societies of the eighteenth and nineteenth centuries, many of which were being overwhelmed by the forces of European imperialism. Rather than trying to compete with the West or slavishly imitating Western thought, however, reformers sought solutions from within the Islamic intellectual tradition.

Revivalist thinkers, most notably Muhammad ibn 'Abd al-Wahhab (d. 1787), believed that Muslims of his time had strayed from the correct path set by the example of the Prophet Muhammad. Thus, the Wahhabis, whose influence is most strongly felt in the Arabian peninsula, maintain that historical misunderstandings and misinterpretations have distorted the true meaning of Islamic texts, allowing the introduction of harmful innovations (*bid'a*). However, the most important strand of reformist thought, which later became known as the Salafiyya movement (derived from the term *al-salaf al-sālih*, or pious ancestors), emerged from nineteenth- and early twentieth-century thinkers, such as Jamal al-Din al-Afghani (d. 1897), Muhammad 'Abduh (d. 1905) and Muhammad Rashid Rida (d. 1935). Troubled by the Islamic world's lack of development in comparison to Europe as well as by its loss of political independence at the hands of European imperialism, they called for a rejuvenation of Islamic thought and practice in order to restore the dignity, unity, and thus the greatness of the Islamic world. Rather than imitating the West, however, they stressed the compatibility of Western science and technology with Islamic, pointing to the earlier contributions of Islamic civilization, which had helped pave the way for European modernity. Moreover, they insisted that reason and faith are compatible. As a result, they called for the rejection of *taqlīd*, blaming this mindset for the stagnation of the Islamic world. As a remedy for this culture of imitation, they emphasized the necessity of *ijtihad*, the antithesis of *taqlīd*, advocating that legal and religious texts must be continuously reinterpreted in order to recapture the dynamism of Islam's glorious past and its ability to confront the changing circumstances of the modern world. Despite its rather liberal beginnings, however, during the twentieth century Salafism and its more conservative cousin, Wahhabism, have often been conflated.

Box 7.1

KEY CONCEPTS IN ISLAMIST THOUGHT—CONT'D

Jihād: from the Arabic root meaning to strive, to exert, or to fight. However, it is important to note that the exact meaning of this word is highly dependent on the context in which it is used. Thus, while the average Western observer may only associate the term *jihād* with terrorism, 'holy war', or a kind of 'crusade' against Western infidels, the term actually works on multiple levels. Typically this concept has been divided into two basic categories in Islamic thought, the 'greater' *jihād* and the 'lesser' *jihād*. The greater *jihād* may express a struggle against the wicked inclinations of one's own soul. This inner struggle for religious perfection may also be reflected in an outward struggle for the moral betterment of the Islamic community as a whole or through efforts to bring new converts to the faith. However, it is the lesser *jihād* that has become a household word the world over. From a legal perspective, the lesser *jihād* is a war waged against enemies residing in the *dār al-harb* (abode of war). It is the only legal form of warfare in Islam. In the past, such warfare could only be called for by state authorities and was highly regulated by Islamic law. In particular, non-combatants were not to be harmed. Moreover, such an action would have been preceded by a call to Islam or treaty. However, in recent decades, in order to justify political struggles against their own co-religionists, Salafi and Wahhabi extremists have branded many Muslims as unbelievers

because of their neglect in adhering to or enforcing Islamic law. This radical shift in the definition of *jihād* has led radical Islamist thinkers to promote the use of violence against secular regimes in the Islamic world as well as against the Western governments that have supported them.

Jāhiliyya: literally the 'state of ignorance', describing the period of Arab paganism preceding the revelation of Islam. During this era, the pristine monotheism of Abraham had given way to idol worship, oppression and decadence. In the twentieth century, Islamist thinkers such as Abu al-'Ala Mawdudi and Sayyid Qutb have used this concept as a metaphor for secular modernity, dubbing it the new *jāhiliyya*. As Qutb explains, Islam is the submission of man to God's 'universal laws'. *Jāhiliyya*, 'on the other hand, is one man's lordship over another'. Therefore, societies or governmental systems based upon man-made values or ideological beliefs as opposed to the divine system created by Islam are considered to be *jāhiliyya*. To remedy this situation, Qutb and others propose the implementation of Islamic law. Using Qutb's logic, radical Islamists have justified military action and terrorist attacks against secular regimes in the Islamic world.

Tawhīd: the pre-eminent doctrine of Islam. *Tawhīd* is the absolute belief in the Unity of God or monotheism.

two generations of Muslims, known as the Companions (those Muslims who knew or met Muhammad), and their Followers. Wahhabi mosques, for example, do not have minarets as they were not included on earlier mosques. Similarly, characteristic Islamic decoration, such as calligraphic script, is not found in Wahhabi mosques. Nor do Wahhabis allow domes on tombs, which is typical of Shia saint veneration tombs.

Wahhabis believe strongly in the concept of *tawhid*, or the oneness of God. Moreover, the Qur'an and the

Hadīth are considered the only sources for understanding God's will. Other sources, such as the commentaries of Islamist jurists, are not acknowledged. This position leaves no room for interpretation, and leads to Wahhabism's rigid and conservative emphasis.

Ibn 'Abd al-Wahhab's ideology was based heavily on the writings of a thirteenth-century Islamist scholar, Ahmed Ibn Taymiyya (1268–1328 AD). Like al-Wahhab, Ibn Taymiyya advocated a literal interpretation of the Qur'an and the oneness of God (*tawhīd*). One of

Ibn Taymiyya's key concepts was the obligation of Muslims to engage in *jihād* (struggle) against leaders who were unbelievers and to remove them from power. In the contexts of Ibn Taymiyya's day, these injunctions were directed toward the Mongol invaders who captured Baghdad in 1258 and established rule over the Middle East. Though they converted to Islam, they still retained some of their own cultural practices, including their legal system, and were not considered by Ibn Taymiyya to be 'true' Muslims. Many Islamists since the eighteenth century have used Ibn Taymiyya's writings to justify revolution against existing governments in the Middle East.

WAHHABISM AND SAUDI ARABIA

Around 1744, Muhammad ibn 'Abd al-Wahhab joined forces with Muhammad ibn al-Saud, who controlled a town near the modern-day Saudi capital of Riyadh. Working together, al-Wahhab and al-Saud were able to conquer and unify the Arabian peninsula. Wahhabi-trained Bedouin solders, known as the Ikhwan, played a pivotal role in the success of al-Saud's military campaigns. In 1932 the Kingdom of Saudi Arabia was formed, combining the regions of the Nejd (central Arabia, around Riyadh), the Hejaz (along the Red Sea coast, including Mecca and Medina) and al-Hasa (in the east).

The close collaboration between the al-Saud family and the Wahhabi religious establishment was embedded in Saudi Arabia's political and religious life. The legal and educational systems are heavily controlled by religious clerics. The King of Saudi Arabia also holds the title of 'Custodian of the Two Holy Mosques', located in Mecca and Medina, and is expected to be a protector and defender of the Islamic faith. The religious establishment routinely issues religious rulings to validate political policy.

The involvement of Osama Bin Laden, formerly a Saudi citizen, and a follower of Wahhabism, in the 9/11 attacks and the leadership of al-Qaeda has brought criticism of Wahhabism as an interpretation of Islam that promotes violence and intolerance. Indeed, non-Muslims are not allowed to practice their religion, and the country's Shiite minority faces discrimination and repression. Of more concern to Western governments is the contention that Saudi Arabia is 'exporting' an extremist brand of Islam through the funding of religious schools (*madrasas*) in various parts of the world, especially in Pakistan. The government of Saudi Arabia, too, faces challenges from religious extremists within its own society. The appearance of a group called al-Qaeda in Arabia, in 2003, which has attacked both foreign workers and state security, illustrates the fact that some in Saudi Arabia feel that the religious establishment needs to return to more stringent values and separate itself from a political leadership seen as corrupt. Specific grievances these militant Islamists have with the Saudi regime include the stationing of Western, 'infidel' troops inside the kingdom.

JAMAL AL-DIN AL-AFGHANI (1839–97)

In the nineteenth century Islamist thought developed many of the concepts and ideological frameworks still significant today. Like Arab nationalism, Islamist thought developed against the backdrop of increasing control by the forces of European colonialism and often deteriorating economic conditions among the popular classes. As Cairo was often the epicenter for the Arab nationalist movements, it was also a center for the development of Islamist thought. Like Arab nationalism, Islamist ideology also supported independence, both from Europe and from native rulers who failed to meet the Islamists' standards of appropriate conduct and adherence to Islam.

Jamal al-Din al-Afghani (1839–97) called for action, in the name of Islam, against the British-backed Egyptian monarchy. An Iranian by birth, al-Afghani moved to Egypt where he came into conflict with the British-installed monarch, Khedive Tawfiq. The core of al-Afghani's message was that the West had been able to achieve superiority over the Islamic world because Islam was in a state of decadence and decay. To resist European domination, the Islamic community needed to unite.

Moreover, the Islamic community needed to reform from within. This included the overthrow of passive Muslim leaders who had allowed Europeans to control their countries. Indeed, al-Afghani visualized the creation of a pan-Islamic nation, united under the leadership of a charismatic leader. Unlike some other Islamist theorists, al-Afghani was willing to utilize Western innovations for his own purposes; they included seeking autonomy for the Islamic world.

Al-Afghani's ideas posed a threat both to the British and to their puppet ruler. Following his expulsion from Egypt, he went to Paris where he co-published a newspaper, *The Firmest Bond*, with Muhammad Abduh, calling for pan-Islamic unity organized around a caliphate. He ended his life under gilded house arrest in Turkey, imprisoned by sultan Abdel Hamid II, who had restyled himself as leader of the Islamic world but found al-Afghani's call for conflict with the West too dangerous.

Al-Afghani's ideas, namely the need for Islam to reform in order to throw off subjugation by the West and reduce the suffering of Muslims, and the role of Islam as a unifying political force against the West and their backers, had a lasting impact on Islamist thought and remain influential today.

MUHAMMAD ABDUH (1849–1905)

In Egypt and Paris, al-Afghani collaborated with Muhammad Abduh (1849–1905), an Egyptian who developed the concept of Islamic modernism. Though many Islamist schools of thought, such as Wahhabism, rejected innovation and openness to other cultures, Abduh's vision was of an Islam free from rigidity and open to modernization. Indeed, he saw no incompatibility between Islam and modernity; it was possible for a person to be both modern and Muslim.

Unlike many Islamic jurists, Abduh argued for the reopening of the gates of *ijtihad* ('interpretation'). He believed strongly in the power of human reasoning to apply Islam to a new situation, rather than to follow tradition unquestioningly. However, innovations did need to be consistent with the standards set in the Qur'an, the Hadīth and the practices of the Rightly Guided Caliphs. Though against blindly following tradition, Abduh revered the Islam practiced by the *al-Salaf al-sāllih* ('pious forefathers or ancestors') as rational and true. His works mark the beginning of the Salafist movement.

Though later theorists would transform the use of the term Salafiyya and Salafist Islam to exclude the potential for innovation within Islam, Abduh cited the practices of the forefathers to support his call for an adaptable Islam.

Abduh was very influential in Egypt, publishing numerous books and serving as the editor of Cairo's official government newspaper. He supported the modernizing initiatives begun under Muhammad Ali, including those that broadened the curriculum in religious schools. Abduh's support for the Egyptian nationalist movement, his criticism of Britain's role in Egypt and his involvement in the Urabi Revolt caused his exile 1882. For part of his exile he joined al-Afghani in Paris and published a journal that called for Muslims to unite against Western imperialism. Abduh eventually returned to Egypt and served as the grand mufti of Al Azhar, serving as head of the university and spiritual leader for Sunni Muslims in Egypt and beyond, a judge and an Islamic legal scholar.

RASHID RIDA (1865–1935)

Following Abduh's death, his student, Syrian-born Rashid Rida, continued to expand on Abduh's ideas and himself became a leader in the Islamic modernist movement. Rida published an extensive biography of Muhammad Abduh, as well as a journal, *Al-Manar*, which, over a forty-year period, presented the Salafist case for reform.

HASSAN AL BANNA (1906–49) AND THE MUSLIM BROTHERHOOD

The 1920s was a tumultuous period in Egypt. Britain's control had increased, bringing increased Westernization, especially to the capital. The vast economic gap between those who benefited from colonialism and the poor became more obvious. Competing political ideas – secularism, nationalism and Islamism – attempted to shape Egypt's social and political life.

Against this backdrop, Hassan al Banna, greatly influenced by Rashid Rida, formed the first widespread popular political movement, based on Salafist thought.

Al Banna was deeply opposed to Western intervention in the Middle East and Egypt, and the associated impact of Westernization. Of particular concern was the growing influence of secularism, especially among Egypt's youth, whom he saw turning away from Islam.

In 1928, al Banna founded the Muslim Brotherhood, an Islamic association dedicated to encouraging personal adherence to Islam and charitable works. Like other Islamist movements, the Muslim Brotherhood was a reaction to the growing influence of secularist movements. The Muslim Brotherhood grew quickly; within two years it had established 500 branches throughout the country.

The principles of the Muslim Brotherhood called for a return to Islam, including *sharia* and implementation of Islam through all aspects of life. This call for a return to Islam was combined with an emphasis on issues that concerned the growing masses, including colonialism, education, Arab nationalism, and social inequality. Indeed, the social justice message in al Banna's thought was transformed into action: much aid for the underprivileged, such as medical care, food, education and employment training, was provided through the Muslim Brotherhood. This aid was particularly crucial for the urban poor who had migrated to the cities after World War I. Such practices encouraged widespread support for the Muslim Brotherhood. The Muslim Brotherhood also sent soldiers to fight with the Palestinians following the declaration of an Israeli state – another popular cause in Egypt.

The Muslim Brotherhood's growing influence – by the 1940s its size was estimated at 500,000 – and its growing involvement in political issues soon brought it into conflict with the Egyptian government. Al Banna supported the idea of *jihād* as the duty of every Muslim, including *jihād* against Egypt's British-backed government.

In 1948 the Muslim Brotherhood assassinated Prime Minister Mahmoud Nuqrashi, following his edict to dissolve the Muslim Brotherhood by force. Hassan al Banna was killed the following year, most likely by Egyptian security forces, amid a large-scale crackdown on the organization in which thousands of its members were imprisoned. The organization continued to exist secretly, though its activities were severely curtailed.

Following Egyptian independence, the Brotherhood split into two branches. The first sought to work with the new government to increase gradually the role of religion in politics and society. The second, under the leadership of Sayyid Qutb, pressed for armed revolt against corrupt rulers in the Middle East and the West.

SAYYID QUTB (1906–66) AND THE MUSLIM BROTHERHOOD

Qutb's early career, as a teacher and an administrator in the Egyptian Ministry of Education, gave little indication that he would emerge as one of the most influential Islamist thinkers ever, creating theoretical works on the role of Islam in social and political life that remain highly influential today.

A defining moment in Qutb's life was a two-year stay in the United States, between 1948 and 1950, while working for the Ministry of Education, where he obtained a Master's degree and studied the US educational system. Qutb's impression of life in the US was extremely negative; he saw American society as morally lax and socially unjust. While he was in the United States his book *Social Justice in Islam* was published. In this book, and in another entitled *Milestones*, he laid out his theory of Islamic society based on principles of social justice. This book was widely read (and is still today) and raised Qutb's profile in Egypt.

Following his return from America, Qutb began to work with the Muslim Brotherhood, which shared his goal of creating an all-encompassing Islamic society in Egypt. He quickly assumed intellectual leadership of the organization, publishing numerous books and articles in the Brotherhood's periodicals and becoming editor-in-chief of its official journal. He also resigned from the Ministry of Education.

In 1954 the Muslim Brotherhood attempted to assassinate Gamal Abdel Nasser, leader of the Free Officers who had overthrown the Egyptian monarchy in 1952, making Egypt independent. At the time of the revolution the Free Officers and the Brotherhood had briefly collaborated to mobilize public support for the revolution. The union between the Brotherhood and the Free Officers was short-lived as differences arose over the return to civilian rule, elections, steps for reintroducing the *sharia*, and a proposed treaty to allow Britain to place troops in the Suez Canal zone. As tension increased, the Free Officers grew concerned about potential challenges to their rule by the Brotherhood. In 1954, Qutb was jailed and the dissolution of the Muslim Brotherhood was decreed by the Egyptian government, though Qutb was released and the ban on the Brotherhood was lifted shortly thereafter.

After the assassination attempt, six leaders of the Brotherhood were hanged, and Qutb and thousands of the organization's members were arrested. Qutb served fifteen years in jail, during which time he wrote numerous books. He focused on the condition of *jāhiliyya* in the modern world. Qutb argued that Saudi Arabia and Egypt, as well as other Muslim countries, existed in an immoral and backward state equivalent to that which existed in the Arabian peninsula prior to the advent of Islam, known as *jāhiliyya*. Only through the creation of an Islamic state, by force if necessary, could society emerge from the *jāhiliyya*.

He was released from prison in 1964, only to be rearrested in 1965. He was charged with supporting the overthrow of the Egyptian government. His writings were used as evidence against him. He was hanged in Cairo in 1966. Despite his death, Qutb had a large impact on the growth of Salafist movements in the region. Under his influence the Muslim Brotherhood expanded throughout the region, taking root in the Palestinian territories and in Saudi Arabia, where his brother Muhammad taught for many years.. His ideas, particularly the duty of *jihād* against leaders viewed as illegitimate, has profoundly influenced the Salafist movement, including organizations such as Islamic Jihad and al-Qaeda.

After Qutb's death, the Muslim Brotherhood in Egypt began to follow a more moderate path, choosing a slow Islamization through democracy rather than violence. Many of the Brotherhood's members refused to accept this moderate position and formed new organizations committed to the use of violence. One such organization is the Islamic Jihad (Egyptian branch), which assassinated the Egyptian president Anwar Sadat in 1981, following the historic peace agreement between Egypt and Israel. In the 1990s the Islamic Jihad continued its attacks on Egyptian government officials and Western tourists.

Today the Egyptian Muslim Brotherhood, which has chosen to use elections rather than violence, is viewed with contempt by groups such as al-Qaeda that advocate global *jihād*. Though the Muslim Brotherhood is officially banned in Egypt, in practice the government tolerates its existence. The Brotherhood regularly runs candidates in Egypt's elections, and won 20 percent of the seats in the November 2005 legislative elections. Currently candidates for the Muslim Brotherhood must run as independents, as the Brotherhood is not recognized as a political party. Though now considered moderate, the Muslim Brotherhood does still condone *jihād* under certain circumstances, including when a country is occupied by a foreign power. Therefore *jihād* against the US occupation of Iraq and the Israeli occupation of Palestinian territories are both justified.

KHOMEINI AND ISLAMIC REVOLUTION

With the Islamic revolution in 1979, its spiritual leader, Imam Ruhullah Khomeini, gained the opportunity to establish an Islamic state. Khomeini's ideology was strongly anti-imperialist, against the Pahlavi monarchy, and laid out a blueprint for the establishment of an Islamic state headed by an Imam. The imamate must adhere to God's law, or the *sharia*. Furthermore, in Khomeini's view, Islamist jurists are given responsibility for guiding the community, overturning the traditional Shia perspective that allowed secular kings to exercise political authority while the clerics offered spiritual guidance, while awaiting the return of the hidden Imam. Shias believe that the twelfth Imam who succeeded the eleventh in 874 AD was hidden by God to protect him. One day the hidden Imam will return to guide the spiritual community. Under his theory of *Velayat-i Faqih*, or 'Guardianship of the Islamic Jurists', a single *faqih*, or expert in Islamic jurisprudence, exercises great power. This application of this theory is evident in Iran's governmental structure, which gives ultimate authority to a Supreme Leader, sometimes referred to as an *ayatollah*. A council of Islamic jurists, known as the

Assembly of Experts, further reinforces the role of jurists within the Islamic state. The actual creation of a Shia state is a major departure from traditional Shia theology, which emphasized waiting and enduring, rather than taking action.

The establishment of a Shia Islamic state in Iran emboldened Islamists throughout the region, and spurred Sunni Islamist groups to continue their efforts to establish their own caliphate. Western states reacted with great concern to the Iranian revolution, fearing it could trigger revolution throughout the region.

AFGHANISTAN AND ISLAMIST RESURGENCE IN THE 1990S

In the 1990s the Middle East and North Africa witnessed a wave of violence by Islamist groups throughout the region. From Cairo to Algiers, Islamist militants attacked government targets and Western tourists. Though these attacks were carried out by a wide array of individuals and groups, they often had one thing in common: the shared experience of fighting Soviet troops in Afghanistan. The Soviet Afghan War ultimately created the connections that helped form the global Islamic militant network affiliated with al-Qaeda.

In 1979 the Soviet Union deployed troops to Afghanistan to support a communist-led government recently brought into power through revolution. The Soviet invasion took place at the height of Cold War tensions between the two superpowers. The US, seeking to thwart Soviet expansionism in Central Asia, provided aid and CIA-led military training to an armed Afghan resistance movement. These guerrilla forces, known as the *mujahideen* (literally 'strugglers'), also received support from China, Pakistan, Saudi Arabia and the United Kingdom. Individual Muslims, usually from Arab countries, came to Afghanistan to fight this *jihad* to liberate Muslim Afghanistan from atheist Soviet occupation. The *mujahideen* proved highly effective, and the Soviet occupation grew very costly. So many Soviet lives were lost that the occupation became known as the 'Soviet Union's Vietnam'. In 1989 the Soviet Union withdrew its troops, and Afghanistan descended into civil war.

Box 7.2

THE TALIBAN IN AFGHANISTAN

The name Taliban derives from the Arabic word meaning student. Indeed, most of the Taliban were trained in religious schools inside refugee camps in neighboring Pakistan. The Taliban are Sunni and come primarily from the Pashtun ethnic group inside Afghanistan. Between 1996 and 2001 they were able to consolidate control over much of Afghanistan, which had descended into political chaos after the Soviet withdrawal in 1989. Under their rule, Afghanistan, which had had a monarch prior to the Soviet invasion, became the 'Islamic Emirate of Afghanistan'.

While at first many in Afghanistan welcomed the relief from anarchy that the Taliban brought, their oppressive rule proved to be difficult. The Taliban exercised a particularly strict interpretation of *sharia*.

The most obvious manifestation was the restrictions on women, including requiring the all-concealing *burqa*. The *burqa*, which covered women head-to-toe in heavy folds, leaving only a small mesh window to see through, was rooted in traditional Pashtun culture. Women could not work or attend school beyond the age of 8. The Taliban banned all sorts of activities deemed 'un-Islamic', including music, soccer, television and kite-flying. Religious police patrolled the streets to ensure enforcement. Punishments were harsh and included public execution.

Taliban ideology combined both a strict interpretation of Islam with Pashtun tribal code. It was also influenced by Wahhabism, and the Taliban received financial support from Saudi Arabia and Pakistan.

Box 7.2

THE TALIBAN IN AFGHANISTAN—CONT'D

Osama Bin Laden came to Afghanistan as a 'guest' of the Taliban after being forced out of Sudan in 1996. An alliance was formed between al-Qaeda and the Taliban, with Bin Laden providing finance for the Taliban.

After 9/11 the US demanded that the Taliban turn over Bin Laden and other al-Qaeda leaders to the United States. The Taliban refused, requiring proof of Bin Laden's guilt. Shortly thereafter the United States, the United Kingdom, Canada and a coalition of NATO forces attacked the Taliban and al-Qaeda in Afghanistan. The goal was to remove the Taliban from power, capture Bin Laden, and break up terrorist bases and camps inside the country. By December 2001 the Taliban had been forced out of all the major cities they had controlled. They retreated to the rural areas and continue to operate an insurgency against the NATO troops and newly formed Afghanistan government led by Hamid Karzai. By 2007, it appeared that the Taliban's ability to stage attacks was increasing.

Rashid, A. (2000). *Taliban: Militant Islam, Oil and Fundamentalism in Central Asia.* London: I. B. Tauris.

After the Soviet withdrawal, many of the *mujahideen*, who came from countries such as Egypt and Saudi Arabia, and were known as Arab Afghans, returned home. There they used the military training gained in Afghanistan against their home governments, which they viewed as corrupt and un-Islamic. At the same time, a stricter adherence to Islam was gaining much popular support within societies in which Westernization and modernization seemed to have produced little benefit for the masses. Long before September 11, 2001, militant violence shook the region. In Algeria, the Armed Islamic Group (GIA) attempted to overthrow the non-Islamist government, leading to civil war in which thousands of civilians were killed. In Egypt, a new group, known as Vanguards of Conquest, attacked a tourist bus in Luxor, killing sixty-eight tourists and Egyptian security personnel. The leader of the group was Ayman al-Zawahiri, also the leader of Egyptian Islamic Jihad, who soon after became a key leader in al-Qaeda.

AL-QAEDA AND AL-QAEDISM

The formation of al-Qaeda also has its roots in the Soviet–Afghan war. In the early 1980s, Osama Bin Laden, a member of a wealthy Saudi family, traveled to Peshawar, Pakistan, to support the *mujahideen*. From here he used his vast financial resources to recruit, train and fund the *mujahideen*. Though some have claimed that he received arms from the CIA, this claim has not been substantiated, though there may have been contact between Bin Laden and the CIA. However, it is clear that the CIA and Bin Laden were working toward the same goal – expulsion of the Soviet Union – in Afghanistan. In 1988, Bin Laden formed al-Qaeda (Arabic meaning 'the base'), composed of a network of largely 'Arab Afghans'. Bin Laden has a direct connection with the ideology of Sayyid Qutb, as he studied under Qutb's brother Muhammad in Jeddah.

After the Soviet withdrawal, Bin Laden returned to Saudi Arabia where he came into increasing conflict with the Saudi government. Following Iraq's invasion of Kuwait in 1991, Bin Laden offered to send fighters to defend the Saudi border. This offer was rebuffed by the Saudi monarchy, which allowed US troops to operate from the territory. Bin Laden demanded the withdrawal of US troops from Saudi Arabia, which contains Mecca and Medina, the two holiest cities in Islam. Under growing pressure from Saudi authorities, Bin Laden moved to Sudan in 1991; his Saudi citizenship was revoked in 1994.

In Sudan, Bin Laden was joined by numerous members of his organization, including Ayman Al-Zawahiri, often described as Bin Laden's lieutenant and figuring on video messages utilized by al-Qaeda to communicate with the world. Throughout the 1990s, al-Qaeda, under Bin Laden's leadership, carried out numerous attacks against Western targets. The most high profile include the bombing of the World Trade Center (1993), the bombing of the US embassies in Tanzania and Kenya (1998), and the attack on the USS *Cole* in Yemen (2000). With Sudan under increasing international pressure to move against Bin Laden, he departed in May 1996, returning to Afghanistan, then under Taliban control (Box 7.3).

SEPTEMBER 11 AND THE WAR ON TERROR

On September 11, 2001, four airplanes were hijacked by Islamist militants. Two of the planes crashed into the

---

Box 7.3

THE STATEMENTS OF BIN LADEN

The ideology espoused by Osama Bin Laden lay within the Salafist tradition, and is heavily influenced by the ideas of theorists such as Qutb and Mawdudi. Bin Laden calls for the establishment of a pan-Islamic caliphate. To achieve this, non-Islamic regimes must be overthrown and Westerners and non-Muslims expelled from Muslim countries.

It has been noted that Bin Laden does not have the scholarly credentials or training in Islamic jurisprudence to conduct Qur'anic interpretation or issue decrees. Nonetheless, his ideology has proven attractive to many in the Muslim world, including those who support his goals but object to the use of violence to achieve them.

Bin Laden's messages touch on a variety of themes that appeal across the Muslim world, including the suffering of Muslims at the hands of others:

> This shows our enemies' belief that Muslims' blood is the cheapest and that their property and wealth is merely loot. Your blood has been spilt in Palestine and Iraq, and the horrific images of the massacre in Qana in Lebanon are still fresh in people's minds. The massacres that have taken place in Tajikistan, Burma, Kashmire, Assam, the Philippines, Fatani, Ogaden, Somalia, Eritrea, Chechnya, and Bosnia-Herzegovina send shivers down our spines and stir up our passions. All this

happened before the eyes and ears of the world, but the blatant imperial arrogance of America, under the cover of the immoral United Nations, has prevented the disposed from arming themselves.

> August 23, 1996, Bin Laden 2005: 25

Other pronouncements deal with the betrayal of Palestine, anti-Jewish sentiment and the presence of infidels in the holy land of Arabia.

His appeal to Muslims is to fight a defensive war (*jihād*) against Jews and Crusaders, which is distinct from an offensive war (*harb*). He utilizes both history and Islamic jurisprudence to remind Muslims of their religious duty to wage *jihād*.

> To kill the Americans and their allies – civilians and military – is an individual duty incumbent upon every Muslim in all countries, in order to liberate the al-Aqsa Mosque and the Holy Mosque from their grip, so that their armies leave all the territory of Islam, defeated, broken and unable to threaten any Muslim.
>
> February 23, 1998, Bin Laden 2005: 61

Receptivity to Bin Laden's message within the region has been mixed. A 2005 poll by the Pew Global Attitudes Survey Project found that a high percentage of respondents in some countries indicated that they

Box 7.3

THE STATEMENTS OF BIN LADEN—CONT'D

have 'a lot' or 'some' confidence in Osama Bin Laden: Jordan (60 percent), Pakistan (51 percent), Indonesia (35 percent) and Morocco (26 percent). However, it should be noted that this level of confidence had decreased since a previous poll in 2003. Nor is this level consistent throughout the region; confidence levels in Turkey (7 percent) and Lebanon (2 percent) were quite low.

Bin Laden, O. (2005) *Messages to the World: The Statements of Osama Bin Laden*. Ed. B. Lawrence. Trans. J. Howarth. London: Verso.

Pew Global Attitudes Project (2005) 'Islamic extremism: common concern for Western and Muslim publics'. July 14: http://pewglobal.org/reports/display.php?ReportID=248.

World Trade Center towers, the third into the Pentagon. The fourth plane crashed into a Pennsylvania field when passengers and crew attempted to retake control of the plane. Nearly 3000 people were killed in these attacks, which were the only such attacks ever to take place on US soil. Though Osama Bin Laden did not publicly acknowledge his role in the attacks until 2004, the nineteen hijackers, mostly from Saudi Arabia, were known to be al-Qaeda affiliates.

In the aftermath of the 9/11 attacks, US President George Bush launched the 'War on Terrorism' (also known as the Global War on Terror) to combat al-Qaeda and other global terrorist organizations. Also included in the War on Terror were the states and governments that aided terrorists. President Bush declared:

> And we will pursue nations that provide aid or safe haven to terrorism. Every nation, in every region, now has a decision to make. Either you are with us, or you are with the terrorists. From this day forward, any nation that continues to harbor or support terrorism will be regarded by the United States as a hostile regime.
>
> (White House, September 20, 2001)

On October 7, 2001 the US and the UK launched a bombing campaign in Afghanistan, intent on capturing Bin Laden, destroying al-Qaeda and overthrowing the Taliban regime which had refused to turn Bin Laden over to the US following the attacks. After the air campaign the US and the UK deployed ground forces, and took Kabul, the capital, in November 2001, seriously weakening the Taliban's hold on the country. However, al-Qaeda forces were not routed until the battle at remote Tora Bora in December.

In early 2002 a new provisional government was established in Afghanistan, following a grand council (*loyal jirga*) of the major factions in Afghanistan. Hamid Karzai was chosen to head the interim government and elected president in 2004. Though a constitution has been accepted, the governing institutions remain weak; a legislature does not yet exist.

Security remains a major issue in Afghanistan, which has seen a resurgence of al-Qaeda's activities since 2002. In January 2006, NATO troops were deployed and took over responsibility for coordinating the International Security Assistance Force, and conducted a series of operations designed to weaken al-Qaeda's forces. In 2007 there were approximately 30,000 United Kingdom, United States and NATO troops in Afghanistan.

In the War on Terror the US government coordinated closely with countries, especially in the MENA region. Jordan and Yemen, and even tiny Djibouti, received increased funding and a heightened military presence. Throughout the Muslim world, however, the War on

Terror has been perceived as a war against Islam, and has contributed to a negative perception of the US within the region. According to a survey by the Pew Global Attitudes Project, in May 2004, 53 percent of Jordanians and 51 percent of Pakistanis believe the real purpose of the war on terror is to target unfriendly Muslim governments and groups.

At the time of writing, Osama Bin Laden has not been captured, despite a $25 million reward offered by the US government. Al-Qaeda continues to operate, utilizing a decentralized network structure, throughout the world. Groups, claiming al-Qaeda affiliation, have appeared throughout the Middle East as well as in Europe, Africa and Asia.

Box 7.4

HEZBOLLAH: THE PARTY OF GOD

Hezbollah (alternative spellings include Hizbullah) is an Islamist militant organization based in Lebanon. Its members are Shia and the group has connections with Iran. The United States and the United Kingdom, among other governments, view it as a terrorist organization. Throughout the Middle East it is viewed by many as a legitimate armed resistance organization. Since 1992, the head of Hezbollah has been Sayyid Hassan Nasrallah.

The formation of Hezbollah lay in the imbalance of political power between the Maronite Christian population, favored under the National Pact, and the Shia population. During the Lebanese civil war the country's confessional groups each formed militias in an attempt to gain a monopoly on power. In particular, Hezbollah fought against the Maronite militia, the Phlange. This was not the first armed conflict between the two. In 1919, when Lebanon became free of Ottoman control, the Maronites and French troops battled the Shia. The establishment of Hezbollah, which appeared in the 1980s, was aided by the Iranian revolution which brought Khomeini into power. Iran has provided Hezbollah with training, weapons, money and ideological influence.

The goals of Hezbollah at first included establishing an Islamic government in Lebanon, a goal they have since 'abandoned temporarily'. They also sought the withdrawal of Israeli troops from southern Lebanon, which they occupied in 1982, and Israeli withdrawal from the Golan Heights and from Shebaa Farms. Shebaa Farms is a small disputed area, seized by Israel from Syria in the 1967 war but claimed by Lebanon. Hezbollah also sought the release of Lebanese prisoners held by Israel and the return of Palestinian refugees.

Hezbollah views Israel as an illegitimate state, a stance that increases its popularity in the region. Attacks on Israel over the years have evolved from suicide bombing of military targets – Hezbollah are thought to be the first to use this technique – to targeting civilian areas with Katyusha rockets. The rockets have short-range capability (12.7 mi./20.4 km) and therefore do not threaten Israel's largest cities. The ongoing conflict between Hezbollah and Israel escalated in 2006 into large-scale warfare (see Chapter 11).

The overwhelming popularity of Hezbollah among the Shia in Lebanon, and their growing influence, can be attributed both to the historically disenfranchised position of the Shia in Lebanese society and their growing demographic power. Despite making up approximately 20 percent of the population, the Shia exercised little political power and held only 3.2 percent of senior civil service jobs. Between 1956 and 1976 the Shia population tripled from 250,000 to 750,000. By the 1980s the Shia were thought to be the largest confessional group in Lebanon. The majority of Shia were poor; their lives in rural southern Lebanon were in stark contrast to the cosmopolitan atmosphere of Beirut. Hezbollah's poverty-alleviation programs, in areas where government services were scarce, encouraged loyalty. The withdrawal of Israeli forces from southern Lebanon in 2000 was a further victory for them.

Box 7.4

HEZBOLLAH: THE PARTY OF GOD—CONT'D

fourteen seats (out of 128) in parliament and gained representation in the cabinet in 2005. Their extensive social-support program runs hospitals and clinics, serving many who otherwise could not afford care. They also own a television station, al-Manar.

The relationship between Hezbollah and the government of Lebanon is uneasy. Hezbollah is able to muster large numbers of supporters, who turn out in the street to back their causes. But Hezbollah's continued attacks on Israel, for which all of Lebanon paid a high price in the summer of 2006, have raised concerns about allowing an armed militia to operate inside Lebanon, and calls to disarm Hezbollah are increasing. And yet Hezbollah increased its political power in the new unity government formed in July 2008. Members of Hezbollah now control 11 out of 30 seats in the cabinet and head up the ministry of Labor.

Hamzeh, A. (2004) *In the Path of Hizbullah*. Syracuse, NY: Syracuse University Press.

SUMMARY OF MAIN POINTS

- The ideology of modern Islamist militant groups has its roots in Islamist thought of the eighteenth and nineteenth centuries.
- Islamist ideology, like secular nationalism, was often a response to colonialism and foreign domination.
- Wahhabism is a type of Sunni Islam, founded in Saudi Arabia, and based on return to a more 'pure' form of Islam.
- The Egyptian Muslim Brotherhood, under the leadership of Sayyid Qutb, attempted to overthrow the Egyptian government. Today it seeks change through electoral processes.
- The Iranian revolution created a Shia theocracy and sparked fears it would spread.
- The Taliban created a Sunni Islamic state based on strict interpretation of the the Qur'an and traditional Pashtun values.
- Al-Qaeda, and Bin Laden, crafted an ideology that addressed many of the grievances of Muslims worldwide.

QUESTIONS FOR DISCUSSION

1 What role do concepts such as 'innovation' and 'interpretation' play in religious thought in Christianity and Judaism?
2 What tensions are created in Saudi Arabia because of the close relationship between Wahhabism and the government legitimacy?
3 In what ways are the ideas of Islamists such as Abduh, Rida and al Banna similar to those of secular nationalists? Different?
4 How did the ideas of Qutb transcend Egypt and become popular throughout the Islamic world?
5 What was the relationship between the Taliban and al-Qaeda?
6 Why would Bin Laden's message appeal to many in the Islamic world, including those who do not support his use of violence?

SUGGESTIONS FOR FURTHER READING

Barber, B. (1996) *Jihad vs. McWorld: How Globalism and Tribalism Are Reshaping the World*. New York: Ballantine Books. In this popular and influential book, the author examines how religious and ethnic identifications are on the rise in the face of widespread globalization.

Berman, P. (2003) 'Philosopher of Islamic terror'. *New York Times*, March 23. Discusses the content of Sayyid Qutb's ideology and its impact on current militant Islamist groups.

Hiro, D. (1990) *Holy Wars: The Rise of Islamic Fundamentalism*. New York: Routledge. An early work on comparative Islamic fundamentalism. Covers Egypt, Saudi Arabia, Iran and Afghanistan. Easy read.

Kepel, G. (2002) *Jihad: The Trail of Political Islam*. Cambridge, Mass.: Harvard University Press. This groundbreaking work on political Islam traces its rise, beginning in the 1970s, and the link with militant global militant movements.

Kepel, G. (2003) *Bad Moon Rising: A Chronicle of the Middle East Today*. London: Saqi Books. In this brief, very readable account, the noted French scholar of political Islam discusses his encounters with Islamism on a tour of the region shortly after 9/11.

Mamdani, M. (2005) *Good Muslim, Bad Muslim: America, the Cold War and the Roots of Terror*. New York: Doubleday.

An accessible and easy-to-comprehend look at the development of political Islam by a well-known scholar. Chapter 4, on Afghanistan, is of particular note.

Murphy, C. (2002) *Passion for Islam. Shaping the Modern Middle East: The Egyptian Experience*. New York: Scribner. Written by an award-winning journalist, this book explores the reasons for the rise of political Islam in Egypt.

Pew Global Attitudes Project (2007) 'America's Image in the World', March 14: http://pewglobal.org/commentary/display.php?AnalysisID=1019.

Qutb, S. (1953) *Social Justice in Islam*. Trans. John B. Hardie. Oneanta, NY: Islamic Publications International. Details his comprehensive theory of an Islamic society.

Tibi, B. (2002) *The Challenges of Fundamentalism: Political Islam and the New World Order*. Berkeley, Calif.: University of California Press. This volume explores the relationship between Islam and globalization in the latter part of the twentieth century. For more on the concept of the Islamic state, see Chapter 8.

PART III

CONTEMPORARY ISSUES AND CHALLENGES

8

ECONOMIC CHALLENGES

Despite windfall profits for the MENA's oil-producing countries in recent years, the Middle East and North Africa region, as a whole, faces a wide variety of economic challenges. On the global level the region lags behind, in both its share of world exports and its share of global gross domestic product (GDP). Only the sub-Saharan African region has lower economic growth than the MENA. Indeed, Pamuk (2006: 810) notes that the 'gap between the Middle East and high income regions of the world is roughly the same today as it was in 1913'. Furthermore, despite rising oil prices, the region has not kept pace with growth posted by other less developed regions, including Latin America. To be fair, the region did post impressive overall growth rates between 2001 and 2006. However, much of this growth was the result of unusually high oil prices and has had little impact beyond the Gulf oil-producing states.

DEMOGRAPHIC TRAP

A demographic 'trap', created by high population growth rates, undermines the region's overall economic situation and creates enormous social challenges. With a present population of about 430 million, the region has the world's second-fastest-growing population, lagging only behind sub-Saharan Africa. In the latter part of the twentieth century, its population increased fourfold (Population Reference Bureau 2007).

In fact, with a regional population growth rate of 2 percent, the region's population will continue to double approximately every thirty-four years. The rapid population growth rate is a function not only of the large number of children being born, but also of the decrease in death rates as medical advances and improved hygiene, especially in the period after World War II, resulted in extended life expectancy (Table 8.1).

With such rapid population growth, young people dominate the region's population. One in every three people living in the region is between the ages of 10 and 24. Demographers speak of a 'youth bulge' in reference to these countries' population pyramids. These young people need services, such as schools and, more importantly, jobs. Job creation lags greatly behind the growing demand; unemployment around the region ranges from 12 percent to –20 percent; and underemployment, whereby occupants hold lower-level or part-time jobs, runs even higher. This large number of young people who have few future prospects is a growing concern for the region and for the West alike.

The rate of population growth in the region has decreased in recent decades, from 3.2 percent in the mid-1980s to 2.7 percent between 1990 and 1995, to 2 percent in 2005. Sharp declines in fertility are a primary reason for this decrease. Fertility is typically measured by the Total Fertility Rate (TFR), which is the average number of children born to a woman during her

Table 8.1 Demographic profiles of MENA countries

Country	Economic growth rate	Population growth rate	Total Fertility rate
Algeria	5.0	2	2.8
Bahrain	1.0	1	2.8
Egypt	6.0	2	3.1
Iraq	N/A	N/A	4.8
Jordan	5.0	2	3.7
Kuwait	8.0	3	2.4
Lebanon	1.0	1	1.9
Libya	4.0	2	3.4
Morocco	2.0	1	2.5
Oman	2.0[1]	1	3.4
Qatar	3.0[1]	5	2.8
Saudi Arabia	7.0	3	4.5
Sudan	8.0	2	4.0
Syria	2.0	2	3.5
Tunisia	4.0	5	2.0
UAE	8.0	3	2.2
West Bank/Gaza	6.0	3	5.0
Yemen	3.0	3	6.2
Iran	3.0	1	2.0
Israel	3.0	2	2.8
Turkey	3.0	1	2.2
Middle East/NA	2.0	2	3.0
Sub-Saharan Africa	6.0	2	5.0
UK	2.0	1	2.0
USA	2.0	1	2.0

[1] denotes 2004 WDI data. All annual GDP growth rates 2005, WDI. N/A = data not available.

Sources: Total fertility rates from Population Reference Bureau (2007), except for Sudan, West Bank/Gaza, Middle East and North Africa, sub-Saharan Africa, UK, and USA from World Development Indicators (2005).

reproductive life. In 1960 the MENA's total fertility rate stood at about seven; by 2006 it had declined to three. A number of countries throughout the region, most notably Egypt, Tunisia and Iran, have launched aggressive family planning campaigns in an effort to slow their population growth. However, the TFR remains high in places, especially in the Arabian peninsula: Yemen (6.2), Saudi Arabia (4.5) and Oman (3.4). The lack of medical supplies, including contraception after Iraq's invasion of Kuwait, may be a contributing factor in Iraq's high TFR (4.8).

From a Western perspective the decision by women to have large numbers of children may seem irrational.

However, within the Middle East, as well as in much of the lesser-developed world, childbearing brings crucial economic and social benefit to the family. Within an agriculture-dominated society, children are an important source of labor for the family farm, helping to tend the fields and animals from even a very young age. Lacking any social security system, grown-up children are necessary to support the elderly. In the Middle East, family is the primary societal unit and the principal source of one's identity; having large numbers of children helps secure women's role within the family. Though birth control is acceptable within Islam, religious beliefs, according to which a child is considered to be a blessing from God, also contribute to high fertility rates. With increasing urbanization throughout the region, and mass migration of people from the countryside to the city, the economic incentive to have large families has been reduced, but the tradition of large families continues in many areas.

Despite the decline in fertility rates in recent years, the region's population will continue to increase owing to 'demographic momentum' as the large number of young females enter their childbearing years and have children. By 2050, the region's population is expected to exceed 700 million.

RAPID URBANIZATION

With the growth of the region's population, its cities have swelled. The region now hosts many cities well above the million mark (Table 8.2). Cairo's vast metropolitan area may hold as many as 16 million people. It is far larger than the country's second-largest city, Alexandria (3.9 million) – a condition known as urban primacy, whereby one city, often the capital, is 'abnormally' large and dwarfs all others in the urban hierarchy. The population of Istanbul, at over 10 million, greatly exceeds that of Ankara (3.6 million, established by Ataturk as Turkey's new capital). In recent decades Tehran (7.1 million) has grown very large. These vast mega-cities contain large areas inhabited by the urban poor, such as Cairo's Imbaba neighborhood and south Tehran. Often these are newly arrived migrants, part of the large rural-to-urban influx that has characterized the region in the period since the end of World War II. Both high

Table 8.2 Large cities of the Middle East and North Africa (2007 estimated population)

Cairo, Egypt	16 million (7.9 million)[1]
Istanbul, Turkey	1.2
Tehran, Iran	7.1
Riyadh, Saudi Arabia	4.4
Alexandria, Egypt	3.9
Ankara, Turkey	3.6
Casablanca, Morocco	3.2
Khartoum, Sudan	2.2
Rabat, Morocco	1.7
Algiers, Algeria	1.5
Aleppo, Syria	1.5
Damascus, Syria	1.5
Amman, Jordan	1.3
Beirut, Lebanon	1.3
Tripoli, Libya	1.1
Fez, Morocco	1.0

[1] Though the population of Cairo governorate is only 7.9 million, the population of the metropolitan area is thought to exceed 16 million.

Source: www.worldgazetteer.com. Accessed July 22, 2007.

Table 8.3 Urban profiles of MENA countries

Country	% Population urban	Urban population growth rate	Population growth rate
Algeria	63	3	1
Bahrain	63	3	1
Egypt	43	2	2
Iraq	67	2	N/A
Jordan	82	3	2
Kuwait	98	3	3
Lebanon	87	1	1
Libya	85	2	2
Morocco	59	2	1
Oman	72	1	1
Qatar	72	1	5
Saudi Arabia	81	3	3
Sudan	41	4	2
Syria	51	3	2
Tunisia	65	2	1
UAE	77	5	5
West Bank/ Gaza	72	3	3
Yemen	27	5	3
Iran	67	2	1
Israel	92	2	2
Turkey	67	2	1
Middle East/ NA	57	2	2
Sub-Saharan Africa	35	4	2
UK	90	1	1
USA	81	1	1

N/A = data not available.

Source: All figures 2005, World Development Indicators.

rates of natural increase among urban dwellers and large-scale migration combine to create massive urban growth.

Indeed, the number of urban dwellers in the Middle East has increased by about 100 million in the last thirty-five years and is expected to increase to over 350 million by 2025. Despite the image of tents and camels, over half (57 percent) the region's population now lives in cities. The level of urbanization is particularly high in the Gulf countries, where agricultural land is nearly nonexistent (Table 8.3).

The loss of jobs in the Middle East's agricultural sector, and declining farm income, is a major factor causing people, especially young people in search of jobs, to migrate to the city. The perception of greater employment opportunities and access to more educational opportunities attract migrants from the rural areas. Often, however, migrants' employment expectations cannot be met, either because they lack the skills required for urban jobs or because jobs are not available. Rather than return to the rural area, they reside in poor sections of the city. The large influx of migrants in the last sixty years has greatly overburdened the region's cities. The infrastructure, both social and physical, is stretched, and many cities have failed to keep pace with the demand for housing. The presence of large numbers of migrants, often unemployed, who lack roots in the city is a major concern for social and political stability.

THE REGION'S HUMAN CAPITAL

In 2002 the publication of the Arab Human Development Report focused attention on the shortcomings of human capital development in the region and its impacts.

Though the report was controversial, it offered one of the most comprehensive and well-researched assessments of the region. In essence it tried to answer this question: Why is this oil-rich region falling behind?

The study noted the demographic issues detailed above and further noted that the region's growth in income per head is lower than in all regions except sub-Saharan Africa.

The AHDR argued that three major 'deficits' were responsible for the region's stagnation. These deficits were in three areas: freedom, knowledge and gender equality.

Constraints on civil society and the media are at the root of the region's 'freedom' deficit. Though many countries in the region have the trappings of democratic society, such as elections, they do not truly function as democracies. Power is tightly controlled by the central authority, and often there is little accountability or checks and balances. In these systems officials are appointed not on the basis of their skills or on merit but on their loyalty or political connection. The lack of an independent media thwarts attempts to expose corruption. Such political patronage has significant economic consequences and lowers overall economic efficiency.

Though many applauded the AHDR's willingness to confront the 'freedom deficit', which was well known but little talked about, the political uses of the freedom deficit have added further controversy to the report. Following the report's publication, the Bush administration used the freedom deficit, and others, to justify its new interventionist policies in the region designed to bring about 'democratization', which ranged from political aid to regime change in Iraq. (This issue is explored more deeply in Chapter 10.) As a result, supporters of the AHDR found it increasingly difficult to implement its suggested changes.

Noting that the Arab region was once the center of global knowledge, the report points to a current 'knowledge' deficit. The region produces little scientific research and has very low levels of information

Box 8.1

OIL AND THE SAUDI WELFARE STATE

The 1970s oil boom dramatically transformed Saudi Arabia's society. The once primarily rural, Bedouin society, characterized by animal pastoralism and loyalty to tribe, became a heavily urbanized, settled culture. The Saudi government invested heavily in infrastructure, building sleek modern cities and creating institutions such as universities and hospitals.

The Saudi royal family used oil revenue to ensure that the Saudi population was well taken care of. Citizens received subsidies and often held government jobs that required very little work. The country relied on foreign workers to provide the skilled and manual labor needed to transform the country. No longer did Saudis lead the self-reliant Bedouin life; rather they became dependent on a luxurious, government-supported lifestyle.

Large population increases over the past three decades, to 23.5 million (including 6 million workers),

and flat oil prices left Saudi Arabia unable to sustain its social welfare system. Per capita income dropped from a high of $18,000 in 1981 to $8424, rebounding to $15,711 in 2005 following sharp rises in oil prices after 9/11. The result was an increase in the number of Saudi citizens living in absolute poverty and an overall decline in the standard of living. By 2002, Saudi Arabia was running a $12 billion budget deficit. Government services, such as education and healthcare, were in decline. Universities, for example, could accept less than half of those seeking admittance. Unemployment worsened, especially among young males, while simultaneously the government attempted to reduce dependency on foreign workers by 'saudization' of their jobs.

There is growing concern over the links between the economic situation, the rise of religious extremism and the lack of support for the royal family in Saudi Arabia. The majority of the 9/11 attackers were Saudi citizens,

Box 8.1

OIL AND THE SAUDI WELFARE STATE—CONT'D

and recent years have seen violent clashes between groups affiliated to al-Qaeda and the Saudi government. A recent report by an international think-tank (International Crisis Group 2004: 11) noted the instability in the kingdom:

> Over time, insufficient job creation, an ill-adapted educational system and anachronistic economic structures, particularly when coupled with the sight of thousands of Princes enjoying lavish lifestyles, risk further undermining the regime's support base.

Rising oil prices, up from $10–30 a barrel in the 1980s to $60 a barrel in 2005, have increased Saudi oil income by 48 percent. The high prices are a result of a number of factors including the chaos in Iraq, unexpectedly high international demand (especially from the US and China), production cuts by OPEC to keep prices high, instability in Nigeria and Venezuela, and attacks on oil workers in Saudi Arabia. The Saudi royal family is using the oil windfall to bolster support for the regime. In August 2005, for example, the government announced a 15 percent salary increase for all government employees.

International Crisis Group (2004) 'Can Saudi Arabia reform itself?'. July 14.

Moore, B. (2006) 'Iraq's oil and the Saudi welfare state'. *Energy Bulletin*, March 23.

technology. Approximately 0.6 percent of the population uses the Internet, and only 1.2 percent owns computers (*The Economist* 2002). The report calls for significant investment in education, especially at the higher levels and the infrastructure to expand knowledge acquisition and communication. A few countries are already taking action. Egypt, for example, initiated a project in 2001 to provide a free dial-up service to all its citizens. Access to the Internet is provided free by multiple providers; no password is needed: and users are charged only for a local telephone call. At the same time, however, countries such as Tunisia and Saudi Arabia continue to block access to websites they find objectionable. In the case of Tunisia, users report being unable to access sites such as Amnesty International; in Saudi Arabia blocked pages range from the sexually explicit to those offering health advice to women and some popular culture sites.

The third deficit focuses on the lack of gender equality for women, with an emphasis on political empowerment, access to education, and involvement in the workforce. The report notes that two-thirds of the region's 65 million illiterate adults are women, and that rates of illiteracy are higher than those found in poorer countries (*The Economist* 2002). By failing to improve the status of women, the region is vastly under-utilizing its available human capital and lags behind other regions in competitiveness (Table 8.4).

Arab countries have shown the most rapid improvements in female education of any region; female literacy rates have tripled since the 1970s (AHDR 2002: 3). This progress has often been the result of national project targets – specifically increased enrollment of girls in primary and secondary school. However, levels of illiteracy remain high; more than half of Arab women are illiterate. Female literacy is particularly low in rural areas, where girls' participation in school, even when compulsory, lags. Often girls are kept out of school in order to help at home, or the price of uniforms and books proves prohibitive. Continuation of their education on to the secondary level in rural areas is often problematic as it may require travel to a different village.

The often low quality of the education throughout the region undermines the region's competitiveness in the global economy. The educational system is often

Table 8.4 Female literacy and labor force participation

Country	Literacy rate adult female %	Literacy rate adult male%	Female labor force participation %
Algeria	60	80	38
Bahrain	60	80	31
Egypt	59	83	22
Iraq	64	84	N/A
Jordan	85	95	29
Kuwait	91	94	25
Lebanon	N/A	N/A	36
Libya	N/A	N/A	27
Morocco	40	66	29
Oman	74	87	24
Qatar	74	87	24
Saudi Arabia	69	87	18
Sudan	52	71	25
Syria	74	86	40
Tunisia	65	83	31
UAE	81.7[1]	76.1[1]	39
West Bank/Gaza	88	97	11
Yemen	N/A	N/A	31
Iran	70	84	41
Israel	96	98	59
Turkey	80	95	27
Middle East/NA	61	81	31
Sub-Saharan Africa	53	70	63
UK	99[1]	99[1]	69
USA	99[1]	99[1]	70

Literacy rates are for people aged 15 and above. Literacy figures from 2006, World Development Indicators.
[1] indicates 2003 data from *CIA World Factbook*.
Female labor force participation equals percent of female population aged 15–64, 2005 figures from World Development Indicators.

based on rote memorization and lacks 'hands-on' or critical thinking skills. The educational infrastructure needs greater resources, including education technology and even basic supplies. In some countries, because of the youth bulge, schools must operate three shifts, with a shortened school day, to accommodate all students.

Finally, the report advocates increasing women's economic participation. Female labor-force participation remains low, despite increasing educational attainment among women. In 2006 the overall percentage of women in paid employment was about 30 percent, well below the global average of 52 percent (Population Reference Bureau 2007). Similarly, female rates of unemployment far exceed those of males. With job creation a major challenge for the region, increasing women's participation will require specific policies to remove gender bias from the workplace. Greater participation by women in the workforce could potentially improve the region's productivity, in the same way that the youth bulge contributed to the economic boom in East Asia (Population Reference Bureau 2007).

PREPAREDNESS FOR THE GLOBAL ECONOMY

As mentioned at the start of this chapter, the Middle East's position in the global economy has not improved over the last century. In terms of trade, the region has declined over the last fifty years. Throughout the 1990s, exports from the region, including both oil and non-oil, grew by only 1.5 percent – far below the global average of

Table 8.5 Economic structure

Country	Agriculture (% GDP)	Industry	Manufacturing	Services	Per capita GNP, $
Algeria	8	61	6	30	7,062
Bahrain	8	61	6	30	21,482
Egypt	15	36	17	49	4,337
Iraq	5^2	84^2	1^2	10^2	N/A
Jordan	3	30	19	68	5,530
Kuwait	0^2	59^2	3^2	40^2	26,321
Lebanon	6	22	14	71	5,584
Libya	N/A	N/A	N/A	N/A	N/A
Morocco	14	30	17	56	4,555
Oman	2^1	56^1	8^1	42^1	$15,146^1$
Qatar	2^1	56^1	8^1	42^1	N/A
Saudi Arabia	4^1	59^1	10^1	5^1	15,711
Sudan	34	30	7	37	2,083
Syria	23	35	30	41	3,808
Tunisia	12	29	18	60	8,371
UAE	2	56	N/A	42	25,514
West Bank/Gaza	N/A	N/A	N/A	N/A	N/A
Yemen	13	41^1	4^1	45^1	930
Iran	10	45	12	45	7,968
Israel	N/A	N/A	N/A	N/A	19,480
Turkey	12	24	14	64	8,407
Middle East/NA	12	40	14	48	6,126
Sub-Saharan Africa	17	32	14	52	1,994
UK	1	26	15^1	73	33,238
USA	1	22^1	14^1	77^1	41,890

All data World Development Indicators, 2005, except those indicated with [1], which are 2004, and [2], which are 2000.

6.0 percent (AHDR 2002: 4). The region produces few manufactured goods for the global market, and intra-regional trade is very low (Table 8.5).

Many countries in the MENA are heavily reliant on their agricultural sectors, both for export income and for employment. In countries such as Egypt, Turkey and Jordan, agricultural production has traditionally been done by family farmers working small plots of land. Today, with a growing emphasis on agriculture for export to markets in the European Union, there is growing pressure to consolidate land holdings into larger plots operated by commercial farms. In some countries, such as Egypt, land reform measures have encouraged consolidation, leading to more efficient farms but creating more rural unemployment.

These countries' weak manufacturing sectors are a legacy of both colonial policy and attempts during the independent period to develop domestic manufacturing.

When the economies of the region were under external control by European states, the development of local manufacturing capacity was prohibited. Resources from the Middle East, such as cotton, were instead transported back to Europe for manufacturing and processing, stimulating job growth there. At independence, therefore, these countries had little or no manufacturing capability and were heavily dependent on imports of everything from machinery to soap to packaged foods.

Following independence, new governments adopted import substitution policies to reduce their dependence on foreign goods and foster their own manufacturing industry. Egypt and Turkey were among the earliest to embrace this policy, which was eventually embraced by Syria, Iraq, Tunisia and Algeria. State-led development through import substitution was consistent with the then popular ideologies of Ba'athism and Arab socialism. Government-owned factories were opened to manufacture everything from cars and televisions to pasta and toothpaste. Unfortunately, these products were often inferior in quality to those produced in the West and sometimes costlier.

Though important substitution policies often led to a stagnation or decline in the standard of living of workers and peasants (Beinin 1999), the policies, and accompanying populist rhetoric, were in place for a number of decades. In the 1970s, characterized by rising oil prices and increased international lending to the region, most states began to acknowledge the shortcomings of import substitution. However, their economies remained heavily burdened with inefficient state industries.

STRUCTURAL ADJUSTMENT AND THE MIDDLE EAST

In the 1980s, with the end of the bipolar state system, the region became more inexorably tied to global capitalism. International lending institutions such as the International Monetary Fund and the World Bank, as well as the world's only superpower, the United States, began to advocate policy for the region's economic reform. The so-called 'Washington Consensus', based on neo-liberal economic ideas, focused on the development of private enterprise and an export-oriented development strategy. For many countries in the region, this meant dismantling their inefficient government-run companies and scaling back their bloated government bureaucracies. Such programs, designed to send these economies through a 'structural adjustment' process, also lifted regulations on trade originally designed to protect domestic industries and cut back government debt.

The activities undertaken under structural adjustment were extensive. Public (government-owned) companies were privatized, sold to both local and foreign investors. Systems such as banking and telecommunications, once controlled entirely by the government, were opened up to competition. These policies were often both difficult to implement and had negative repercussions on portions of the population.

Box 8.2

ISLAMIC FINANCE

Recent decades have witnessed the growth of 'Islamic banks' in the Middle East as clients turn toward banking option that are consistent with their faith. Islamic banks offer products such as checking and savings accounts, loans and credit cards.

Specifically, Islamic law prohibits usury, the payment of interest. To buy a car, for example, the bank will purchase the car on behalf of the individual and sell it to them at a higher price, giving the bank a profit but avoiding interest. Typically the individual is allowed to pay the bank in installments, and the bank holds the title until the vehicle is fully paid for.

Similarly, savings accounts do not generate interest. Rather, clients with savings accounts are given a share of the bank's profits generated by loans and other activities, in proportion to the amount they have in the bank.

Islamic law also prohibits investing in any activities that are forbidden under the *sharia*. Such activities include the sale of alcohol or pork. Islamic banks can offer their clients investment choices, such as mutual funds or bonds, which are guaranteed to be consistent with Islamic law.

Though Islamic banks are popular in the region, they represent a very small part of the global financial system. However, interest in Islamic finance is growing in the West, with an increasing number of business schools now offering this specialization. Institutions such as City University of London, Rice University and Harvard University offer courses or workshops on the subject.

Di Meglio, F. (2007) 'A fresh take on Islamic finance'. *Business Week Online*, March 27.

Privatization, for example, often proceeded slowly as few investors were available to purchase the government-run companies. Many of the companies, saddled with obsolete or inefficient equipment, were simply unattractive investments, especially when compared to the private firms being created in the new open economic climate. Privatization also often meant a reduction in the workforce as private investors sought to increase productivity and reduce costs.

Structural adjustment also required a reduction in the state's social welfare role. Subsidies, or government discounts, on everything including gasoline, sugar and cooking oil were eliminated or slashed. Government services such as healthcare were also cut back. Though many, especially the investor class, benefited from structural adjustment, its policies often caused economic hardship in the lower and middle classes. Eventually, however, increased economic growth over the long term was expected to help improve the living standard across all economic groups.

Many Middle Eastern countries, with the assistance (and often insistence) of the international financial community, initiated structural adjustment programs in the late 1980s and 1990s. Only now are these countries, such as Egypt, beginning to see a payoff in the form of higher economic growth.

FREE TRADE AND THE MIDDLE EAST

In the era of capitalism-based globalization, free trade has become the slogan of the West and its financial institutions. Truly free trade means that there is no impediment to the flow of goods and services across national boundaries. Tariffs and quotas that were put in place to protect domestic industry need to be removed under a free trade regime. For example, policies that place high tax on imported cars to protect local car producers need to be eliminated.

According to free-trade advocates, increased trade leads to higher growth and income, thereby reducing unemployment and poverty. The removal of obstacles to free trade was often tied to economic packages Middle Eastern countries sought from Western governments to alleviate their large debts.

And, indeed, there is no doubt that the Middle East and North Africa's trade performance continues to lag. In some countries barriers to free trade remain in place. Recently, the fostering of free trade has taken on a political as well as an economic dimension. Believing that free trade, by reducing poverty, can reduce terrorism, the United States has brokered free trade agreements with a number of countries in the region. Those countries seeking a free trade agreement with the US agree to

---

Box 8.3

ISRAEL: POVERTY AMID WEALTH

In many ways the Israeli economy is quite different from that of her neighbors. Its per capita GNP of $25,864 (2005) exceeds even that of some oil-exporting countries. Israel's economy is well diversified, with healthy industrial and manufacturing sectors. Israel produces high-quality products that enjoy access to European and Western markets. With a wealth of human capital, Israel's high-tech sector is globally competitive. Major firms such as Motorola and IBM operate facilities in Israel. And yet, amid Israel's relative economic wealth, and recent economic growth, the gap is widening between the rich and the poor. A 2006 report by Israel's National Insurance Institute found an increase in the country's poor population from 15 percent of families in the 1990s to a current 20.3 percent. The poverty line is calculated at NIS 4500, or $937.50 a month. Among developed countries only the US has a higher level of income inequality.

Of greater concern may be the impact of poverty on children, as now one in three of Israel's children live in poverty, an increase of 50 percent since 1988. Israel now leads all developed countries in rates of child poverty.

Box 8.3

ISRAEL: POVERTY AMID WEALTH—CONT'D

Poverty is highly concentrated among Israeli Arabs and ultra-Orthodox Jews, both of whom tend to have large families. Critics of Israel's economic policies that have focused on reducing social services and cutting governmental costs argue that the rising poverty figures are a result of policies that have benefited the higher classes while pushing the middle class toward poverty.

Poverty is even more pervasive within the West Bank (currently occupied by Israel) and Gaza (formally occupied by Israel until September 2005).

The official Palestinian poverty line is calculated at NIS 1800 ($410 a month). This is the equivalent of less than two dollars a day. Various estimates of the level of Palestinian poverty exist. A World Bank survey in 2003 estimated that 38–51 percent of the population lived below this poverty line. Furthermore, the very poorest have depleted their economic reserves and are suffering from malnutrition.

Madslien, J. (2006) 'Economic boom belies Israeli poverty'. BBC News, March 27: http://news.bbc.co.uk /2/hi/business/4833602.stm (accessed 25 July 2007)

National Insurance Institute (Israel) (2004) *Annual Survey 2002–2003*, April.

The World Bank and Palestinian Central Bureau of Statistics (2004) *Deep Palestinian Poverty in the Midst of Economic Crisis*, October: http://unispal.un.org/ unispal.nsf/2ee9468747556b2d85256cf60060d2a6/ 8487d551dc4e35ff85256f7000626989/$FILE/Deep %20Palestinian%20poverty.pdf (accessed July 25, 2007)

cooperate with the US on foreign policy and security issues, in exchange for preferential access to the US market. Currently the US has agreements with Israel (signed 1985), Turkey (1991), Jordan (2001), Egypt (2004), Morocco (2004), Bahrain (2004) and Oman (2004), and there are others in the planning stages. The number of US bilateral trade agreements with countries in the region has risen dramatically since the attacks of September 11, 2001, with the goal of a region-wide agreement by 2013.

Critics, however, question whether or not the Middle East, given the current state of its economies, can prosper in a free trade environment, or perhaps will only lag further behind. If free trade increases the region's disparity with the rest of the world, more instability and violence could be created (Looney 2005). Critics cite the difficulties encountered by other countries with free trade agreements, many of them more developed than those in the Middle East, whose current links to the world economy are weak. Many countries in the region are not even members of the World Trade Organization, the body that oversees global trade. Though free trade agreements with the US may at first seem both politically and economically attractive, the region's great distance from the US will entail longer transit times and higher transportation costs, making the US only a remote trading partner.

OIL ECONOMIES AND THE CHALLENGE OF DIVERSIFICATION

While the non-oil-producing countries of the region work to create strong economic bases, the oil-exporting countries face a different, though in some ways similar, challenge: to diversify their economies. The oil-exporting countries are composed largely of GCC members: Bahrain, Kuwait, Oman, Qatar, Saudi Arabia and the United Arab Emirates. Diversification is the attempt to develop non-oil sectors of their economy including non-oil exports and non-oil revenue sources. Such diversification is intended to guard against the day when oil supplies are depleted as well as act as a buffer against the enormous volatility associated with oil prices.

Box 8.4

THE MAGHREB: PERILOUS GATEWAY TO EUROPE

The distance between Morocco and the coast of Spain is only ten miles. Even more attractive to migrants seeking a foothold in Europe are the Spanish enclaves of Ceuta and Melilla, located on the coast of Morocco. They are surrounded by two razor-wire fences, and migrants risk death to gain entry.

Morocco is a major gateway for migrants from sub-Saharan Africa seeking jobs, escape from violence, and better lives in Europe. The migrants come from many countries: Senegal, Gambia, Sierra Leone, Liberia, Mali, Sudan, Cameroon and others.

The number of migrants entering North Africa is growing; an estimated 65,000–120,000 migrants from sub-Saharan Africa enter the Maghreb each year. Libya is the major crossroads for these migrants; 70 percent migrate through the country each year. A further 20–30 percent make their way through Algeria and Morocco. A smaller number attempt to cross via the Mediterranean. The use of false papers and tourist visas is a common method for gaining entry into Europe.

North African countries now host large immigrant communities of people from sub-Saharan Africa who are unable to emigrate to Europe but do not want to return home. The size of these communities varies from 1.5 million in Libya to 100,000 in Mauritania and Algeria, and tens of thousands in Tunisia and Morocco.

The passage of sub-Saharan African migrants through the Maghreb to Europe is a major source of friction between European governments and countries such as Morocco. European countries apply pressure to North African governments to combat this migration and accept the migrants back into the Maghreb if they are caught in Europe. North African countries, such as Morocco and Tunisia, have implemented new laws against 'irregular immigration' and human smuggling. Europe and North Africa are also cooperating on border controls.

The treatment of migrants or suspected migrants is of major concern to human rights organizations. Migrants face arbitrary arrest, deportation, harassment and possible torture. The rights of migrants to request asylum are often denied. Incidents such as the killings of five men by law enforcement officials as they attempted to climb the razor-wire fence into the Spanish enclave of Ceuta in 2005 demonstrate the risks to migrants.

Amnesty International (2005) 'Spain/Morocco: migrant rights between two fires', October 3: http://web.amensty.org/library/print/ENGEUR410112005.

de Haas, H. (2006) 'Trans-Saharan migration to North Africa and the EU: historical roots and current trends'. *Migration Information Source*, November 1: http://www.migrationinformation.org/Feature/print.cfm?ID=484.

The GCC countries have attempted to develop heavy industry, and have been successful in the area of petrochemicals. Emphasis has also been placed on bolstering their small agricultural sectors, but the lack of water – many of them are reliant on desalinized water – is a hindrance. In some places, such as Bahrain and the UAE, the financial services sector has been an area of growth.

Moves to attract international visitors have been especially strong in the UAE. Dubai is nearing construction of the world's tallest building. Exclusive high-end resorts line the country's beautiful beaches, leading to an incongruous mixing of bikini-clad foreigners and veiled citizens. Dubai has become an international 'city of spectacle', hosting sporting events with outrageous prize money. In the waters off its shores, they have even created artificial marine environments, stocked with a gold bar each day for a lucky diver to find.

Overall, the GCC countries have made progress in diversifying their economies. A UN report notes a steady

Table 8.6 GCC economic diversification

Contribution of the oil sector to GDP, 1977–98 (Percentage)

Country	1977	1981–5	1986–90	1991–5	1996–8
Bahrain	27	23.3	12.8	15.7	16.8
Kuwait	61	61.4	37.2	37.5	38.7
Oman	61	60.3	47.2	39.1	37.7
Qatar	N/A	64	34.7	33.9	38
Saudi Arabia	63	42.8	28.9	35.2	34.4
United Arab Emirates	59	48.9	38.1	37.6	28.2

Source: United Nations Economic and Social Commission for Western Asia, 'Economic diversification in the oil-producing countries: the case of the Gulf Cooperation Council', January 10, 2001. http://www.escwa.org.lb/information/publications/edit/upload/ed-01-1-e.pdf
Please see original source for detailed statistical sources.

decline in oil's contribution to GDP since the 1970s. In addition to growth in industry and services, non-oil exports have risen steadily, though the dramatic rise in oil prices in late 2007 could change this ratio (Table 8.6).

The Gulf diversification process in some ways mirrors structural adjustment, in that privatization of government firms and a reduction of subsidies are included in the process. In the Gulf, however, greater amounts of investment capital are available to purchase government firms, and the population is wealthier and better able to withstand cuts in subsidies.

ECONOMIC CHALLENGES: A LINK WITH RADICALISM?

There is no doubt that the economic failure of Arab socialism, characterized by central planning, government-owned companies and guaranteed employment, has bolstered the influence of Islamist ideology.

Box 8.5

CHINA'S GROWING INVOLVEMENT IN THE MIDDLE EAST

Historically, China has had very little involvement in the Middle East. Its great distance from the region and superpower dominance did little to encourage interaction. In recent decades China has begun to flex its economic and demographic muscle, and has adopted more activist foreign policies. It has forged closer relations with the Middle East. Chinese–Middle East relations are deepening each year and becoming more important.

China's new interest in the Middle East is based upon a number of factors. First, given US hegemony over the region after the end of the Cold War, China may be establishing a foothold to forestall complete US dominance of the region.

More important to the rapidly expanding Chinese economy is the region's oil supply. The Middle East is now China's fourth-largest trading partner. With its enormous economic expansion, China became a net oil importer in 1993. By 2003, China's oil demand stood at 5.5 million barrels per day, and China is the second-largest international consumer of oil after the United States. The Middle East now supplies more than half of China's oil imports, provided mostly by Saudi Arabia and Iran.

Iran is a particularly close trading partner and signed a bilateral energy cooperation agreement in 2004. Under it, China will purchase 10 million tons of oil each year for twenty-five years and participate with Iran

> **Box 8.5**
>
> ## CHINA'S GROWING INVOLVEMENT IN THE MIDDLE EAST—CONT'D
>
> in oil exploration and development as well as in the construction of power plants and cement factories. China is also becoming increasingly active in providing oil services in GCC countries as well as in other parts of the Arab World.
>
> Of major concern to the West are China's arms sales to the region, and specifically to Iran. China began supplying Iran with weapons during the Iraq–Iran war when the US backed Iraq.
>
> Iran's continued international isolation, particularly as a result of its nuclear program, will likely strengthen its relationship with China. In the US, there are concerns that China will provide Iran with chemical,
>
> nuclear and biological weapons. Earlier, China had plans to sell missiles to Syria and nuclear research technology to Algeria; both deals were cancelled following US pressure and bad press. It should be noted, however, that Chinese arms sales to the region are minuscule compared to the weapons provided by the US.
>
> Liangxiang, J. (2005) 'Energy first: China and the Middle East'. *Middle East Quarterly*, Spring.
>
> Rubin, B. (1999) 'China's Middle East strategy'. *Middle East Review of International Affairs Journal*, March.

Moreover, the economic transition from an agriculture-based society to an urban economy based on industry and services has, historically and globally, always been traumatic and associated with social upheaval (Richards 2002).

Militant Islamists have been able to capitalize on the region's current economic and social upheaval. According to Richards (2002: 31): 'Today's basic profile for a violent militant is a young man with some education who may also have recently moved to the city. Such young people are often unemployed or have jobs below their expectations.' The violent radicalism that spread through the region in the 1990s typically centered on poor urban areas.

Globalization may also be contributing to the growth of militant radicalism. Global communications, such as the Internet and television, have made young people in poor countries deeply aware of the differences between their lives and those portrayed in Western television and film. There is a new and growing 'expectation gap' between what these young people can expect to have and what they desire. The Internet has also greatly facilitated the spread of militant ideas across national borders.

> ## SUMMARY OF MAIN POINTS
>
> - Second only to sub-Saharan Africa, the Middle East and North Africa lags behind in economic growth.
> - Demographic challenges, especially a 'youth bulge', both demand and hamper significant economic growth.
> - The region's cities have grown dramatically in recent decades, receiving large numbers of immigrants from rural areas.
> - Deficits in 'freedom', 'knowledge' and 'gender equity' have been identified as barriers to economic growth.
> - Economies in the region are undergoing transformation to become more competitive in a global system dominated by capitalism and free trade.
> - Economic insecurity and associated social instability may be a strong contributing factor in the increase of militant violence in the region.

QUESTIONS FOR DISCUSSION

1 In what way does the demographic profile of the Middle East and North Africa differ from that of the US or the UK? Are there any possible advantages to the MENA's demographic profile?
2 What policies could be adopted to lower fertility rates in the MENA?
3 What challenges do rural migrants face when they reach the city?
4 In what way does the US endorsement of the Arab Human Development Report hinder acceptance of its conclusions?
5 Globalization produces both 'winners' and 'losers'. What is the likelihood that the MENA will be able to compete effectively in a global economy characterized by free trade and capitalism?
6 What are the links between globalization and the spread of ideas?

SUGGESTIONS FOR FURTHER READING

Beinin, J. (1999) 'The working class and peasantry in the Middle East: from economic nationalism to neoliberalism'. *Middle East Report*, Spring. Details the transition in Middle Eastern economies from state-led socialism to market capitalism.

The Economist (2002) 'Self-doomed to failure'. July 4. Offers a brief summary of the Arab Human Development Report.

Looney, R. (2005) 'US Middle East economic policy: the use of free trade areas in the war on terrorism'. *Mediterranean Affairs*, 16: 102–17. Assesses attempts by the Bush administration to link free trade agreements with security cooperation in countries in the Middle East and North Africa.

Martin, J. (2006) 'After the oil…'. *The Middle East*, February. A brief examination of attempts to diversify the region's economies.

Noland, M. and Pack, H. (2004) 'Islam, globalization and economic performance in the Middle East'. *Institute for International Economic Policy Brief* PB04-4, June. Assesses the role of Islam in the region's economic performance, attitudes toward globalization and the region's demographic challenges.

Pamuk, S. (2006) 'Estimating economic growth in the Middle East since 1820'. *The Journal of Economic History*, 66: 809–28. A highly detailed academic analysis of the Middle East's economic growth prior to and after independence.

Population Reference Bureau (2007) 'Challenges and opportunities – the population of the Middle East and North Africa'. *Population Bulletin*, 62: 2. This short report lays out the region's demographic challenges, with numerous easy-to-comprehend charts and tables.

Richards, A. (2002) 'Socioeconomic roots of Middle East radicalism'. *Naval War College Review*, 55: 22–39. Explores the connection between the tremendous economic challenges facing the region and the rise of radical Islam.

Richards, A. and Waterbury, J. (1996) *A Political Economy of the Middle East.* Boulder, Colo.: Westview Press. A comprehensive history of the region's economic development both during the colonial period and after independence.

United Nations Development Programme (2002) *Arab Human Development Report: Creating Opportunities for Future Generations.* New York: UNDP. A groundbreaking report that investigated the region's failure to thrive economically and the social and political aspects of relative underdevelopment.

United Nations Economic and Social Commission for Western Asia (2001) *Economic Diversification in the Oil-producing Countries: The Case of the Gulf Cooperation Council,* January 10: http://www.escwa.org.lb/information/publications/edit/upload/ed-01-1-e.pdf. Detailed statistical assessment of the GCC countries' attempts to reduce their economic dependence on oil in the latter half of the twentieth century.

9

THE ARAB–ISRAELI CONFLICTS: A CONFLICT RESOLUTION PERSPECTIVE

This chapter examines the conflict between Israel and the Arabs, and particularly the Palestinians, from a conflict resolution perspective. The emphasis is on understanding the issues that must be resolved to achieve a final peace settlement, past conflict resolution efforts and the current state of the conflict.

DEBUNKING THE MYTHS

Any discussion of the conflict between the state of Israel and its Arab neighbors must first address commonly held misconceptions. These 'myths' are perpetuated by the media as well as by those involved in the conflict as they attempt to gain support for their cause within the international community. Because the history of the conflict is so poorly understood by most people, these 'myths' go unchallenged and have become part of everyday discourse or conversation about the conflict.

1. *The Middle East conflict is thousands of years old.*
Typically this is expressed as 'those people have been killing each other for thousands of years'. Over the course of its history, particularly during the age of pre-modern

empires, the Middle East has experienced considerable violence. As in Europe and Asia, warfare was the common means of expanding empires and controlling territory. During much of this time pagans, Christians, Jews and, later, Muslims lived in the Middle East. Conflict was generally not defined along religious lines; in fact, some of the most long-lived conflicts were between Muslim empires. Throughout this time a small but constant Jewish presence existed.

The current conflict is approximately sixty years old, and dates to the creation of the state of Israel in 1948 and the decades of European Jewish immigration that preceded it. In the nineteenth century Europe established political and economic control over many areas in Africa and the Middle East. At the time, colonialism was considered acceptable, though it ignored the rights of the current inhabitants. In 1917 the British government granted the Jewish people the right to create a 'homeland' in the territory of Palestine, which they controlled via the League of Nations. Both the Arabs living in the mandate, today known as the Palestinians, and Arabs in surrounding states, such as Syria, Egypt and Jordan, opposed the creation of a state, populated largely by European Jewish immigrants, in Palestine.

As the colonial period drew to a close after World War II, Britain withdrew from Palestine. Jewish settlers created the state of Israel in 1948, and warfare ensued between Israel and neighboring states. War broke out again in 1967 and 1973 when Arab states attacked Israel. Ending the conflict means resolving the claims resulting from these three wars.

2. *Religious hatred is the reason for the conflict.*
Though there is clearly a religious dimension to the conflict, its primary focus is land. The Jewish connection to Palestine is based on their historical and spiritual connection to the area, and the memory of the forced expulsion of Jews under the Romans in the second century AD, which dispersed the Jewish community into two thousand years of Diaspora. It is more useful to view the conflict between Israelis and Palestinians as one of competing nationalist visions, in which each seeks to create a state within a very small territory.

Clearly religion is important; and Jerusalem as well as surrounding areas are of significance to Judaism, Christianity and Islam. Some people, on both sides, are unwilling to compromise what they see as divine providence in order to achieve resolution of the conflict.

Both hard-line Israeli settlers and Islamist extremists may be willing to die rather than to compromise for peace.

Religion is also used by parties in the conflict to achieve political advantage and achieve support for their position. Some Israelis, for example, frighten Christian Zionists with images of a Muslim-controlled Jerusalem. Some Muslims publish anti-Semitic cartoons to encourage condemnation of Israel. However, the root of this 'religious' conflict is political. There is no inherent anti-Semitism in Islam; and both Judaism and Islam, along with Christianity, share a common forefather, Abraham. Prior to the creation of Israel, thriving Jewish communities existed throughout the Middle East. Many Jews took refuge in North Africa after the Catholic reconquest of the Iberian peninsula and the introduction of the Spanish Inquisition. Today, synagogues in Cairo, Tunis and other cities stand under heavy guard to protect them from attack, and the once sizable Jewish communities in these countries have withered. A particularly unfortunate outcome of the current Middle East conflict is the loss of religiously mixed communities, especially in the area known historically as Palestine.

Box 9.1

CHRISTIAN ZIONISM

In the United States and some other countries, strong, and often unconditional, support for Israel comes from the Christian community. This at first may seem unusual, given the significant theological differences between Judaism and Christianity, but the partnership of convenience allows both to pursue their goals.

One reason Christians support Israel is the status of Jews, like Christians, as God's 'chosen people'. Another is the belief, held by some Christians, that the return of Jews to the Holy Land, and particularly Jewish control over Jerusalem and all of Palestine, is necessary to fulfill biblical prophecy. To some, reconstruction of the Temple in Jerusalem by the Jews is a necessary prerequisite to the End of Days (or End Times),

which precede the second coming of the Messiah (Jesus Christ). At the End Times, or Rapture, Christians expect that many Jews will convert to Christianity, accept the Messiah and ascend into heaven; those who do not will perish in hell along with other unbelievers.

Events in the latter part of the twentieth century, specifically the establishment of the state of Israel, have led some Christians to support the same goals as Jewish Zionists, but for very different reasons. Christian Zionism is particularly strong among Protestant evangelical groups, the largest of which is the Southern Baptist Convention which has over 16 million members. Some groups provide political and economic support to Israel. Believing that Israel

Box 9.1

CHRISTIAN ZIONISM—CONT'D

must control all of the West Bank, large sums of money are raised to support the building of settlements. Numerous organizations, such as Christian Action for Israel and Christians United for Israel, encourage Christian support for Israel. While popular Christian ministers such as Jerry Falwell and organizations such as the Moral Majority help build popular support for Christian Zionism, support for Israel is controversial within the evangelical community, and other organizations work against uncritical support for Israel.

Within the US political system, Christian evangelicals have gained considerable political power in recent years, and have advocated stronger US support for Israel. This support is consistent with their belief in pre-millennialism, which states that the return of Jesus Christ will precede a thousand-year reign of peace. Man, however, is unable to bring about a peaceful world. In recent years membership in evangelical churches has swelled, making them a potent force in electoral politics. For example, 'by 2003 there were more Southern Baptists than Methodists, Presbyterians, Episcopalians, and members of the United Church of Christ combined' (Mead 2006). According to the National Election Pool exit poll, Bush received 78 percent of the vote among white evangelicals in the 2004 election, an increase of 10 percent over the 2000 election. Though only 23 percent of the American population are white evangelicals, they have become increasingly effective in maintaining a narrow agenda and have shifted their support primarily to the Republican Party.

Mead, W. (2006) 'God's Country?' *Foreign Affairs*, September–October.

The Pew Research Center for People and the Press (2004) 'Religion and the presidential vote: Bush's gains broad-based', December 6: http://people-press.org/commentary/display.php3?AnalysisID=103.

3. *Attempts to end the conflict are pointless.*

Actually, significant progress toward the eventual resolution of the conflict has been made. Peace treaties between Israel and both Egypt and Jordan were concluded in 1979 and 1994 respectively. And it is extremely unlikely that any Arab state will today launch an attack against militarily superior Israel.

Progress has even been made to resolve the Israeli–Palestinian conflict. Until the early 1990s there was no formal contact between the state of Israel and the Palestine Liberation Organization (PLO), which represented the interests of the Palestinians.

Under the Oslo Accords the Israeli government recognized the PLO as the legitimate representative of the Palestinian people, and the PLO recognized the right of the state of Israel to exist and formally renounced terrorism.

In the last fifteen years, dozens of meetings have taken place between Israeli and Palestinian officials, academics and representatives to discuss means to end the conflict. Numerous agreements have been drafted, though none has ended the conflict.

THE 'CONFLICTS': ISRAEL, THE ARAB STATES AND THE PALESTINIANS

There is no single 'conflict' in the Middle East; rather there is a series of conflicts between specific Arab states and the Palestinians and the state of Israel. The differing names applied to these conflicts sometimes cause confusion.

The Arab–Israeli conflict is a broad term that refers to the unresolved issues, largely involving territory, between Israel and Egypt, Jordan, Syria and the Palestinians that resulted from the 1967 war. By the end of this war, Israel had expanded its territory greatly, seizing the Golan Heights from Syria, Sinai from Egypt and the West Bank

Box 9.2

THE ISRAELI-JORDANIAN PEACE

In 1994, Jordanian prime minister Abdelsalam al-Majali and Israeli prime minister Yitzhak Rabin signed the peace treaty that ended the state of war that had existed between the two countries since 1948. The treaty was the result of extensive secret negotiations, carried out by King Hussein of Jordan, the elder statesmen of the Arab world.

King Hussein had led Jordan since 1952, and had fought against Israel in the 1967 war, during which Jordan lost control over the West Bank and East Jerusalem. Despite this, King Hussein had adopted an increasingly pragmatic approach to Israel, noting that geography forced the two nations to deal with each other. Indeed, Hussein may have attempted an agreement with Israel earlier, had there not been a need to maintain Arab solidarity with the Palestinians against Israel. Jordan's population contains a large number of Palestinians.

The conclusion of the Oslo Accords, which were designed to lead to the creation of a Palestinian state, opened the door for King Hussein to move forward with peace with Israel. Over time, he and Yitzhak Rabin formed a close friendship, facilitating the negotiations. President Bill Clinton also promised Jordan debt relief if it agreed to end its state of belligerency with Israel as well as warmer relations between the US and Jordan, which had soured owing to Jordan's support of Iraq.

Mindful of the limited nature of the Israeli–Egyptian peace, the Israeli–Jordanian peace treaty is an extensive document, designed not only to normalize relations between Israel and Jordan, but also to create relations between the two peoples. The treaty addressed necessary issues such as territory and mutual defense. It also included provisions for economic cooperation, scientific and cultural exchange, and cooperation on the environment and health issues. Direct air travel was established between the two countries, as well as phone lines and postal links. Article 11 of the agreement specifically banned 'hostile or discriminatory propaganda against each other'.

For a short time after the signing of the peace treaty there was reason to be optimistic that the peace would have a broad societal impact in both countries. Israeli tourists flocked to visit Jordan's famed ancient city of Petra. Economic cooperation, in trade and manufacturing, was established. Sadly, the increasing violence between Israel and the Palestinians since 2000 has hindered attempts to foster real societal relationships between Israelis and Jordanians. Though today the security relationship, always the bedrock of the peace agreement, remains strong, the relationship between the citizenry is nonexistent.

Within five years of the peace treaty, its main architects, Hussein and Rabin, were both dead. Hussein died of cancer in 1999, and was likely already ill during the peace negotiations. Rabin was assassinated, on November 4, 1995, while attending a massive peace rally in Tel Aviv, by an Orthodox Jewish extremist who opposed the Oslo Accords.

Stewart, D. J. (2007) *Good Neighbourly Relations: Jordan, Israel and the 1994–2004 Peace Process.* London: I. B. Tauris.

from Jordan. Ceasefires secured an end to the military conflict (Map 9.1).

Peace treaties were signed, which normalized relations, between Egypt and Israel in 1979 and between Jordan and Israel in 1994. As a result of the peace treaty, the Sinai peninsula was returned to Egypt, with the exception of the Gaza Strip. In 1988, Jordan had renounced its claim to the West Bank, ceding it to the Palestine Liberation Organization, so this territory was not included in the Israel–Jordan peace.

To date a peace agreement has not been signed between Israel and Syria, though extensive negotiations

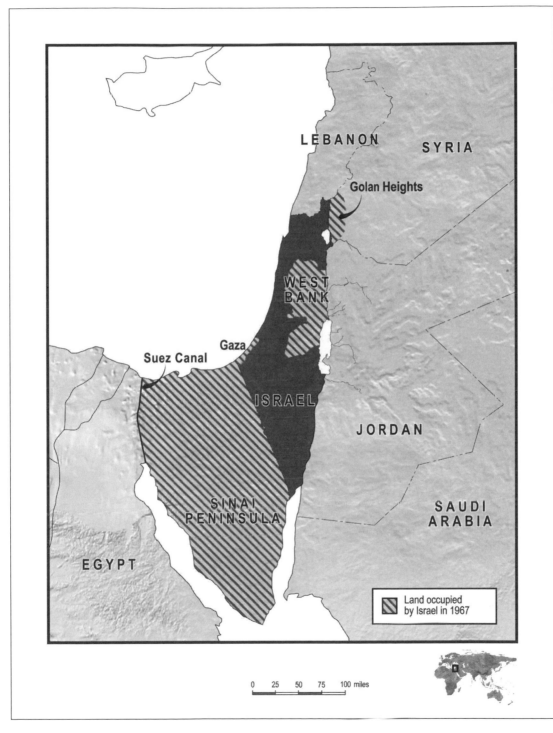

Map 9.1 The occupied territories

Box 9.3

ARIEL SHARON AND THE GAZA WITHDRAWAL

On September 12, 2005, the Israeli government completed its withdrawal from the Gaza Strip, concluding its thirty-eight-year control over the territory and ending its military rule there. With the end of its military rule, Israel pulled its last 3000 troops from Gaza. Israel retains control over the Gaza Strip's borders and controls the passage of Palestinians between the Gaza Strip and the West Bank.

In the weeks prior to the withdrawal of the Israeli military, all Israeli settlers were removed. Though many had chosen to leave voluntarily, accepting compensation packages from the government, some settlers mounted extensive protests and had to be forcibly removed. Prior to the evacuation, there were twenty-one settlements in the Gaza Strip, with a population of nearly 9000. Four settlements in the northern West Bank were also evacuated at this time. As they withdrew, the settlers destroyed the infrastructure in the settlements, rendering it unusable by Palestinians.

The driving force behind the Gaza withdrawal, also known as the unilateral disengagement plan, was Israeli prime minister Ariel Sharon. When he first announced the plan in 2004, it was met with rejection by the public. Eventually an amended disengagement plan, and compensation for the relocated settlers, was approved. The months before the withdrawal saw large protests in Israel against the disengagement.

The unilateral disengagement plan represented a radical departure from Israel's earlier policy of settlement-building to claim territory for Israel and provide for its defense. Even more surprisingly, Ariel Sharon had been the major architect of the settlement program, even choosing the locations for specific settlements. Sharon's highly successful military and political career began at the age of 20 when he led a military unit in the 1948 war. Sharon was known for often brutal tactics. In 1982, as minister of defense, he led Israel's occupation of southern Lebanon. He was found to be indirectly responsible for the massacre of between 800 and 3500 Palestinian civilians in two refugee camps: Sabra and Shatila.

By 2004, Sharon had come to believe that continuing to hold on to Gaza was not in the interests of Israel's security and that the disengagement would give Israel diplomatic advantage in the international community.

On January 4, 2006, Sharon suffered a massive stroke and fell into a coma. His duties were assumed by then acting prime minister Ehud Olmert. He remains in a persistent vegetative state. With Sharon's incapacitation and the death of PLO chairman Yasser Arafat, each the other's arch-nemesis, two of the dominant personalities in the Israeli–Palestinian conflict are now silent.

'Israel completes Gaza withdrawal'. BBC News, September 12, 2005: http://news.bbc.co.uk/2/hi/middle_east/4235768.stm.

Prusher, I. (2006) 'Sharon's legacy of controversy'. *The Christian Science Monitor*, April 12, p. 10.

have taken place and the two parties have reportedly come close, at times, to a resolution. The main issue is continued Israeli control of the Golan Heights. Like the West Bank and Sinai, the Golan Heights has played an important role as a security buffer against potential Syrian attack in the decades following the 1967 war. Syria has demanded Israeli withdrawal from the entire Golan Heights, which has been heavily settled by Israelis and was formally annexed in 1981. Approximately thirty-three settlements, with a total population of over 18,000, have been built in the Golan, many of them in the southern section. Though most of the Syrian population, largely of Druze origin, fled or were expelled during the war, a handful of 'Syrian' villages remain.

The Israeli–Palestinian conflict, which is by far the most active in the region, refers to the conflict between Israel and the Palestinians over the territories of the West Bank and the Gaza Strip, occupied by Israel in 1967. In 2005, Israel withdrew from the Gaza Strip and removed its settlements. Today, the primary representative for the Palestinian people in negotiations with Israel is the Palestinian National Authority (PNA), an elected body established under the Oslo Accords. Currently the PNA is headed by President Mahmoud Abbas. Until the creation of the PNA , the Palestine Liberation Organization served as the official representative of the Palestinians. However, the PLO still receives considerable international recognition; and its members, including those in its affiliated political party, Fatah, dominate the PNA.

TWO PEOPLES – TWO NARRATIVES

At the root of the conflict is the desire by two different groups of people each to have a state, in which they are the majority population, within a very small geographical area. For the last sixty years Israeli nationalism and Palestinian nationalism have been mutually exclusive. Each party believes passionately in its own nationalist narrative and works to convince the world that its narrative is 'right' and the other's is 'wrong'. For the Israelis, the creation of Israel is the saga of carving a Jewish homeland, for a persecuted stateless people, out of a barren and undeveloped land. The same event, to Palestinians, is the *nakba*, or disaster, and means the loss of ancestral homes and agricultural groves, and the violent uprooting of entire communities. A single event can be interpreted differently when viewed through the prism of one's nationalism.

Though it is unlikely that Israelis and Palestinians will ever fully accept each other's narrative, conflict resolution is still possible as long as both parties can find enough common ground and accept parts of the other's narrative. Clearly the Israeli and Palestinian people hold a wide range of opinions about the conflict and about each other. While some people work actively to bring about resolution, others seek to continue the conflict or view violence as the only possible means to achieve the vision set forth in their narrative.

It is important to realize that there is very little 'unbiased' news or writing about the Middle East conflict. Language is a very important aspect of the conflict; through language each side tries to gain advantage for its own narrative. Statements such as 'there are no Palestinian people' and references to the West Bank as 'Judea and Samaria' are designed to refute the other's potential claims and undermine conflict resolution efforts. Similarly, referring to Israelis as 'Jews' or 'Zionists', and failing to recognize Israel, perpetuates the conflict. Both the current Israeli and Palestinian governments have mutually recognized each other, and have committed themselves to the idea of two states within the current territory. Fernea and Hocking (1992) point out that the use of neutral terminology indicates gradual acceptance of the other party's legitimacy and opens the door for nationalist narratives that are not mutually exclusive.

CENTRAL ISSUES IN THE CONFLICT: TERRITORY

The primary issues that need to be addressed in order to resolve the Israeli–Palestinian conflict include: territory, refugees, compensation and the status of Jerusalem. Only then can the 'just and lasting peace' called for in United Nations Security Council Resolution 242, passed in the aftermath of the 1967 war, be reached. However, each of these issues is quite complex, and finding a solution that satisfies the concerns of both the Israelis and the Palestinians has proved elusive. When Palestinian and Israeli negotiators speak of the treaty that will end the conflict, they use the term 'final status agreement', which indicates that all issues between the two parties are resolved, and nothing has been put off for a future agreement.

UN resolution 242 calls for the 'withdrawal of Israeli armed forces from territories occupied in the recent conflict', which include the West Bank, the Gaza Strip and East Jerusalem. East Jerusalem was officially annexed, contrary to international law, by Israel on June 11, 1967, placing it under Israeli law, jurisdiction and

Box 9.4

YASSER ARAFAT: THE STRUGGLE FOR THE PALESTINIAN NATION

Many words have been used to describe Yasser Arafat: freedom fighter, terrorist, corrupt official, nationalist, peace negotiator …. His reputation was controversial, to say the least. To Palestinians, even to those who disagree with his stances or methods, he was the driving force behind the Palestinian nationalist movement, and the international face of the Palestinian struggle.

Much of Arafat's (b. 1929) early life, including his birthplace and family origin, is shrouded in myth. He grew up in Egypt, and attended Cairo University, an environment which fostered his strong nationalist position. Though he attempted to enter Palestine during the 1948 war to fight against Jewish forces, like other volunteer guerrilla forces, he was turned back at the Egyptian border.

In 1959, Arafat formed Fatah, an acronym standing for The Palestinian National Liberation Movement, and based it in Jordan. Fatah was dedicated to the liberation of Palestine and the establishment of an independent Palestinian state. In the 1960s, Arafat, and Fatah, became the primary representative of the Palestinian people. In 1964 the Arab League formed the Palestine Liberation Organization (PLO), in part to challenge Arafat's monopoly of the Palestinian cause. Its charter explicitly called for the destruction of Israel. By 1970, Arafat had become supreme commander of the Palestine Liberation Army, the armed branch of the PLO.

During the 1970s, Palestinian militant groups connected to Arafat adopted increasingly violent tactics to highlight the Palestinian cause and attack Israel. The hijacking of three international airlines, and the PLO's attempt to carve out an autonomous area inside Jordan, increasingly brought it into conflict with the monarchy. In September 1970 they were forced to leave Jordan, and relocated in Lebanon.

From Lebanon, the PLO continued its attacks on Israel, including the attack and killing of eleven Israeli athletes at the Munich Olympics. In 1982, Israel, under the leadership of defense minister Ariel Sharon, invaded Lebanon to attack the PLO. Under a US-brokered agreement, Arafat and the PLO were allowed to leave Lebanon, and were transported into exile in Tunis in US ships. Tunis remained the PLO headquarters until 1993 when the Olso Accords paved the way for the return of Arafat and the PLO to the Occupied Territories.

Arafat had directed the Palestinian team in the secret negotiations at Oslo. Prior to signing the Olso Accords, Arafat, in his role as chairman of the PLO, had officially recognized Israel and renounced the use of violence. In 1994, Arafat received the Nobel Peace Prize, along with Israelis Shimon Peres and Yitzhak Rabin. In 1996, Arafat was elected president of the Palestinian Authority, the body created under Oslo to allow Palestinian self-rule in the occupied territories. He won the vast majority of votes, but the victory was marred by the failure of Hamas, the dominant Islamist party and Fatah's rival, to participate.

The US and Israel grew frustrated with Arafat in the aftermath of Oslo. His unwillingness to participate in Oslo, his support for the *intifada*, and his inability or unwillingness to stop armed attacks on Israel led to his marginalization in any potential peace process by the United States.

On October 25, 2004, Arafat fell ill; his condition quickly worsened, and he was flown to Paris for medical treatment. He died on November 11. The exact cause of his death is still not known.

Kimmerling, B. and Migdal, J. (2003) *The Palestinian People: A History*. Cambridge, Mass.: Harvard University Press.

administration. The West Bank and the Gaza Strip were not annexed but administered by the Israeli Civil Administration. The 'Green Line', or armistice line, established after the 1948 war also marks the border between Israel and Jordan and Egypt prior to the 1967 war (Map 9.2).

In recent years the desirability of creating a Palestinian state has become accepted as a component of the peace agreement between the Israelis and the Palestinians. What is not agreed upon is the exact territory this state will include. Dispute centers largely on the West Bank. From the Palestinian perspective, Israeli withdrawal from 100 percent of the pre-1967 territory is the most desirable. From the Israeli perspective, this is untenable as large Israeli housing developments (termed 'settlements' by Palestinians and 'neighborhoods' by Israelis) have been built inside the Green Line, especially in the area around Jerusalem. While dismantling many of the approximately 145 settlements and 130 outposts built by Israel inside the West Bank may take place following a peace agreement, Israel will probably not give up large neighborhoods near Jerusalem such as Ma'ale Adumim. Though residents of settlements and outposts deep in the West Bank typically move there for religious or ideological reasons, with a goal of claiming land they see as their birthright, residents of the so-called neighborhoods in the Jerusalem area tend to be secular and move there for the economic benefits. The Israeli government offers these 'economic settlers' low mortgage rates and grants to move into the occupied territories.

Further complicating the territory issue is the construction of a security barrier along and inside the Green Line by Israel (Map 9.3). The Palestinians refer to it as the racial segregation wall or apartheid wall, and in places the barrier is a wall 25 feet high. Most Israelis refer to it as the security fence, and for much of its length the barrier is a 150-feet-wide multi-layer system of fences. Many news agencies and the international community use the somewhat neutral term 'barrier'. Though the idea for a physical barrier to provide security for Israelis had existed since the 1990s, the movement to erect the barrier grew following high-casualty suicide bombings during the al-Aqsa *intifada*.

The barrier runs for approximately 436 miles, and cuts deep into the West Bank to include Israeli neighborhoods in the West Bank. The route of the separation barrier is controversial, even inside Israel. In 2004 the Israeli Supreme Court determined that parts of the route violated Palestinian human rights, and sections were re-routed. The separation barrier has had extremely negative consequences for the Palestinian population. Palestinians who live near the barrier have found themselves separated from their agricultural land, jobs and neighbors, and they can no longer move freely within the West Bank. Critics argue that the barrier is in effect a 'de facto' border and is an attempt by Israel unilaterally to determine the borders of a future Palestinian state. Data suggest, however, that the barrier has increased security for the Israeli population, dramatically reducing attacks and suicide bombings on Israelis.

Current conflict resolution efforts between Israel and the Palestinians acknowledge that the Palestinians will likely not receive 100 percent of the pre-1967 land. Instead, the parties now talk in terms of 'land swaps'. In this formulation, the Palestinians will receive an area of land equivalent in size to the pre-1967 West Bank area. Israel may trade some land on its side of the armistice line for some land it will not give up inside the Green Line. In practical terms the Palestinians currently control about 90 percent, if not a little more, of the original area inside the Green Line. The actual area of territory that needs to be decided upon is quite small, but of crucial importance. If the Palestinians agree to give up some area inside the Green Line, what will they get in return?

From the Palestinian perspective it is important that the future Palestinian state, of which the West Bank is part, be composed of territory that is contiguous (i.e. attached) and that the land is of equivalent quality to any land given up. Finally, any agreement on territory must also include a means to connect the two parts of the Palestinian state, the West Bank and Gaza. How to connect these parts, while maintaining Israeli security, has resulted in proposals ranging from tunnels to elevated highways.

CENTRAL ISSUES IN THE CONFLICT: REFUGEES AND COMPENSATION

After the 1948 Arab–Israeli War, there were approximately 711,000 Palestinian refugees. The United Nations

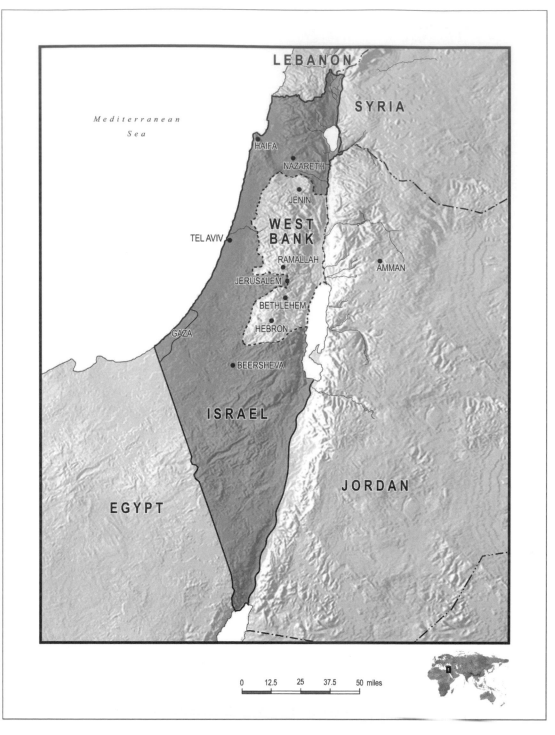

Map 9.2 Israel's 1949 Green Line

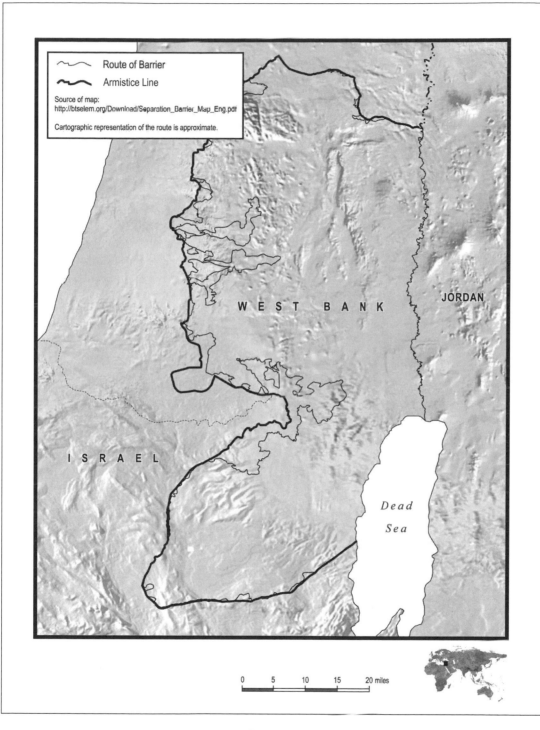

Map 9.3 Route of the Israeli separation barrier

Relief and Works Agency for Palestinian Refugees in the Near East (UNRWA) was created to provide educational and medical aid and support for the refugees. Palestinian refugees, according to UNRWA, 'are persons whose normal place of residence was Palestine between June 1946 and May 1948, who lost both their homes and means of livelihood as a result of the 1948 Arab–Israeli conflict'. As of December 2006, the number of refugees and their descendants was 4.44 million.

The refugees live primarily in the West Bank and Gaza and in neighboring Arab countries. Many of the refugees live in the fifty-eight camps that were established to house them temporarily but have now been in place for decades. A relatively small number of Palestinians have been able to migrate to Europe, North America and other parts of the world (Table 9.1).

The return of these refugees was called for in United Nations General Assembly Resolution 194, passed in December 1948, which states that

> the refugees wishing to return to their homes and live at peace with their neighbors should be permitted to do so at the earliest practicable date, and that compensation should be paid for the property of those choosing not to return and for loss of or damage to property which, under principles of international law or in equity, should be made good by the Governments or authorities responsible.

Under the Absentee Property Law, passed by Israel, property formerly belonging to refugees was confiscated and transferred to Israeli citizens. Much property, especially in Arab villages, was destroyed, so the return of Palestinians to the actual houses they, or their forefathers, once inhabited is impossible for many.

The refugee issue is one that is very emotionally charged for both Israelis and Palestinians. Many Palestinian families still carry the keys to homes they once inhabited that are now inside Israel. For many Palestinians, there is a need for Israel to acknowledge the events of the Arab–Israeli war and admit their role in Palestinian suffering. This is problematic from an Israeli point of view, in part because it contradicts the Israelis' nation-building myth of 'a land (Palestine) with no people for a people with no land (Jews)'. To acknowledge responsibility for the Palestinian refugees could create a legal precedent relating to compensation and, to some Israelis, undermine the legitimacy of the state in the eyes of the international community.

The actual return of 4 million Palestinian refugees and their descendants to Israel is unlikely ever to happen. Israel will not agree to it, and many Palestinians do not want it. The return of 4 million Palestinians would disrupt the demographic balance inside Israel, where Jews are the majority, and threaten its character as a Jewish state. Presently there are approximately 6.5 million Israelis, of which 1.3 million are Israeli Arabs. Both Israeli Arabs and Palestinians have higher birth rates than Israelis – a further concern for Israel's desire to maintain a Jewish majority.

Though the right to return is very important to Palestinians, it seems highly unlikely that many of them would actually seek to move to Israel and live under Israeli law. A 2003 survey by the Palestinian Center for Policy and Survey Research found that only 10 percent of the refugees in the West Bank, the Gaza Strip, Jordan and Lebanon would prefer to live in Israel under Israeli law. Rather, most Palestinians would prefer to receive compensation and live either in the new Palestinian state to be formed in the West Bank and Gaza or remain in their current host country.

Though there is by no means a common understanding between Israelis and Palestinians over how to resolve the refugee issue, a likely formulation may be one whereby Israel recognizes Palestinian suffering, but does not accept responsibility for it, and provides

Table 9.1 Location of Palestinian refugees

Country	Refugees total	Camps	Refugees in camps
Jordan	1,858,362	10	328,076
Lebanon	408,438	12	215,890
Syria	442,363	9	119,055
West Bank	722,302	19	186,479
Gaza Strip	1,016,964	8	478,272
Egypt	70,245		
Saudi Arabia	240,000		

Source: United Nations Relief and World Agency, http://www.un.org/unrwa/publications/index.html, accessed August 27, 2007.

compensation. In some formulations, a small number of refugees, primarily the surviving members who were dislocated in 1948, would be allowed into Israel.

CENTRAL ISSUES IN THE CONFLICT: JERUSALEM

Because of its spiritual significance, all three monotheistic faiths have their significant holy places in Jerusalem; the status of Jerusalem is treated as a separate subject within final status talks. Jerusalem contains not only holy sites but also Jewish and Arab neighborhoods (both Christian and Muslim).

It would be difficult, if not impossible, to divide the holy places within Jerusalem's old city. In many cases the sites share walls and other physical structures. The most significant holy places are: the Temple Mount/Haram as Sharif, the Western Wall, the Dome of the Rock, the al-Aqsa mosque and the Church of the Holy Sepulchre (Map 9.4).

The Temple Mount is the holiest site in Judaism. It is known to Muslims as the Haram as Sharif or 'noblest sanctuary'; only Mecca and Medina are considered holier. For Jews the Temple Mount is the site of the first and second Jewish temples. According to the Talmud, the world was created from a foundation stone in the Temple. It is also the site where Abraham offered his son in sacrifice to God.

For Muslims, the gold-covered Dome of the Rock marks the site of Muhammad's night journey. According to Islamic tradition, Muhammad ascended into the heavens and met the prophets, including Moses, as well as God (Allah). On this night journey he convinced Allah to allow humankind to pray only five times a day, instead of fifty. Nearby is the al-Aqsa mosque, which literally translated means 'the furthest mosque'.

Below the Temple Mount/Haram as Sharif complex lies the Western Wall. It is also known as the Wailing Wall. This retaining wall dates to the time of the second Jewish temple, and functions as a large outdoor synagogue, with segregated areas to allow male and female worshippers to pray.

Located nearby, though not part of the Temple Mount/Haram as Sharif complex, is the Church of the Holy Sepulchre, which marks the site of Jesus Christ's crucifixion and burial.

It is likely that any arrangement for Jerusalem in the final status agreement will reflect the current status quo arrangement. At present, Israeli authorities have control over Jewish holy places and Palestinian authorities control Muslim holy places. The most holy core of the old city is jointly administered by representatives of the three major faiths.

OTHER ISSUES

Beyond these major issues a number of other details will need to be worked out, including the use of environmental resources, such as water that originates in Palestinian areas but is drawn by Israel inside its territory. But of primary concern for both Israelis and Palestinians is the assurance of mutual security for both parties.

A SHORT HISTORY OF CONFLICT RESOLUTION EFFORTS

In the sixty years since the 1948 Arab–Israeli war, the Arabs and Israelis have made considerable progress in resolving the conflicts between them. And, though issues remain to be resolved between Israel and Syria and Israel and the Palestinians, these previous agreements have laid the groundwork for an eventual final status agreement between Israel and the Palestinians.

1979 Camp David Accords

These Accords led directly to the 1979 Israel–Egypt peace treaty, which ended the state of belligerency between the two states. Israel and Egypt had fought three wars since 1948.

The Accords were the result of intensive effort by President Jimmy Carter to renew the Middle East peace process when he took office in 1977. In the first year of his presidency he met with the heads of state of Egypt and Israel, as well as of Jordan and Syria. At the same time, Egyptian president Anwar Sadat, frustrated by the slow pace of negotiations and seeking US economic aid to bolster Egypt's economy, made an unprecedented visit to Israel, giving a speech in the Knesset. He was the first Arab

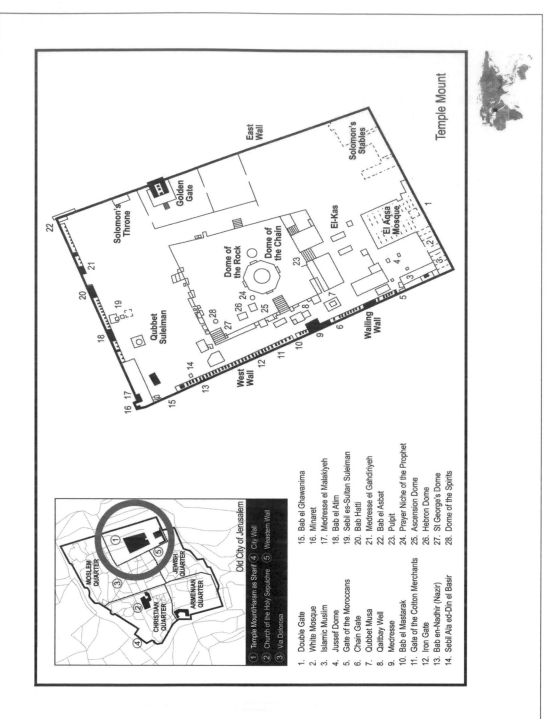

Map 9.4 The Temple Mount/Haram as Sharif complex

leader ever to visit Israel, thereby implicitly recognizing the country. As a result of Sadat's actions, direct bilateral talks were initiated between Egypt and Israel.

Under the agreement, Israel agreed to give up Sinai, which it had seized during the 1967 war, including the Abu-Rudeis oil fields in western Sinai. A permanent ceasefire was declared along the Israeli–Egyptian border. In return, Egypt agreed to normalize diplomatic relations with Israel. This established the precedent of 'land for peace' by which Israel gives up land it occupied in armed conflict subsequent to the establishment of the state of Israel, in return for diplomatic acceptance in the region. Both Egypt and Israel benefited economically from the peace; each receives billions of dollars a year in economic aid and grants from the US as well as access to US military equipment. The Camp David Accords also established the United States as the region's primary 'peace-broker'.

Sadat was severely criticized by the Arab world for concluding a peace with Israel without resolving the Palestinian issue. The peace ultimately led to Sadat's assassination by members of an Islamist militant group, Egyptian Islamic Jihad.

The peace between Israel and Egypt has been criticized as a 'cold peace', meaning that it exists only between the two governments; there is no real relationship between the people of Egypt and the people of Israel. It is important to remember that the treaty has not been violated, even in times of great tension between the two countries.

Madrid Peace Conference

There was little progress in Middle East peace negotiations during the 1980s. In the aftermath of the 1991 Gulf War, which found the Arab states and Israel on the same side of the conflict, the international community attempted to reinvigorate the Middle East peace process. The Madrid Conference, hosted by the Spanish government, brought together representatives of Israel, Syria, Lebanon and Jordan as well as of the Palestinians. Though the Madrid Conference itself did not lead directly to any new agreements, secret bilateral talks, initiated at the conference, led to major breakthroughs. These included the contacts between Israel and Jordan that led to the peace agreement between

them. While the formal negotiating track established between the Israelis and the Palestinians at the Madrid Conference failed to make progress, secret negotiations ultimately led to the Oslo Accords.

The Oslo Accords

The Oslo Accords are officially called the Declaration of Principles on Interim Self-government Agreements. They were the result of secret direct negotiations between Israelis and Palestinians, held at a time when it was technically illegal for Israelis to meet with Palestinians, and sponsored by the Norwegian government. The Oslo Agreement was officially signed in Washington, DC, on September 13, 1993, and marked by historic handshakes between Israeli prime minister Yitzhak Rabin and PLO leader Yasser Arafat.

The Olso Accords were designed as an interim step, to install Palestinian self-rule in parts of the West Bank and Gaza Strip during a five-year period in which a final status agreement between the Israelis and the Palestinians would be concluded. As a result, the Oslo Accords did not address issues such as refugees and the final borders between the two parties.

The Accords included mutual recognition between the two parties. The Palestine Liberation Organization recognized the right of the state of Israel to exist and renounced terrorism, violence and its desire to destroy Israel. Israel recognized the Palestine Liberation Organization as the legitimate representative of the Palestinian people.

Under the Oslo Accords, Israel agreed to withdraw from portions of the West Bank and Gaza Strip, turning them over to Palestinian self-government under a newly created Palestinian Authority. Three different zones were created: Area A zones, in which the Palestinian Authority had full control; Area B zones, in which the PA exercised civil control but Israel exercised security control; and Area C zones, in which Israel exercised full control, though not over Palestinian civilians. Area C areas included Israeli settlements (Map 9.5).

The Oslo Accords created a period of relative peace and optimism in Israel and the Palestinian territories which lasted from 1993 until the al-Aqsa *intifada* in 2000. Frustration at the inability to move from the interim Oslo

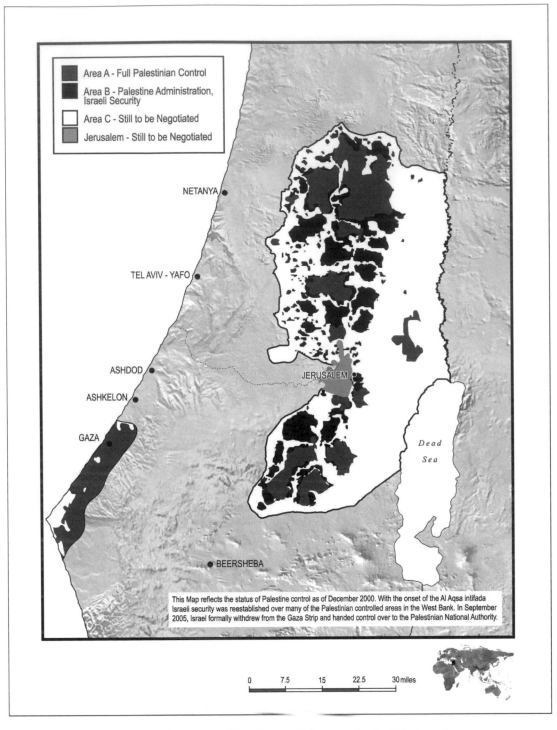

Area A - Full Palestinian Control

Area B - Palestine Administration, Israeli Security

Area C - Still to be Negotiated

Jerusalem - Still to be Negotiated

NETANYA

TEL AVIV - YAFO

ASHDOD

ASHKELON

GAZA

JERUSALEM

Dead Sea

BEERSHEBA

This Map reflects the status of Palestine control as of December 2000. With the onset of the Al Aqsa intifada Israeli security was reestablished over many of the Palestinian controlled areas in the West Bank. In September 2005, Israel formally withdrew from the Gaza Strip and handed control over to the Palestinian National Authority.

0   7.5   15   22.5   30 miles

Map 9.5 Palestinian- and Israeli-controlled areas under the Oslo Accords

Agreement into successful final status talks contributed greatly to the rising tension between the two parties prior to the onset of the *intifada*. Both sides undertook actions that created distrust during the Oslo period; Palestinian groups such as Hamas continued to call for the destruction of Israel, while Israel rapidly expanded its settlement-building – a move that Palestinians saw as an attempt to influence final border talks. The Oslo Accords had a mixed legacy. While they succeeded in finally bringing the two parties face-to-face, they failed to bring about a peace settlement, and as a result may have deepened the distrust between Israelis and Palestinians at both the governmental and the societal level. A common criticism of this 'incremental' approach to resolving the conflict is that it delays discussion of the major issues to some indeterminate time in the future, contributing to distrust and insecurity among the parties.

Camp David II

In July 2000, US president Bill Clinton, who had overseen the historic handshake on the White House lawn between Rabin and Arafat, attempted to broker a final status agreement between Israel and the Palestinians. He convened a summit at Camp David, where President Carter had successfully brokered the Israeli–Egyptian peace, inviting Israeli prime minister Ehud Barak and Yasser Arafat, now chairman of the Palestinian Authority.

The summit ended in failure, and probably contributed to the onset of the al-Aqsa *intifada*. President Clinton was criticized for trying to force the parties into an agreement before he left office, when clearly significant differences existed in the two parties' positions. The Israelis and the Palestinians hold very different beliefs about what happened at Camp David, with each side accusing the other of failing to negotiate in good faith. Disagreement over the status of Jerusalem and resolution of the Palestinian refugee problem ultimately caused the parties to abandon negotiations.

The Road Map

In 2002, after two years of worsening violence, a 'quartet' made up of the United States, the European Union, Russia and the United Nations drafted a plan designed to end the violence and lead to a permanent status agreement. In this document the principle of an independent Palestinian state was explicitly endorsed by the United States.

The Road Map had three phases. The first centered on the cessation of violence, elections in Palestine and a freeze on settlement expansion. In the second phase, a Palestinian state with provisional borders was to be established and an international conference convened to provide economic support for the Palestinian economy and foster negotiation on a variety of issues including refugees. In the final stage an international conference would be convened to negotiate a final status agreement including the issues of territory, Jerusalem and refugees.

Under the Road Map a Palestinian prime minister, Mahmoud Abbas, was appointed – in part to lessen the influence of Yasser Arafat, who was distrusted by both the US and Israel. Following his appointment, the details of the Road Map were released on April 30, 2003.

The Road Map was never fully implemented. Indeed, both parties fell short of achieving the goals set in phase one. Violence between the two parties did not cease, and Israel did not withdraw from Palestinian areas it had reoccupied during the *intifada*. Though the quartet still considers the Road Map to be a viable document, and occasional attempts are made to restart the Road Map process, no real progress has been made.

The Geneva Accord

Not all attempts at a final status agreement have been government-led. In fact, for years groups of Palestinian and Israeli academics, retired security officials, activists and politicians have met to hold 'unofficial' negotiations. Known as 'track-two talks', the agreements formed in these meetings are not binding on either government. However, track-two talks are an important way for the two sides to exchange ideas.

The Geneva Accord, also known as the Draft Permanent Status Agreement, was a joint effort led by an Israeli politician, Yossi Beilin, and Yasser Abed Rabbo, a former minister in the Palestinian Authority. It was launched, amid much fanfare, at a ceremony in Geneva on December 1, 2003.

Under the Geneva Accord, a Palestinian state would be established and the Palestinians would recognize Israel as the homeland of the Jewish people. The Palestinians would get most territory inside the Green Line, with the exception of areas around some Israeli 'neighborhoods' in Jerusalem. Israel would agree to accept an unspecified number of Palestinian refugees; Israel would have ultimate control over the total number admitted.

Neither the government of Israel nor the Palestinian Authority endorsed the Geneva Accord, though it received considerable support from the populace.

THE PRESENT SITUATION

The present situation in Israel and Palestine is quite bleak. Violence and casualties have increased dramatically since 2000 and the onset of the second Palestinian *intifada*. The term *intifada* is literally translated as 'shaking off' and is considered by many Palestinians to be a legitimate form of armed resistance to Israeli occupation. The first Palestinian *intifada* took place in 1987 and lasted until 1993 when the Oslo Accords were reached. Tactics in this mass uprising included strikes, boycotts of Israeli products, and attacks on Israeli soldiers, mainly by children throwing stones. Israeli soldiers responded largely with rubber bullets and water cannons. During the first *intifada* approximately 160 Israeli soldiers and 1100 Palestinians were killed.

During the Oslo period violence diminished greatly; but, by 2000, Oslo was in tatters, the Camp David summit had failed, and tension between Israel and the Palestinians was very high. The second *intifada*, also known as the al-Aqsa *intifada*, began in September 2000 and was triggered by a controversial visit of Ariel Sharon, head of the Likud Party, to the Temple Mount/al-Aqsa, accompanied by hundreds of Israeli riot police, which sparked a Palestinian riot and a harsh Israeli security response. Some in Israel contend that the uprising was pre-planned, and Sharon's visit was only an excuse – a charge the Palestinians deny. Some Israelis and Palestinians argue that Sharon intended to provoke violence through his visit. In any event, the *intifada* reflects the growing despair within Israel and Palestine, and the rising tension between the two parties.

The al-Aqsa *intifada* continues today; it is characterized by much higher casualty figures than the first *intifada*. Suicide bombers and assault helicopters have replaced stones and bullets. According to B'Tselem, an Israeli human rights organization, 4873 Palestinians were killed by Israeli security forces and Israeli civilians between September 29, 2000 and September 30, 2008; 1061 Israelis were killed by Palestinians, including suicide bombers.

The al-Aqsa *intifada* is marked by the increasing use of tactics that harm civilians. Palestinian militant groups have conducted extensive suicide bombing campaigns, on targets such as cafés, buses, malls and nightclubs inside Israel. While there were only thirteen suicide bombings during the 'Oslo' years of 1993–2000, the incidence increased sharply after 2000. In 2001 there were thirty-five attacks, reaching a high of sixty in 2002. Casualties from suicide bombings totaled 545 between 2000 and 2006; rates of injury were much higher. By 2006, after construction of the security barrier, the number of suicide bombings had dropped to five.

The use of suicide bombing is controversial within Palestinian society, with some people supporting it as an act of religious martyrdom, or as a means to overcome Israel's vastly superior military power, and others condemning it. It can also be seen as an indicator of growing desperation and a lack of hope among Palestinian youth. During the *intifada*, Israel has increasingly utilized 'targeted assassination' against suspected militants. Often this is done by firing missiles from a helicopter into a car or building containing the militant. Unfortunately, nearby civilians are often killed or wounded in these attacks. Palestinians also accuse Israel of 'collective punishment', punishing Palestinian society as a whole for the actions of a small minority of militants. Collective punishment measures include the Israeli closure of the West Bank and Gaza Strip, prohibiting Palestinians from moving between the two or moving around within the West Bank. The closures restrict Palestinian mobility, making it difficult or impossible to reach jobs or essential medical care.

With the lack of progress on a jointly negotiated final status agreement, unilateral approaches by Israel now characterize the Israeli–Palestinian relationship. Both the separation barrier and the Gaza withdrawal are examples of such approaches. As of fall 2008, there had been little attempt by the international community to reinitiate negotiations. The electoral victory of Hamas, which now has a significant role in the Palestinian Authority's governing structure, and internal conflict between Hamas and Fatah further deter attempts to negotiate a settlement. The impact of the Hamas victory is discussed in more detail in the next chapter.

SUMMARY OF MAIN POINTS

- The conflict between Israel and certain Arab states is not 'ages old'; rather, it has been in existence for less than a hundred years.
- Competing nationalist visions, not innate religious hatred, is the dominant factor in the conflict.
- In recent decades substantial progress has been made on resolving the conflicts between Israel and the Arab states; including peace treaties with both Egypt and Jordan.
- Both Israel and the international community support the creation of a Palestinian state on territory in the West Bank and the Gaza Strip.
- Three of the most challenging issues that must be resolved to achieve a peace agreement between Israel and the Palestinians are: territory, refugees and control over Jerusalem.
- At present there is little real negotiation taking placed between Israel and the Palestinians; unilateral actions, such as the 'separation barrier', now dominate.

QUESTIONS FOR DISCUSSION

1 In what ways do the media shape the public's view of conflict in the Middle East?
2 What role do religion and nationalism play in the Israeli–Palestinian conflict?
3 How has the relationship between Israel and its Arab neighbors changed in the last sixty years?

4 Are there possible compromises on the issues of territory, refugees and Jerusalem that will satisfy both Israel and the Palestinians?
5 What are some of the positive and negative impacts of the Oslo Accords?
6 What are the impacts of so called unilateral approaches, such as the Gaza withdrawal and the separation barrier?
7 What should be the role of the international community, and specifically the US and the UK, in resolving the Israeli–Palestinian conflict?

SUGGESTIONS FOR FURTHER READING

Agha, H. and Malley, R. (2001) 'Camp David: the tragedy of errors'. *The New York Review of Books,* August 9. Written by a member of the US team at Camp David (Malley) and a Palestinian academic, this article explores the problems that undermined the negotiations, even before they started. See also Grinstein, G. and Ross, D. (2001) 'Camp David: an exchange', *The New York Review of Books.* September 20, which is a response to Agha and Malley's article, written by an Israeli official involved in the negotiations (Grinstein) and a former US diplomat. Finally, see 'A reply' by Agha and Malley, *The New York Review of Books*, September 20, 2001.

Agha, H., Feldman, S., Khalidi, A. and Schiff, Z. (2004) *Track-II Diplomacy: Lessons from the Middle East.* Cambridge, Mass.: MIT Press. Co-written by Palestinian and Israeli academics with extensive track-II experience, this book gives unprecedented insight into the role of 'diplomacy without diplomats' in Middle East peace negotiations.

Amnesty International (2007) *Israel and the Occupied Territories.* Annual Report: http://thereport.amnesty.org/eng/Regions/Middle-East-and-North-Africa/Israel-and-the-Occupied-Territories. An annual summary of violence, closures and other events in the West Bank and Gaza Strip.

Barghouti, M. (2003) *I Saw Ramallah.* Cairo: American University in Cairo Press. A personal account of the author's return from the West Bank after thirty years in exile. The author is a poet.

Beilin, Y. (1999) *Touching Peace: From the Oslo Accord to a Final Agreement*. London: Weidenfeld & Nicolson. A personal account by the primary Israeli architect of the Oslo Accords of the negotiations and breakthrough at Oslo.

B'TSELEM, The Israeli Information Center for Human Rights in the Occupied Territories. Documents human rights violations in the Occupied Territories and maintains statistics on settlements, casualties, destruction of property and separation barrier. www.btselem.org.

Dempsey, J. (2000) 'Four killed as Sharon visit sparks violence in Jerusalem'. *The Financial Times* (London), September 30. Reports the visit of Ariel Sharon to the Temple Mount that marks the onset of the al-Aqsa *intifada*.

Fernea, E. and Hocking, M. (eds) (1992) *The Struggle for Peace: Israelis and Palestinians*. Austin, Tex.: University of Texas Press.

Foundation for Middle East Peace. Non-profit organization based in Washington, DC, that seeks a 'just resolution' to the Middle East conflict. Collects current data on Israeli settlements: http://www.fmep.org/settlement_ifo/stats_data/golan_heights_settlements.html.

Geneva Accord: www.geneva-accord.org. A website devoted to increasing support for the unofficial Geneva Accord.

Hinchcliffe, P. (2007) *Conflicts in the Middle East since 1945*, 3rd edn. London: Routledge. Examines the conflicts from a broader perspective and their regional and global impact. Newly published and up-to-date.

Laqueur, W. and Rubin, B. (eds) (2001) *The Israel–Arab Reader: A Documentary History of the Middle East Conflict*.

6th edn. New York: Penguin Books. Collection of source documents on the Middle East, such as United Nations resolutions and agreements between states.

Moore, M. (2004) 'Israeli court orders changes in barrier'. *The Washington Post*, July 1. Reports decision by the Israeli Supreme Court to order rerouting of sections of the barrier because it violated Palestinians' rights.

Morris, B. (2001) *Righteous Victims: A History of the Zionist–Arab Conflict, 1881–2001*. New York: Vintage Books. Written by one of Israel's best-known revisionist historians, this book examines the relationship between Zionism and the creation of a Palestinian identity.

Palestinian Center for Policy and Survey Research (2003) 'Results of PSR refugees' polls in the West Bank/Gaza Strip, Jordan and Lebanon'. July 18: http://www.pcpsr.org/survey/polls/2003/refugeesjune03.html (accessed September 7, 2007). Results of a survey of Palestinian refugees and their attitudes toward various right-of-return options.

Shlaim, A. (1995) *War and Peace in the Middle East: A Concise History*. New York: Penguin. Offers a critical assessment of American foreign policy and its role in shaping the development of the region.

Shlaim, A. (2001) *The Iron Wall: Israel and the Arab World*. New York: W. W. Norton. Chronicles the evolution of Israel's policy toward the Arab world from 1948 to 1998.

Shulman, D. (2007) *Dark Hope: Working for Peace in Israel and Palestine*. Chicago, Ill.: University of Chicago Press. A moving account of an Israeli activist's efforts to alleviate Palestinian suffering under Israeli occupation.

Tessler, M. (1994) *A History of the Israeli–Palestinian Conflict*. Bloomington, Ind.: University of Indiana Press. An exhaustive and in-depth history of the conflict from its roots to the first *intifada* in 1988.

10

CIVIL SOCIETY, MEDIA AND DEMOCRATIC REFORM

The Middle East and North Africa region lags behind other regions in the development of civil society. In general, this means that the state dominates public life; there are few institutions beyond state control. Institutions that foster the development of a civil society – namely a public that is actively engaged and able to participate in governance – include media organizations, non-governmental organizations, and advocacy groups. In the Middle East and North Africa, such institutions are often absent, or their actions are tightly constrained by government. Civil society is considered a key prerequisite for the creation of participatory governance and democratic practices. There tends to be a strong association between the level of civil society development and issues such as respect for human rights, freedom of the press and democracy. In recent years, democratic reform in the Middle East has been a focus of attention, owing largely to a shift in US government policy to promote democracy region-wide.

MEASURING CIVIL SOCIETY

It is difficult to measure the level of civil society development in any country. There is no common, precise definition of civil society, though most agree that it is composed of voluntary social organizations.

A non-partisan, US-based non-governmental organization, Freedom House, publishes an annual report that measures freedom in every country in the world. Two aspects are assessed: political rights and civil liberties. A score is assigned for each characteristic, ranging from 1, indicating high presence of these characteristics, to 7, indicating their absence. The country's final 'freedom status' score is based on an average of the two characteristics. Countries are rated as 'Free' (score 1.0–2.5), 'Partly Free' (score 3.0–5.0) or 'Not Free' (5.5–7.0).

In the MENA, only one country, Israel, is rated as 'Free'. Founded largely by immigrants from Europe, Israel follows many of the traditions of Western democracy and civil society development, though it lags behind the United States and the United Kingdom (Table 10.1).

Seven countries are rated 'Partly Free': Bahrain, Jordan, Kuwait, Lebanon, Morocco, Turkey and Yemen. It is interesting to note that many of these countries – Bahrain, Jordan, Kuwait, and Morocco – are monarchies and yet they have a higher level of freedom than most countries that have a parliamentary or presidential system. And, indeed, Gulf countries, such as Bahrain and Kuwait, have taken important steps in recent years to increase participation in governance.

Table 10.1 MENA: Freedom in the World 2007

Country	Political rights	Civil liberties	Status
Algeria	6	5	Not Free
Bahrain	5	5	Partly Free
Egypt	6	5	Not Free
Iraq	6	5	Not Free
Jordan	5	4	Partly Free
Kuwait	4	5	Partly Free
Lebanon	5	4	Partly Free
Libya	7	7	Not Free
Morocco	5	4	Partly Free
Oman	6	5	Not Free
Qatar	6	5	Not Free
Saudi Arabia	7	6	Not Free
Sudan	7	7	Not Free
Syria	7	7	Not Free
Tunisia	6	5	Not Free
UAE	6	6	Not Free
West Bank/Gaza	N/A	N/A	N/A
Yemen	5	5	Partly Free
Iran	6	6	Not Free
Israel	1	2	Free
Turkey	3	3	Partly Free
United Kingdom	1	1	Free
United States	1	1	Free

Source: Freedom House, www.freedomhouse.org/template.cfm?page=372&year+2007 (accessed September 21, 2007).

Most countries in the region – twelve – are rated 'Not Free'. This includes Gulf monarchies that have little or no mechanism for popular participation, such as Saudi Arabia and Qatar, as well as regimes such as Libya, where Qaddafi has led since 1969. What may be surprising is the large number of countries with presidential systems, which often include an elected parliament, on the 'Not Free' list. In countries such as Egypt, Tunisia and Algeria, elections are held regularly, but the participation of political parties is tightly constrained. In Iran, too, a president is elected by the people, but true power is held by the country's religious leadership.

The controversial Arab Human Development Report (AHDR) also notes the stunted level of civil society in the region, and notes specifically the distinction between having institutions and laws to protect civil society in place. The AHDR cites a 'freedom deficit', which:

undermines human development and is one of the most painful manifestations of lagging political development. While de jure acceptance of democracy and human rights is enshrined in constitutions, legal codes and government pronouncements, de facto implementation is often neglected and, in some cases, deliberately disregarded.

(AHDR 2002: 2)

'Freedom' is clearly a multi-faceted concept. Many factors contribute to the overall level of freedom one experiences within a society.

HUMAN RIGHTS

The concept of human rights refers to those rights that are considered to be basic and fundamental to every human being. Included in these rights are the rights to life, freedom, fair legal processes and freedom of thought. Human rights can be guaranteed or protected by state governments through the passage and implementation of laws. Such laws may include those that preclude unreasonable search and seizure, prohibit torture, and allow the freedom of assembly and of demonstration. Many, if not most, governments in the Middle East and North Africa lag behind in guaranteeing their citizens' human rights. In some cases the state consistently violates their citizens' human rights.

The United Nations monitors and promotes human rights around the globe. In 1948 the UN General Assembly passed the Universal Declaration of Human Rights, a non-binding document that laid out a set of basic rights each individual should be guaranteed. Included are such rights as freedom of thought, of movement and of religion. Subsequent to this declaration, the UN has passed a number of conventions (again, non-binding) in which states voluntarily pledge to guarantee certain human rights. Among the most significant are the International Convention on Economic, Social and Cultural Rights, the International Convention on

Table 10.2 UN conventions ratified by MENA countries

	Convent. economic, social and cultural rights	Convent. civil and political rights	Convent. against torture	Convent. against forms discrimination against women	Convent. against racial discrimination
Algeria	1989	1989	1989	1996	1972
Bahrain	–	–	1998	2002	1990
Egypt	1982	1982	1987	1981	1969
Iraq	1976	1976	–	1986	1970
Jordan	1976	1976	1991	1992	1974
Kuwait	1996	1996	1996	1994	1969
Lebanon	1976	1976	2000	1997	1971
Libya	1976	1976	1989	1989	1969
Morocco	1979	1979	1993	1993	2003
Oman	–	–	–	–	2003
Qatar	–	–	2000	–	1976
Saudi Arabia	–	–	1997	2000	1997
Sudan	1986	1986	–	–	1977
Syria	1976	1976	2004	2003	1969
Tunisia	1976	1976	1988	1985	1969
UAE	–	–	–	–	1974
West Bank/Gaza	–	–	–	–	–
Yemen	1987	1987	1991	1984	1972
Iran*	1975	1975	–	1979	1968
Israel*	1991	1991	–	1991	1979
Turkey*	1997	2003	2006	1985	2002
United Kingdom*	1976	1976	2003	1986	1969
United States*	1970	1992	–	1980[1]	1994

Data with * indicate ratified date, from the Office of the High Commissioner for Human Rights, http://www.ohchr.org/english/countries/ratification/3.htm.

[1] Note that the US signed the convention but has not yet ratified it.

Source: United Nations Development Program, Arab Human Rights Index, www.arabhumanrights.org/en/ratification/index.asp?id=1 (accessed September 22, 2007).

Civil and Political Rights, the Convention against Torture, the Convention on the Elimination of All Forms of Discrimination against Women, and the International Convention on the Elimination of All Forms of Racial Discrimination. Table 10.2 gives the date the associated protocols came into force in MENA countries.

The International Convention on Economic, Social and Cultural Rights was adopted by the UN General Assembly in 1966. The convention provided for basic economic, political and social freedoms, including the right to self-determination. The convention included the right to fair wages, social security and a decent living. Free and compulsory primary education, and provision for higher education are included in the protocol. With the exception of the Gulf monarchies, all countries in the region have adopted this convention.

The International Convention on Civil and Political Rights was also adopted by the UN General Assembly in 1966. Its protocol includes restrictions on the use of the death penalty, bans on cruel and unusual punishment, on slavery, and on the use of arbitrary arrest and detention. The protocol guarantees access to due judicial process and equality before the courts. Freedom of thought and the right to peaceful association are also included.

Article 25 includes provisions that are key for the development of democratic societies, including:

(a) To take part in the conduct of public affairs, directly or through freely chosen representatives.
(b) To vote and to be elected at genuine periodic elections which shall be by universal and equal suffrage and shall be held by secret ballot, guaranteeing the free expression of the will of the electors.
(c) To have access, on general terms of equality, to public service in his country.

The Convention against Torture, passed by the UN General Assembly in 2002, defines torture broadly as severe mental and physical pain. Parties to the protocol pledge to prevent torture and to prosecute any acts of torture under criminal law. Victims of torture also have the right to seek redress and compensation for their suffering. The protocol also establishes a Committee against Torture to monitor the activities of signatory states.

Most of the countries in the region have ratified this protocol with the notable exceptions of Iran and Israel. Also note that the US has not ratified this protocol.

The Convention on the Elimination of All Forms of Discrimination against Women was passed by the General Assembly in 1979. It seeks to eliminate discrimination against women, which it defines as:

> any distinction, exclusion or restriction made on the basis of sex which has the effect or purpose of impairing or nullifying the recognition, enjoyment or exercise by women, irrespective of their marital status, on a basis of equality of men and women, of human rights and fundamental freedoms in the political, economic, social, cultural, civil or any other field.

Member states pledge to eliminate all forms of discrimination and create equality in their legal systems.

Finally, the Convention on the Elimination of All Forms of Racial Discrimination was passed by the General Assembly in 1965. It seeks to eliminate discrimination based on race, color, descent, or national or ethnic origin.

AN 'ISLAMIC DECLARATION OF HUMAN RIGHTS'

A number of countries in the Middle East, though ratifying various UN protocols, felt that the UN-sponsored Universal Declaration on Human Rights was based on a secular foundation and failed to address the cultural values of non-Western countries. When the UDHR was passed in 1948, most countries in the Middle East were not yet independent and provided no input into the document. Citing the need for Islamic countries to be in compliance with Islamic law, the fifty-seven members of the Organization of Islamic Conference adopted the Cairo Declaration on Human Rights in Islam.

The Cairo Declaration forbids any discrimination on the basis of race, religion, sex, status, language, political affiliation, or other characteristics. It covers many of the same issues incorporated in the UDHR such as freedom of expression, prohibition of arbitrary arrest and torture, and the right to work. However, all rights in the declaration are subject to Islamic law, *sharia*.

Of particular note are the provisions concerning women, who are granted 'equal human dignity'. The document provides for a variety of protections for women, including the right to marriage and to financial independence. But critics note that all rights granted to women must be in agreement with the *sharia* and women have 'certain duties to perform', though they are not defined.

DE FACTO HUMAN RIGHTS

It is important to distinguish between the formal adoption of human rights legislation in a country and the de facto, or actual, human rights practices. In the MENA there is often a large gap between human rights in law (*de jure*) and in practice. For example, Saudi Arabia is a signatory to the protocol banning discrimination against women, and yet women cannot drive and the government enforces covering in public. Human Rights Watch, Amnesty International and the US State Department all monitor human rights activity

Box 10.1

IRAN: DETAINING IRANIAN-AMERICANS

Iran's detention and persecution of visiting Iranian-American scholars and journalists has raised concerns within the US government and international human rights organizations. In 2007, Haleh Esfandiari and Parnaz Azima, who both hold dual US and Iranian citizenship, were detained on security-related charges.

Esfandiari is a professor and co-director of the Middle East program at the Woodrow Wilson International Center for Scholars. On December 30, 2006, while visiting her ailing 93-year-old mother, she was held up at knifepoint and her passports confiscated as she prepared to leave the country to return to the US.

She was imprisoned and interrogated for months in Tehran's notorious Evin prison. She was questioned extensively about her work at the center and charged with attempting to form a network of Iranians to carry out a 'soft revolution'. At the end of August 2007, she was released on bail, and allowed to return to the United States, though the charges against her have not been dropped.

Azima, a journalist with the US-sponsored Persian-language Radio Farda, was detained and charged with disseminating propaganda. Like Esfandiari, she

was in Iran to visit her mother. Currently she is also free on bail. Two other Iranian-Americans were imprisoned in Iran on charges related to national security: Kian Tajbakhsh, a consultant with the Soros Foundation Open Society Institute, and Ali Shakeri, a founding board member of the Center for Citizen Peacebuilding at the University of California, Irvine. They were released on bail hours before Iranian President Mahmoud Ahmadinejad addressed the UN General Assembly on September 25, 2007.

These incidents, and the death of a Canadian-Iranian photojournalist, Zahra Kazemi, at the hands of interrogators in 2003, have led to an international outcry. The detentions of Iranian-Americans are also part of ongoing diplomatic sparring between the United States and Iran.

'US academic held in Iran freed on bail'. *USA Today*, August 21, 2007: http://www.usatoday.com/news/world/2007-08-21-iran-detainee_N.htm (accessed September 29, 2007).

Wright, R. (2007) 'US faults detention by Iran of dual citizens'. *The Washington Post*, May 10.

in the region. Recent concerns raised in their reports include: the detention of Iranian-Americans in Iran, the closure of a prominent human rights organization in Egypt and prison terms for newspaper editors there, prison beatings in Jordan, the holding of political prisoners in various countries, and abuse of migrant workers. Actions by both armed Palestinian groups and Israeli security forces continue to violate human rights, and especially those of civilians.

MEASURES OF PRESS FREEDOM

Each year, Reporters sans frontières (Reporters Without Borders) examines press freedom violations for

168 countries around the world. A fifty-question survey is used to create a relative ranking for each country. Countries in the Middle East and North Africa consistently rank near the bottom of the index; only countries such as Cuba, China, Turkmenistan and North Korea display less press freedom. Within the region Saudi Arabia and Iran post the lowest scores. Ironically, some Gulf countries – Kuwait, Qatar, Oman and the UAE – post some of the highest rankings. Israel, at a ranking of 50, has the highest ranking, surpassing even that of the United States (53).

Violence in Lebanon, including politically associated bombings and the Israeli military attack in 2005, substantially eroded press freedoms; the country's rank

Box 10.2

SAUDI ARABIA: THE ABUSE OF MIGRANT WORKERS

Many of the Gulf countries, such as Saudi Arabia and the United Arab Emirates, are heavily dependent on expatriate labor to fill jobs. While some of the expatriates are Westerners who have highly specialized managerial and technical jobs, the vast majority are poor, uneducated workers from Asia and South Asia filling menial jobs such as construction workers or maids.

Often these migrant workers face abuse by their employers and have little power either to escape or to stop the abuse. Women are particularly vulnerable as they work in isolation inside private homes. Once workers arrive in the Gulf their passports are typically held by their employers until they complete their service contract. Workers can be deported without cause. Workers often have few avenues of recourse through their own embassies because remittances – money that these workers send back to their home country – are often a very important part of the national economy. Sometimes they are unable to reach their diplomatic representatives, and have been detained and tried without their embassy's knowledge.

The abuse of migrant workers, though well known throughout the region, are usually ignored until a high-profile incident brings it briefly into the public spotlight. The recent killing of two female Indonesian domestic workers in Saudi Arabia is one such incident.

In August 2007, the two Indonesian workers were beaten to death by their Saudi Arabian employers, who accused them of practicing 'black magic' on their teenage son. According to Human Rights Watch, abuse of Saudi Arabia's 2 million female workers, predominantly from Indonesia, Sri Lanka and the Philippines, is routine. The forms of abuse include underpayment, and physical, mental and sexual abuse. In some cases the domestic workers are impregnated by their employers; in others they have been locked up and deprived of food. If the women are able to bring an accusation against their employers, they often face accusations of theft, adultery or witchcraft. Most cases of abuse are thought to go unreported.

As of July 2007, the Indonesian embassy had 500 women in a shelter it operates for abused workers.

Human Rights Watch has urged the Saudi Arabian government to take action to end the climate in which employers can abuse migrants with impunity. An important step would include conducting fair investigations into suspected cases of abuse and quickly informing the worker's diplomatic representatives when a case is suspected. The passage of labor laws to protect domestic workers has also been urged.

Human Rights Watch (2007) 'Saudi Arabia: migrant domestics killed by employers', August 17: http://hrw.org/english/docs/2007/08/17/saudia16699_txt.htm).

dropped from 56 to 107 in five years. The Reporters sans frontieres 2006 report noted increasing freedom in Morocco, but concerns over press freedoms in Tunisia where secret police spied on and intimidated domestic and foreign journalists during the 2005 World Summit on the Information Society.

The organization Freedom House also found that the MENA had the lowest regional rates on their Press Freedom Index. Only one country, Israel, is rated as 'Free'; Turkey is the only country rated 'Partly Free'.

All other countries in the region are 'Not Free'. Throughout the region the press faces extensive legal restrictions, including laws against criticizing the country's leadership, especially in the Gulf monarchies. 'Emergency' laws and anti-terrorism legislation are also used to curtail freedoms. Their 2006 report noted specifically concerns in Libya, Tunisia, Syria, and Israel and the Occupied Territories. Like Reporters sans frontières, they noted the negative impact of increased violence in Lebanon on freedom of the press.

Table 10.3 Measures of press freedom in the Middle East and North Africa

Country	Reporters sans frontières rank (2006)	Freedom House score (2005)	Freedom House rank (2005)
Algeria	126	61	Not Free
Bahrain	111	72	Not Free
Egypt	133	61	Not Free
Iraq	154	71	Not Free
Jordan	109	61	Not Free
Kuwait	73	56	Not Free
Lebanon	107	60	Not Free
Libya	152	96	Not Free
Morocco	97	61	Not Free
Oman	N/A	70	Not Free
Qatar	80	61	Not Free
Saudi Arabia	161	79	Not Free
Sudan	139	??	
Syria	153	84	Not Free
Tunisia	148	83	Not Free
UAE	77	65	Not Free
West Bank/Gaza	134	86	Not Free
Yemen	149	81	Not Free
Iran	162	84	Not Free
Israel	50	28	Free
Turkey	98	48	Partly Free
United Kingdom	28	19	Free
United States	53	16	Free

Source: Reporters sans frontières, Press Freedom Index, 2006, http://www.rsf.org/rubrique.php3?id_rubrique=639 (accessed September 22, 2007).
Freedom House, Freedom of the Press 2006, http://www.rsf.org/rubrique.php3?id_rubrique=639 (accessed September 22, 2007.

To create the Freedom of the Press Index, the legal, political and economic environment affecting the media in each country is assessed. A total score between 0 and 30 indicates that a country's media are 'Free', between 31 and 60 is 'Partly Free', and 61 and greater indicates 'Not Free'.

JOURNALIST DEATHS IN IRAQ

The widespread deaths of journalists in Iraq is a new concern affecting press freedoms. The organization, the Committee to Protect Journalists, recorded thirty-four deaths in Iraq in 2006, the most ever recorded in a single country. Worldwide, the total number of journalists killed was fifty-five.

Of the thirty-four journalists killed in Iraq, thirty-two were Iraqi. This in part reflects the fact that fewer Western journalists are working in Iraq. Those who do are confined to the 'Green Zone' and rely on reports from Iraqi correspondents. Of the Iraqis killed, only four were killed in an 'act of war', such as getting caught in cross-fire or an explosion. The rest were murdered; in many cases they were threatened prior to their death. Three were kidnapped and then killed. Overall, since the US invasion in April 2003, ninety-two journalists have been killed, along with thirty-seven support personnel such as translators and administrative staff. Increasingly, the perception of journalists as non-combatants protected under the Geneva Convention has eroded.

NEW MEDIA – NEW OPPORTUNITIES

Despite the restrictions on media throughout the Middle East and North Africa, new forms of media are beginning to create greater access to information. With the explosive spread of satellite television and the Internet, people in the region now have access to media beyond state-controlled television, radio and newspapers.

For decades, governments in the Middle East controlled all access to various forms of the media. Nightly broadcasts on state-owned television consisted of little more than footage of the head of state greeting visiting foreign dignitaries. In some countries even fax machines were controlled by the government. In the last decade, satellite television, independent newspapers, the Internet and blogs have supplanted former 'official' sources of news.

The creation of al-Jazeera satellite television in 1997 marked a key moment in new media expansion. Based in Qatar, the channel offered an exciting new mix of debate-oriented talk shows and critical news coverage. Al-Jazeera's influence in the region quickly grew. Its coverage of the al-Aqsa *intifada* in 2000 offered a welcome alternative to the constrained and, some would

Box 10.3

AL-JAZEERA: OPENING THE MIDDLE EAST'S AIRWAVES

Until recently, media in the Middle East have been tightly controlled. Government-run newspapers continue to be routinely censored in many countries, and state-controlled televised news often consists of footage of the head of state greeting foreign dignitaries.

The spread of Internet access and satellite television in the 1990s created new forms of media in the region, which are able to circumvent government control. Though the repression of independent (i.e. non-state-controlled) media still continues in most Middle Eastern countries, new media outlets are changing the way the Middle East sees the world – and the way the world sees the Middle East.

In 1996 a new, Arabic-language satellite television station, al-Jazeera, was launched from its headquarters in Doha, Qatar. Funded by the emir of Qatar, al-Jazeera shook up the airwaves with its often controversial coverage that contained dissenting views rather than the official viewpoint of any one government. It was the first Arab channel to allow Israelis to appear on air, speaking in English or Hebrew, and extensively covers Israeli issues – a practice that has led to criticism from the Arab public and governments. It has also been critical of Arab governments, including that of its sponsor, Qatar.

Al-Jazeera became widely popular in the Middle East and spurred the development of other satellite channels such as al-Arabiya and the Middle East Broadcasting Center, both based in Dubai, and the Beirut-based Lebanese Broadcasting Center.

Al-Jazeera grew quickly and expanded its coverage to include a channel in English and channels focused on sport, live political broadcasts, children's programs and documentaries. Its Arabic news channel has an estimated 40–50 million viewers; its English new channel has approximately 100 million. The English channel maintains bureaux in Doha, London, Kuala Lumpur and Washington, DC, and maintains a web presence at http://english.aljazeera.net/.

Miles, Hugh (2006) 'Think again: al Jazeera'. *Foreign Policy*, July–August.

argue, pro-Israeli coverage by Western-based channels such as CNN.

Al-Jazeera was soon joined by other independent satellite channels, most notably the Dubai-based al-Aribiya. In addition, national independent television stations such as Lebanon-based MBC and Zein TV are now delivered across the region via various satellite packages. Even the militant group Hezbollah operates its own station.

The Internet and blogs have been another important media source in the region. Despite control over sites such as Hotmail and Google in some countries, governments have largely been unable to control unrestricted access to the Internet. Internet cafés have become ubiquitous throughout the region, providing affordable access to many. Hundreds of blogs exist, many of them written in English and designed to bring situations inside the Middle East to the attention of the rest of the world.

The impact on the flow of news in the region has been extraordinary. One measure of the influence of these new forms was the inability of the United States to control the flow of information out of Iraq during the 2003 invasion. This was a major contrast with the 1991 Gulf War when the US had total control over all coverage. New media technologies and controversial issues such as Iraq have helped to create a 'new Arab public'. According to Lynch (2006: 2–3):

> The new public rejects the long, dismal traditions of enforced public consensus, insisting on the legitimacy of challenging official policies and proclamations. This has created an expectation of public disagreement, an expectation vital to any

meaningfully pluralistic politics. The new public has forced Arab leaders to justify their positions far more than ever before, introducing a generally new level of accountability to Arab politics.

Much of the new media, and al-Jazeera, has been met with suspicion and hostility by the Bush administration. Critics argue that it is a mouthpiece for terrorists and anti-American sentiment; and, indeed, Osama Bin Laden would often release his 'messages to the world' by sending a tape to al-Jazeera. Others, including many academics, point out that the new media offer crucial insights into Middle Eastern society not offered by other venues. Stations like al-Jazeera also provide viewers in the Middle East with insights into the West. Al-Jazeera, for example, provided coverage of the Republican and Democratic national conventions in 2004.

To counter the influence of the new Arab media in the region, the United States created its own television station to broadcast directly to the Arab world. Al-Hurra (meaning 'the Free One') is funded by the US Congress and broadcasts from Virginia. Its first year of operation, in 2004, was estimated to cost $62 million. The station, which is commercial-free, broadcasts news summaries and programs such as 'The Body Human' and 'Big Boutique in the City' in an attempt to draw viewers away from al-Jazeera and al-Aribiya. However, the station has failed to attract a substantial number of viewers. Respected Middle East expert William Rugh noted in testimony before the US Senate in 2004 that al-Hurra failed to attract viewers because 'it was perceived as a US government-run, not just government-funded, station; its coverage of US domestic news was not in depth, and its coverage of news in the Middle East, including in US-occupied Iraq, lagged behind that of other channels'.

Radio Sawa, the administration's other attempt to reach the Middle Eastern masses, has fared slightly better. Its programming, featuring a mixture of Arab and Western pop music, is popular, especially among young people. It seems to be the radio station of choice among taxi drivers throughout the region. However, its news summaries are perceived as controlled by the US government; and listeners often change the dial when they come on.

DEMOCRATIC REFORM IN THE REGION

The Bush administration's public diplomacy effort, which produced al-Hurra and Radio Sawa, was but one part of a much larger US policy to encourage democratic reform in the Middle East. In the aftermath of the 9/11 attacks, creating democracy in the region was expected to undermine the influence of radical and militant Islamists, and was part of an overall pre-emptive attack on terror.

This approach marked a major shift in US policy toward the region, which had previously placed emphasis on the stability of governments in the region, regardless of their level of democratization and civil society development. In fact, many of the key US allies, such as Egypt and Saudi Arabia, have limited civil society participation in governance. The other main components of US policy included securing a steady supply of oil and ensuring Israeli military predominance by providing military and economic aid.

In September 2002 the US adopted a new National Security Strategy, which called for 'supporting moderate and modern government, especially in the Muslim world, to ensure that the conditions and ideologies that promote terrorism do not find fertile ground in any nation' (National Security Council 2002). But by June 2004 reform in the Middle East had become a central policy focus; the US launched a number of programs such as the Middle East Partnership Initiative (MEPI) and the Greater Middle East Initiative. These programs sought to 'close the freedom gap to strengthen civil society, expand political participation, and lift the voices of women' (US Department of State 2002). This included attempts to strengthen political parties, strengthen independent media and reform the judiciary. In reality, these projects were often very limited, and very little funding was awarded.

A further barrier to US-led political reform was the chilly reception it received from governments in the region. They saw the reforms as a US attempt to mobilize their populations directly, without going through existing governmental structures. And, indeed, the US launched the policy following little consultation with the region's governments, including close allies. Governments and people in the region also viewed the policy as one that the US applied unequally, allowing undemocratic allies to continue their policies while forcing reform on countries that the US saw as problematic.

But the biggest blow to the US attempts to bring democracy to the region was dealt by Iraq. In support of the invasion, the administration argued that the removal of Saddam Hussein would quickly result in a democratic Iraq, which would 'unleash a democratic tsunami across the Islamic world' (Ottoway 2002). As it became increasingly clear that mere stability, much less democracy, was hard to achieve in Iraq, support for democratic reform plummeted amid rising criticism of the US within the region. In recent years the administration has quietly abandoned its ambitious reform program.

THE HAMAS ELECTORAL VICTORY

The recent electoral victory of the Islamist militant group Hamas in Palestinian parliamentary elections illustrates the reality of democratization in the Middle East and North Africa; it is likely to result in increasing political participation by Islamist political parties (the majority of which, unlike Hamas, are non-violent).

In 2006 the Palestinian legislature, known as the Palestinian Legislative Council, held its first elections since 1996 (elections had been delayed during rising violence and the al-Aqsa *intifada*). The primary political parties were Fatah, the long-time secular party of

---

Box 10.4

ENOUGH! EGYPT'S KIFAYA MOVEMENT

Kifaya is an Arabic word meaning 'enough'. It is also the name a grassroots coalition of political activists adopted for their organization, the Egyptian Movement for Change. Their message to the Egyptian people was one of 'enough of the current political system'.

The Kifaya movement, more formally known as the Egyptian Movement for Change, galvanized the Egyptian political scene after its formation in 2004. The movement had its roots in the anti-US Iraq war protests that erupted in Egypt in advance of the US invasion. Much anger was directed against the Egyptian government, considered by protesters to be an uncritical ally of the US.

The Kifaya movement contains a diversity political groups – leftists, Islamists, nationalists – brought together by their mutual opposition to Egypt's long-serving president, Hosni Mubarak. Of particular concern to the movement is the potential for Mubarak, who has no vice-president, to ensure that his son Gamal is Egypt's next president. Kifaya applied pressure for multi-party presidential elections. Mubarak has run unopposed in five presidential referendums since 1981 when he became president following his predecessor's

assassination. The Kifaya movement also seeks to get rid of the emergency laws, in effect since 1981, that limit civil liberties and restrict political participation.

The call for multi-candidate elections was bolstered by pressure from the Bush administration, which sought to bring political reform to the region in the aftermath of 9/11. An unusual show of political activism including rallies and protests further heightened the call for political reform. Many of the participants in the protests were students, who had grown up in an atmosphere in which demonstrations and protests were not allowed under the emergency laws. The last significant protests in Egypt were in the 1970s and were focused on Israel. According to human rights organizations, protesters were attacked by plainclothes policeman while riot police watched.

In May 2005, the Egyptian public approved a constitutional referendum to allow multi-candidate presidential elections. The amendment to the constitution, however, contained multiple measures to ensure that few, if any, political parties would be able to field candidates in the election. Protests mounted in the aftermath of its passage.

Box 10.4

ENOUGH! EGYPT'S KIFAYA MOVEMENT—CONT'D

Against this backdrop, the Egyptian government imprisoned Ayman Nour in January 2005. Nour was founder of the Al Ghad (Tomorrow) Party and the most promising challenger to Mubarak in an election. Nour had played a pivotal role in the formation of Kifaya and its operations. Nour was arrested on a charge that he forged signatures in order to form Al Ghad. The move caused US Secretary of State Rice to postpone her visit to Egypt in protest. Nour was released in March 2005, following much US pressure.

In September 2005, Egypt held its first-ever multi-party elections for president. Mubarak easily won re-election to another six-year term with 88.6 percent of the vote. Of the ten other candidates for president, Ayman Nour won the highest percentage of the vote: 7 percent. Two months later he was sentenced to five years in prison – a move criticized by the United States.

Since the 2005 election the Kifaya movement has struggled to maintain its momentum. The movement suffers from a number of problems including lack of internal cohesion. The members of the movement are held together by their mutual dislike of Mubarak, but offer no alternative platform or solutions after his potential removal. Given the diversity of the membership, agreement on solutions to Egypt's economic and social problems could be elusive. The movement has also been criticized for not really being grassroots but, rather, anchored in the culture of Cairo elites and therefore having limited appeal to the broad spectrum of Egyptian society.

Fattah, H. (2005) 'Egypt puts off reformer's trial, letting him run against Mubarak'. *New York Times*, July 7.

Slackman, M. (2005) 'Anti-Mubarak protesters clash with police in Cairo'. *New York Times*, July 31.

Yasser Arafat and the traditional PLO leadership, and Hamas, also known as the Islamic Resistance Movement. The current president of the Palestinian Authority, Mahmoud Abbas, is a member of Fatah. With 132 parliamentary seats at stake, Hamas won by a clear majority, claiming seventy-six seats to Fatah's forty-three. The victory gave Hamas the right to form a new cabinet under Abbas and appoint a prime minister.

The election results were an enormous shock to Fatah, the United States and Israel. The results have seriously complicated efforts to resolve the Israeli–Palestinian conflict and have plunged the Palestinian government into crisis. Hamas does not recognize the two-state solution to the conflict and, until 2006, officially included calls for the destruction of Israel in its manifesto. Shortly after the election, both the US and the EU suspended all aid to the Palestinian Authority. Hamas has long launched attacks on Israel, and in the months after

the election captured an Israeli soldier, adding further strain to relations with Israel.

In the aftermath of the election, armed conflict broke out between Hamas and Fatah and their supporters, causing fears of a Palestinian civil war. In January 2007, Hamas and Fatah signed a ceasefire and formed a unity government. The unity government was short-lived, and Hamas continued to attack Israel in retaliation for its attacks on Gaza. In June 2007, Palestinian president Abbas declared a state of emergency and dissolved the Hamas-dominated government – a further blow for democratic reform in the region.

ISLAMIST PARTIES IN THE MIDDLE EAST AND NORTH AFRICA

Yet, despite the experience with Hamas, which presents a unique case given the backdrop of the Israeli–Palestinian crisis, Islamist parties, especially moderate ones, often have significant potential to increase civil society participation in governance in the Middle East and North Africa. The Islamist parties tend to be highly organized with a strongly committed membership. In addition to having broad social networks, the Islamic duty of *zakat*, or giving of alms, ensures that they are well funded. In some cases, such as the Egyptian Muslim Brotherhood, the Islamist parties support numerous female candidates.

In a number of countries, such as Jordan, Islamic parties play an important role as opposition parties, offering alternative solutions and opinions to those of the parties that have traditionally backed the government. Throughout the region, however, Islamist parties are often banned from participating in local or national elections, in some cases membership in these organizations is considered illegal and their members imprisoned. For example, the Egyptian Muslim Brotherhood is not a formally approved political party; it runs its candidates as independents.

A notable exception is the Gulf where, in these heavily traditional societies, Islamist parties dominate.

Box 10.5

DEMOCRATIZATION IN THE GULF: ISLAMISTS WIN, WOMEN LOSE

In recent years much of the democratic reform in the region has taken place within the Gulf monarchies, which have typically provided little or no formal mechanism for public participation in governance. In most cases, women have historically been excluded from political processes. The limited expansion of political participation in the Gulf has resulted in increasing strength for Islamist parties, who now form the main opposition parties, and few gains by women.

In tiny Bahrain's 2006 parliamentary elections, Islamist candidates won most of the seats for the 40-member legislative body. In Bahrain, Islamist parties of various types dominate the political landscape, though a small number of liberal/nationalist groups exist. Shias make up two-thirds of the country's population; Shiite candidates won seventeen seats, considerably more than the pro-government Sunni Islamist bloc that support the kingdom's traditional Sunni leadership. Some analysts were concerned that the election results reflected growing sectarianism in the Gulf, with people increasingly identifying themselves as 'Shia' or 'Sunni', rather than as Islamist or Bahraini.

Though eighteen women ran for office in the Bahraini elections, only one woman won a seat. She ran as a pro-government independent candidate, in an unopposed race.

Women won the right to vote in Kuwait in May 2005, and exercised this right for the first time in Kuwait's 2006 parliamentary elections. Of the 249 candidates, twenty-eight were women. None won a seat, though 57 percent of Kuwait's eligible voters are women. This reflects a current reality in Middle Eastern politics: the reluctance of women to vote for women. Though no candidate won a seat, a woman was appointed to the Kuwaiti cabinet as minister of planning and administrative development, the first-ever female member. Her appointment was challenged by Islamic conservatives and representatives of traditional tribal society who oppose women's participation in politics. This reflects another interesting reality of Middle East politics: in some cases the ruling families in Gulf monarchies are more liberal than much of their population and traditional political supporters. As in the Bahraini elections, Islamist candidates, and their allies, were able to establish majority control over the legislature, and prominent liberals lost their seats. The election results will likely mean more conflict between the parliament and the often

---

Box 10.5

DEMOCRATIZATION IN THE GULF: ISLAMISTS WIN, WOMEN LOSE—CONT'D

more progressive government led by the al-Sabah family.

In 2005, Saudi Arabia held its first-ever elections for seats on municipal councils. Though there were over 1800 candidates for the 592 seats, none was a woman, and women were not allowed to vote. The elections, which took place in stages during a period marked by al-Qaeda-related violence in the kingdom, were dominated by conservatives – though this is a misleading term, as a 'liberal' strand of politics does not exist inside Saudi Arabia.

Gause, G. (2007) 'Bahrain parliamentary election results: 25 November and 2 December 2006'. *International Journal of Middle East Studies*, 39: 170–1.

Kifner, J. (2003) 'Islamic traditionalists sweep liberals in Kuwaiti elections'. *New York Times*, July 7.

SUMMARY OF MAIN POINTS

- The MENA region consistently ranks very low in measures of civil society development and 'freedom'.
- Though signatory to many UN conventions on human rights, implementation of human rights legislation is uneven throughout the region.
- Media, including print and television, are often tightly controlled.
- In the last decade, new forms of media, such as satellite television and the Internet, have created greater access to information.
- The post-9/11 US-led political reform program failed to achieve significant change in the region.
- Democratization in the region is likely to lead to greater influence of Islamist parties and, in some cases, a continued lack of representation by women.

QUESTIONS FOR DISCUSSION

1 What historical and political factors limit civil society development in the Middle East and North Africa?
2 Are some countries more likely to expand civil society participation than others? Which ones? Why?
3 Is the concept of human rights a universal concept? Or is it culturally determined? Is the 'Islamic' concept of human rights the same as the Western one?
4 How are the new media reshaping the Arab public?
5 What were the barriers to the US-led political reform program?
6 What role are Islamist parties likely to play in democratization of the region? What is the potential impact of participation by Islamist parties?

SUGGESTIONS FOR FURTHER READING

Abootalebi, A. (1998) 'Civil society, democracy and the Middle East'. *Middle East Review of International Affairs*, 2: 46–59. Discusses barriers to civil society development and democratization in the Middle East.

Diamond, L., Plattner, M. and Brumberg, D. (2003) *Islam and Democracy in the Middle East*. Baltimore, Md: Johns Hopkins University Press. Collected essays on civil society and democratization based on experiences of numerous countries in the region.

Lynch, M. (2006) *Voices of the New Arab Public: Iraq, Al-Jazeera, and Middle East Politics Today*.

New York: Columbia University Press. Ground-breaking study of how new media, such as al-Jazeera, has awakened debate and dissent in the Arab world.

Miles, H. (2005) *Al Jazeera: The Inside Story of the Arab News Channel That Is Challenging the West*. New York: Grove Press. Examination of the innovative Arab satellite station and its contested relationship with the West, and the United States, in particular.

National Security Council (2002) *The National Security Strategy of the United States of America*, September 17. Articulates the security priorities of the US in the post-9/11 era.

Norton, A. (ed.) (2005) *Civil Society in the Middle East*. Leiden: E. J. Brill. In-depth analysis of civil society in many countries in the region, including Algeria, Iran, Israel, Turkey, Yemen and the Sudan.

Ottaway, M. T., Hawthorne, C. and Brumberg, D. (2002) *Democratic Mirage in the Middle East*. Carnegie Endowment Policy Brief No. 20. Washington, DC: Carnegie Endowment for International Peace. Provides a very critical assessment of the administration's plans for democratic reform in the region.

Rugh, W. (2004) Comments on Radio Sawa and al-Hurra Television. Testimony before the US Senate: http://www.senate.gov/~foreign/testimony/2004/Rugh Testimony040429.pdf. Exposes the limitations of US public diplomacy efforts in the Middle East.

United States Department of State (2002) 'The US–Middle East partnership initiative: building hope for the years ahead', Secretary Colin L. Powell, December 12. Articulates the Bush administration's ambitious plans for democratic reform in the Middle East and North Africa.

Wilson, S. (2006) 'Hamas sweeps Palestinian elections, complicating peace efforts in Mideast'. *The Washington Post*, January 27, p. A1.

The following organizations have websites with extensive information on civil society and human rights in the Middle East and North Africa:

Amnesty International, www.amnesty.org

Committee to Protect Journalists, www.cpj.org

Freedom House, www.freedomhouse.org

Human Rights Watch, www.hrw.org

Reporters sans frontières, www.rsf.org

PART IV

THE FUTURE OF THE REGION

11

THE COMING CHALLENGES: KEY ISSUES TO WATCH

The coming decade is likely to be one of significant volatility and change in the Middle East and North Africa. Both internal factors, such as growing societal debate over the role of Islam and increasing tension between nascent civil society and existing regimes, and external factors, including continued integration into the global economy and the presence of foreign military forces, will contribute to this volatility. This chapter examines the underlying reasons for this instability, and the issues that are likely to dominate inter-state and international relations in the near future.

INSTABILITY IN THE REGION

Despite the popular perception that the Middle East region is constantly embroiled in conflict and is highly volatile, the region has actually been quite stable in the past few decades. Its post-World War II system of independent states is largely unchanged and the last major regional war took place in 1973. Even the Iraqi invasion of Kuwait in 1991 was a short-lived event that had little long-term impact on the region's political

system, though it did help launch the peace process that led to the Israeli–Jordanian peace treaty.

Unlike Latin America, whose post-independence politics have often been characterized by coups, the countries of the Middle East and North Africa have had relatively little change in leadership. Though this has undoubtedly stifled the growth of civil society, it has provided the region with considerable political stability. Many of the leaders who led their countries through independence have ruled for many years. By the time they died, Hafez al-Asad had ruled Syria for 39 years, King Hussein had ruled Jordan for forty-six years, Sheikh Zayed of the UAE for thirty-three, and King Hassan II of Morocco for thirty-eight years. Qaddafi has ruled Libya since 1969 and Mubarak has been Egypt's president for over twenty-six years. Though the sons of many of these leaders have recently come to power, this generation change has resulted in little real alteration of political life. The younger generation have largely continued to implement the policies of their fathers, especially in foreign affairs.

Even the rise of Islamic militancy, which produced armed conflict in the region, especially during the 1990s, had largely been suppressed by the start of the new millennium. In Egypt, the Jamaat al-Islamiyya, which had fought Egyptian security forces in an attempt to overthrow the Mubarak government, renounced violence in 1999 and agreed to a ceasefire. In Algeria, combat between government forces and the Armed Islamic Group (GIA), which sought to create an Islamic state in Algeria, broke out after the government's cancellation of the 1992 elections. Fighting raged for years, causing high casualties among civilians, including 100 expatriates. A 1991 amnesty law, though rejected by the GIA, led most militants to lay down their arms and relative stability is now in place.

Of course the Middle East region has faced destabilizing influences in the past decades, including economic transformation and the continuing Israeli–Arab conflicts. The current period, however, is one of greatly increased instability where the outcomes and potential impacts are difficult to predict.

IRAQ: DESTABILIZING THE REGION

Iraq, of course, is the main reason for the destabilization of the region. The overthrow of Saddam Hussein, the inability to put a stable, functioning government in place, and the continued presence of large numbers of Western (primarily US troops) in the region, have created a number of new dynamics in the region.

The territorial question

The US occupation of Iraq has reopened the territorial question. Not since the San Remo Conference in 1920 has there been such a high potential for the redefinition of state borders in the region. At San Remo, the British Mandate of Mesopotamia was created. This League of Nations mandate combined the Ottoman regions of Baghdad, Basra and Mosul (in 1925) together into a single entity. In doing so, the British created a new territorial entity that eventually, after a failed British-installed monarchy and attacks on occupying British troops, became Ba'athist Iraq.

Iraq's population is predominantly Arab (80 per cent), with a significant Kurdish minority (15 per cent) located primarily in the north, in the former Mosul region. Shia Muslims are the largest religious group, comprising 60 to 65 per cent of the population and located primarily in southern Iraq, around Basra. The Sunni (32 to 37 per cent of the population), located around Baghdad, held power in Iraq until the overthrow of Saddam Hussein. Under Hussein's regime, strong, and often oppressive, force by the central government was used to control Iraq's Shia majority and Kurdish minority. In the absence of a strong central government, each of these groups is seeking the greatest amount of territory and power.

One possible option for solving the internal violence in Iraq is to break Iraq up into three separate sect-based territories. Each group, the Shia, the Sunnis and the Kurds, would have their own territory. As the violence in Iraq continues, this option has gained some popularity, in part because it seems like an easy solution, to let each group live amongst their own kind. Unfortunately, implementation of this option would prove quite difficult. Iraq's major cities are still mixed, with Sunnis and Shias, especially living in the same areas. While there has been a tendency toward more neighborhood homogeneity in recent years, encouraged by attacks on each other, actually dividing the cities could lead to larger-scale ethnic cleansing.

The creation of three federal 'states' inside Iraq could potentially open up the territorial issues more broadly and destabilize neighboring countries. If a 'Kurdistan' were created in northern Iraq, Kurds in neighboring Turkey, where they make up 7 per cent of the population (approximately 10 million), could increase their demands for greater autonomy or inclusion of areas of Turkey with large Kurdish populations in the new Kurdistan. Over the past twenty years Kurds in Turkey have led a violent separatist movement against the Turkish government. An independent Kurdistan could function as a new base for an escalated separatist movement.

The creation of a new Shia-led state in southern Iraq is also a matter for concern. Such a state could be expected to have a close relationship with the only other Shia-dominated state in the region, Iran. Indeed, the

Box 11.1

WHY DID THE US INVADE IRAQ?

Why did the United States invade Iraq and remove Saddam Hussein from power? While the truth may not be known for some decades when presidential archives from the time are declassified, there seem to be multiple motivations for the US invasion of Iraq.

At the time, the Bush administration argued that the invasion was necessary to stop Hussein's weapons of mass destruction program. Indeed, the administration argued that he posed an imminent threat to world peace that could not be met with sanctions or other diplomatic options. It was this argument that convinced the Republican-dominated US Congress to authorize the war on October 16, 2002. War could only be averted, according to President Bush, if Iraq declared and destroyed all its weapons of mass destruction.

The Iraqis replied that they did not have such weapons. Indeed, a 1,500-member Iraq Survey Group, formed by the Bush administration and headed by former UN weapons inspector David Kay, to search for weapons of mass destruction in Iraq in May 2003, issued the following conclusion: 'In the aftermath of Operation Iraqi Freedom, coalition forces failed to uncover production facilities for, or stocks of, weapons of mass destruction.'

It now appears the Bush administration used faulty intelligence to pressure the congress and allies, such as Great Britain, to support the war. Attempts to use intelligence findings to gain support for a war in the United Nations, however, failed.

Similarly, accusations that Iraq was a haven for al-Qaeda terrorists have also proven to be false.

Why did the administration want a war with Iraq? One argument is that the administration believed regime change could be achieved easily, US troops would be greeted as liberators, and a pro-US government would be installed. This would immediately benefit the US, and its major ally in the region, Israel. A pro-American Iraq would allow the US to lessen its dependence on its traditional ally, Saudi Arabia. Perhaps even more importantly, US oil companies could profit from access to Iraq's rich oil fields; Iraq is thought to contain the world's second largest oil reserves, 11 per cent of the global total.

Regime change in Iraq was expected to create a wave of democratization throughout the Middle East. A wave which would presumably benefit the US as pro-American governments took control. However, the failure in Iraq and the US war on terror has undermined democratization in the region.

The decisions of the administration, sadly, were driven by ideology, with little reference to the realities on the ground in the region. They relied on faulty advice from others, such as expatriate Iraqis and some Israeli politicians, who sought regime change in Iraq to serve their own agendas. The US has paid a great price for the miscalculations on Iraq; as of October 2008, 4,115 US soldiers were reported dead and a further 30,182 wounded. And now it is the US, regardless of which party takes control of the presidency following the 2008 elections, which must find a way to solve the Iraq problem.

Danner, M. (2005) 'The secret way to war', *New York Review of Books*. June, 9.

Pillar, P. (2006) 'Intelligence, policy and the war in Iraq'. *Foreign Affairs*, March–April.

Iraqi cities of Najaf and Karbala eclipse those of Iranian cities, such as Qom, for their religious significance in the Shia community. Both are the site of frequent pilgrimages by Shias from around the region. Many of the states surrounding southern Iraq, such as Saudi Arabia and Bahrain, have large Shia populations. Saudi Arabia's Shia-population is centered around the oil-rich Eastern province. Some fear that the presence of a new Shia state could embolden these Shia populations, who have a strong historical sense of their shared persecution at the hands of Sunnis, to seek additional autonomy themselves.

A 'third way' has also been proposed, to keep a unitary Iraq, but to allow each group significant autonomy. Proposed by president emeritus of the Council of Foreign Relations, Leslie Gelb, and US Senator Joseph Biden (Democrat), the five-part plan calls for:

> The first is to establish three largely autonomous regions with a viable central government in Baghdad. The Kurdish, Sunni and Shiite regions would each be responsible for their own domestic laws, administration and internal security. The central government would control border defense, foreign affairs and oil revenues. Baghdad would become a federal zone, while densely populated areas of mixed populations would receive both multisectarian and international police protection.
>
> (Biden and Gelb 2006)

Sunni support for the plan would be based on providing them with a financial incentive to offset the fact that they, unlike the Kurds and Shia, lack significant oil resources.

Empowering al-Qaeda and insurgents

The lack of internal security in Iraq has created a new base for militant activity, and especially for al-Qaeda and al-Qaeda-inspired groups. Despite claims of cooperation between Saddam Hussein and al-Qaeda, there is no evidence to support the idea that Iraq was a harbor for terrorists. Al-Qaeda had no operational presence in Iraq prior to the US. Though Hussein used Islamic rhetoric to justify and garner support for his rule, even adding the words 'God is great' in Arabic to the Iraqi flag, he was a secular ruler who allowed no threats to his rule. In the absence of the Saddam-era security apparatuses that tightly controlled the country, and lack of effective control of Iraq's borders following the US invasion, 'foreign' fighters were able to enter Iraq. Iraq is now the new base for al-Qaeda, which sought a new base of operations following the US military campaign in Afghanistan. Moreover, the 'occupation' of Iraq by foreign, non-Muslim soldiers has been a rallying cry drawing new adherents to al-Qaeda, from both within Iraq and surrounding countries. Since 2003, al-Qaeda-affiliated groups have emerged throughout the region and carried out attacks, primarily in countries allied with the US, including the bombing of a wedding reception at a hotel in Amman, Jordan, and the Egyptian tourist resort of Sharm el Sheikh in 2005.

In reality, 'foreign' forces such as al-Qaeda are responsible for only a small portion of the violence in Iraq; most of the violence is a result of Iraq's descent into sectarian conflict, especially between the Sunni and Shia. Attempts to end the violence through political process have largely failed and US troops have at best been able to contain the level of violence for short periods. Many Iraqis fear that if the US withdraws completely the country will experience heightened levels of violence and ethnic cleansing will take place.

Strengthening Iranian influence

The failure of the US to create a stable post-Saddam Iraq has increased Iran's influence in the region and raised concerns of increasing geo-political power of the region's Shia population overall. Sunni-led countries, such as Jordan and Saudi Arabia, now speak of a 'Shia crescent' running from Iraq, through the Gulf states, to Iran. Iran is exercising considerable influence in Iraq and has deep connections to prominent Shias there. Perhaps the most well known is Muqtada al-Sadr, the son of a major Shia religious figure, who has strongly opposed the US occupation and attempted to form a government. His Mahdi Army, estimated to have over 10,000 fighters, is funded by Iran, and his popularity among Iraq's Shias is in part due to his links to Iran.

The situation in Iraq will continue to dominate the region's politics in coming years and create enormous instability within Iraq as well as surrounding countries. The continuing crisis in Iraq has also undermined the perception of the US in the region. At the end of the 1991 Gulf War, the US had established itself as the supreme military power in the region. The war proved that US policy was backed by credible military force. The occupation of Iraq has revealed limitations on US military strength, particularly against non-state actors, and emboldened them.

OTHER ISSUES TO WATCH

A number of other issues are likely to cause continued conflict among actors in the region and with the international community.

Israeli-Hezbollah confrontation

In July 2006 military conflict erupted between the state of Israel and the militant group, Hezbollah, based in southern Lebanon. The conflict, which lasted thirty-four days, was triggered by Hezbollah rocket attacks on civilians in Israeli border towns, the death of three Israeli soldiers and the capture of two others in a Hezbollah raid. An Israeli attempt to rescue the kidnapped soldiers resulted in the deaths of five others.

In response, Israel launched a massive, and many would argue disproportionate, attack on Lebanon as a whole. The Israeli airforce flew over 12,000 combat missions, severely damaging Lebanon's infrastructure, including its airport and roads. The attacks destroyed power plants, plunging Beirut and much of Lebanon into darkness. Schools, homes and sewage treatment plants were also hit. Israel imposed a naval blockade on Lebanon's ports, to prevent Hezbollah from receiving more missiles from Iran, but which also prevented the civilian population from being able to flee, and sent ground forces into southern Lebanon. Throughout the attack, Hezbollah was able to continue its missile attacks on Israel. The conflict resulted in forty-three Israeli casualties, and the temporary displacement of 250,000 Israelis from the vulnerable border town. Lebanese

---

Box 11.2

TRYING TO BUILD A GOVERNMENT IN IRAQ

After the overthrow of Saddam Hussein and his regime, the United States and its coalition partners established the Coalition Provision Authority to rule Iraq. The CPA assumed responsibility for all governmental functions. Its head, L. Paul Bremer, exercised substantial authority over Iraq's internal and external affairs. He disbanded the Iraqi army and instituted a policy of de-Ba'athification of Iraqi society, banning senior Ba'ath party members from participation in the new Iraq. The CPA was a division of the Department of Defense. In July 2003 the CPA appointed the Iraqi Governing Council, an advisory council composed largely of expatriate Iraqis who had lived outside if Iraq during Hussein's rule and dissidents. The CPA existed from April 21, 2003 until June 28, 2004 when authority for governing Iraq was turned over to the Iraqi Interim Government. US and coalition troops remained in Iraq, however, and were not under Iraqi control.

The Iraqi Interim Government was appointed by the United States and the coalition members, and under the Interim Government sovereignty was officially transferred from the CPA to Iraqis. The Interim Government included a prime minister (Iyad Allawi, considered a moderate Shia with close ties to the US) and a ceremonial president (Sunni). The Interim Government also included two vice-presidents, one Shia and one Kurdish. Members were appointed to fill cabinet positions, such as minister of oil and minister of education. The primary activity of the Iraqi Interim Government was to prepare Iraq to elect a permanent government.

Legislative elections were held in Iraq in January 2005, and the Iraqi Transitional Government took office on May 3, 2005. Shia-led groups dominated the elections, followed by Kurdish parties. Sunni Arabs largely boycotted the elections. The governmental structure put in place was similar to that under the Iraqi Interim Government. The prime minister (Shia) held most authority, alongside a ceremonial president (Kurdish). The deputy prime ministers included a Shia, a Kurd and a Sunni. A transitional National Assembly was elected. On May 20, 2006 the Iraqi Transitional Government was replaced by the first permanent government of Iraq.

Box 11.2

TRYING TO BUILD A GOVERNMENT IN IRAQ—CONT'D

To prepare for the first permanent government, the transitional National Assembly drafted a new constitution for Iraq, which was approved by the population by referendum in October 2005. A general election, to elect the new government and a permanent National Assembly, was held in December 2005.

The current government of Iraq includes a prime minister, Nouri al-Maliki (Shia) and president, Jalal Talabani (Kurd). The two vice-presidents are Tariq al-Hashimi (Sunni) and Adel Abdul Mehdi (Shia). The largest winner in the legislative elections was the United Iraqi Alliance, a Shia coalition that included the Islamic Dawa Party and the Supreme Council for the Islamic Revolution in Iraq (SCIRI), which claimed 128 seats. The Democratic Patriotic Alliance of Kurdistan won fifty-three seats. The Sunni-dominated Iraqi Accord Front won forty-four seats.

The current Iraqi government faces difficulties due to political disputes among the Sunni, Shia and Kurds and the lack of security and continued violence in the country. Despite the existence of a government, the US and coalition forces still exercise much authority in Iraq.

---

statistics record about 1,000 deaths of Lebanese civilians, and the displacement of 974,184 whose homes had been destroyed. Hezbollah claimed it lost only 250 fighters, though Israel claims to have killed 600. A United Nations sponsored ceasefire ended the hostilities and led to the withdrawal of Israeli troops from Lebanon. Though the resolution called for the disarming of Hezbollah, neither the Lebanese government nor the United Nations has been able to do this, a further indication of Hezbollah's influence inside the country.

This conflict is distinctive in that it was not a war with the government of Lebanon or its troops, but against the Islamist party, that is both a political and military force, centered in southern Lebanon. Hezbollah has been a potent force in Lebanese politics since the Lebanese civil war (for more details see Box 7.4). In recent decades Hezbollah has gained power in Lebanese politics. Its support is centered among the poor of southern Lebanon, who have not enjoyed the same economic success as the cosmopolitan Maronites (Christians) of Beirut who have traditionally dominated politics. Hezbollah runs an extensive network of social services, including schools and healthcare, in southern Lebanon, perhaps providing greater support to the poor than the state. With financial assistance from Iran, it runs a satellite television station, Al-Manar (the Lighthouse), and radio station, Al-Nour (the Light).

Despite the heavy damage inflicted on Lebanon, the military operation was, in many ways, a failure and setback for Israel. Israel had expected the conflict to last only a matter of days, believing that the Hezbollah forces would quickly stand down. Instead, the conflict illustrated the strength and effectiveness of Hezbollah, while showing Israeli's inability to suppress a weaker, non-state actor. The massive military attacks, which Israel expected would cause the Lebanese public to turn against Hezbollah, actually had the opposite effect as the Lebanese pulled together in the face of Israeli violence. In the aftermath of the conflict, Hezbollah has gained additional political influence in Lebanon. Within Israel the military attack created considerable controversy and calls for the resignation of Prime Minister Olmert and his handling of the war.

The US–Iran conflict

Iran's recent efforts to develop a nuclear program have brought it into conflict with the international community and the United States. Moreover, the nuclear program may encourage the United States to stage a military attack on Iran.

Iran has long had a nuclear program. Ironically, the program was launched in the 1950s with the help of the United States. Iran's current leadership maintains that the program is focused on peaceful nuclear technology, such as nuclear power, not weaponry. In 2002, Iran announced that it had developed both a uranium enrichment facility and a heavy water facility. Inspections by the International Atomic Energy Agency in 2003 found no evidence of weapons production. In April 2006, Iran announced that it had succeeded in producing enriched uranium, though at a level suitable for a nuclear reactor, not weapons. In recent years Iran has failed to submit required reports to the AIEA of developments in its nuclear program, but by January 2006 the IAEA certified that Iran was complying with required inspections. The Iranian government maintains that their program is focused only on peaceful nuclear technology.

The development of nuclear weapons has become a major rallying cry within some members of the Bush administration for military action against Iran. US intelligence consider Iran about ten years away from developing key ingredient for nuclear weapons, though no evidence was found of a weapons program there is a belief that Iran wants to develop such weapons. One major reason for Iranian weapons is to provide deterrence to the Israeli nuclear threat. Estimates of the Israeli nuclear arsenal range from forty to 400 warheads, but the program, anchored by the Dimona reactor, is secret. Israel has not signed the Nuclear Non-proliferation Treaty, so its facilities are not subject to inspection by the IAEA, a situation that infuriates Iran and other countries in the Middle East who have been pressured to abstain from developing nuclear weapons. The Israeli nuclear program also undermines attempts by the international community to create a nuclear-free zone in the region.

Within the international community sanctions and diplomacy are the current approaches to dealing with Iran. Though the Bush administration has publicly committed itself to diplomatic approaches to Iran, insiders and analysts argue that the administration is intent on a military confrontation with Iran. The goal of the confrontation is not only to thwart the nuclear program but, as in Iraq, to bring about regime change.

Significant military planning for operations against Iran is reportedly already underway, as are secret operations. According to Hersch (2006):

> One former defense official, who still deals with sensitive issues for the Bush Administration, told me that the military planning was premised on a belief that 'a sustained bombing campaign in Iran will humiliate the religious leadership and lead the public to rise up and overthrow the government.'

The bombing campaign could potentially include the use of nuclear tactical weapons by the United States. In any case, if the administration is truly intent on a military confrontation with Iran, it has little time to accomplish it. Clearly 'regime change' is difficult to control once set in process, as the US has learned in Iraq. Regime change in Iran could introduce even greater instability into the region and further empower non-state actors such as terrorist organizations.

SUMMARY OF MAIN POINTS

- The state system in the Middle East has been very stable over the last 50 years.
- The US invasion of Iraq has destabilized the region, creating the possibility of territorial redrawing and creating a base for terrorists.
- With the removal of Saddam Hussein, Iran and the region's Shia population now exercise greater influence.
- The Hezbollah–Israel confrontation illustrates the increasing power of non-state actors in the region; this conflict remains unresolved and will likely resurface.
- Iranian nuclear aspirations may lead to a direct confrontation with the US which is seeking regime change.
- The US is now a major actor in the Middle East, and will remain deeply involved in the region until Iraq is stabilized.

QUESTIONS FOR DISCUSSION

1   What are the options for ending the internal violence in Iraq? What is a post-Hussein Iraq likely to look like?
2   What are the possible impacts of increased Iranian influence in the region?
3   How serious is the potential of a Sunni–Shia divide?
4   In what ways was the Hezbollah–Israel war a setback for Israel?
5   Will US military action undermine Iran's nuclear program?

SUGGESTIONS FOR FURTHER READING

Biden, J. and Gelb, L. (2006) 'Unity through autonomy in Iraq'. *New York Times*, 1 May. Editorial article that introduces the Biden-Gelb federal plan for Iraq.

Federation of American Scientists: http://www.fas.org/nuke/guide/israel/nuke/index.html. Formed by a group of nuclear scientists involved with the Manhattan Project, the website contains information on Israeli nuclear activities.

Hersch, S. (2006) 'The Iran plans: would President Bush go to war to stop Tehran from getting the bomb?' *The New Yorker*, April 17. Details the administration's current activities toward Iran, including clandestine activities and plans for regime change.

International Crisis Group (2007) 'Hezbollah and the Lebanese crisis'. *Middle East Report*, 69, October, 10. Discusses the current role of Hezbollah in Lebanese politics and the conflict with Israel.

International Crisis Group (2006) Iran: is there a way out of the nuclear impasse? *Middle East Report*, 51, February, 23. Discusses options for handling Iran's ambition to develop a nuclear program, and potential for a nuclear weapons program.

Norton, R. (2007) *Hezbollah: A Short History.* Princeton, NJ: Princeton University Press. Analyzes the formation of Hezbollah and its current role in Lebanese politics. Includes a discussion of the 2006 confrontation with Israel.

PlanforIraq.com. A website devoted to the Biden-Gelb plan for Iraq; includes details of the plan and endorsements of the plan.

Valbjørn, M. and Bank, A. (2007) 'Signs of a new Arab Cold War: the 2006 Lebanon war and the Sunni–Shi'i divide'. *Middle East Report*, Spring. Discusses the growing division of the Middle East along, Sunni–Shia lines as sectarian loyalties replace the Arab socialist ideology of previous decades.

BIBLIOGRAPHY

Abootalebi, A. (1998) 'Civil society, democracy and the Middle East'. *Middle East Review of International Affairs*, 2: 46–59.

Abu Lughod, Janet L. (1989) *Before European Hegemony: The World System AD 1250–1350*. Oxford: Oxford University Press.

Agha, H. and Malley, R. (2001) 'Camp David: the tragedy of errors'. *The New York Review of Books*, August 9.

Agha, H., Feldman, S., Khalidi, A. and Schiff, Z. (2004) *Track-II Diplomacy: Lessons from the Middle East*. Cambridge, Mass.: MIT Press.

Amery, Hussein A. and Wolf, Aaron T. (eds) (2000) *Water in the Middle East*. Austin, Tex.: University of Texas Press.

Amnesty International (2007) *Israel and the Occupied Territories*. Annual Report: http://thereport.amnesty.org/eng/Regions/Middle-East-and-North-Africa/Israel-and-the-Occupied-Territories.

Anderson, E. (2000) *The Middle East: Geography and Geopolitics*. London: Routledge.

Anderson, L. (1986) *The State and Social Transformation in Tunisia and Libya, 1830–1980*. Princeton, NJ: Princeton University Press.

Aslan, R. (2006) *No god but God: The Origins, Evolution and Future of Islam*. New York: Random House.

Barber, B. (1996) *Jihad vs. McWorld: How Globalism and Tribalism Are Reshaping the World*. New York: Ballantine Books.

Barghouti, M. (2003) *I Saw Ramallah*. Cairo: American University in Cairo Press.

Bates, D. G. and Rassam, A. (2001) *Peoples and Cultures of the Middle East*. Upper Saddle River, NJ: Prentice Hall.

Beilin, Y. (1999) *Touching Peace: From the Oslo Accord to a Final Agreement*. London: Weidenfeld & Nicolson.

Beinin, J. (1999) 'The working class and peasantry in the Middle East: from economic nationalism to neoliberalism'. *Middle East Report*, Spring.

Berman, P. (2003) 'Philosopher of Islamic terror'. *New York Times*, March 23.

Biden, J. and Gelb, L. (2006) 'Unity through autonomy in Iraq'. *New York Times*, May 1.

Bilefsky, D. (2006) 'Turks seething over French bill; dispute taints pride over Nobel honor'. *International Herald Tribune*, October 16.

Bin Laden, O. (2005) *Messages to the World: The Statements of Osama Bin Laden*. Ed. B. Lawrence. Trans. J. Howarth. London: Verso.

Bosman, J. (2007) 'Novelist endangered by her book'. *New York Times*, February 10.

B'TSELEM, The Israeli Information Center for Human Rights in the Occupied Territories: www.btselem.org.

Central Intelligence Agency (2007) *CIA World Factbook*. Central Intelligence Agency, Office of Public Affairs.

Cleveland, W. (2004) *A History of the Modern Middle East*, 3rd edn. Boulder, Colo.: Westview Press.

Cockburn, A. and Cockburn, P. (1999) *Out of the Ashes: The Resurrection of Saddam Hussein*. New York: Harper Perennial.

Cook, M. (2000) *The Koran: A Short Introduction*. Oxford: Oxford University Press.

Crampton, J. (2006) 'The cartographic calculation of space: race mapping and the Balkans at the Paris Peace Conference of 1919'. *Social and Cultural Geography*, 7: 731–52.

Cutler, I. (2001) *Mysteries of the Desert: A View of Saudi Arabia*. New York: Rizzoli International Publications.

Danner, M. (2005) 'The secret way to war'. *The New York Review of Books*, June 9.

Dawisha, A. (2003) *Arab Nationalism in the Twentieth Century: From Triumph to Despair*. Princeton, NJ: Princeton University Press.

Dempsey, J. (2000) 'Four killed as Sharon visit sparks violence in Jerusalem'. *The Financial Times* (London), September 30.

Derbyshire, J. D. (2000) *Encyclopedia of World Political Systems*. Armonk, NY: Sharpe Reference.

Di Meglio, F. (2007) 'A fresh take on Islamic finance'. *Business Week Online*, March 27.

Diamond, L., Plattner, M. and Brumberg, D. (2003) *Islam and Democracy in the Middle East*. Baltimore, Md: Johns Hopkins University Press.

Doran, M. (2004) 'The Saudi paradox'. *Foreign Affairs*, January–February.

Dresch, P. (2005) *A History of Modern Yemen*. Cambridge: Cambridge University Press.

Ebadi, S. (2004) 'The Progressive interview: Shirin Ebadi'. Interview by Amitabh Pal. *The Progressive* (September), 35–9.

The Economist (2002) 'Self-doomed to failure'. July 4.

Esposito, J. L (2005) *Islam: The Straight Path*. Oxford: Oxford University Press.

Fattah, H. (2005) 'Egypt puts off reformer's trial, letting him run against Mubarak'. *New York Times*, July 7.

Federation of American Scientists: http://www.fas.org/ nuke/guide/israel/nuke/index.html.

Fernea, E. (1995) *Guests of the Sheikh: An Ethnography of an Iraqi Village*. New York: Anchor Books.

Fernea, E. and Hocking, M. (eds) (1992) *The Struggle for Peace: Israelis and Palestinians*. Austin, Tex.: University of Texas Press.

Fisk, R. (2005) *The Great War for Civilisation: The Conquest of the Middle East*. New York: Vintage Books.

Foundation for Middle East Peace: http://www. fmep.org/settlement_ifo/stats_data/golan_heights_settle ments.html.

Fromkin, D. (1989) *A Peace to End All Peace: Creating the Modern Middle East, 1914–1922*. New York: Holt.

Frye, R. (1975) *The Golden Age of Persia: The Arabs in the East*. New York: Barnes & Noble.

Gause, G. (2007) 'Bahrain parliamentary election results: 25 November and 2 December 2006'. *International Journal of Middle East Studies*, 39: 170–1.

Geneva Accord: www.geneva-accord.org.

Halliday, F. (2005) *The Middle East in International Relations: Power, Politics and Ideology*. Cambridge: Cambridge University Press.

Hamzeh, A. (2004) *In the Path of Hizbullah*. Syracuse, NY: Syracuse University Press.

Held C. C. (2006) *Middle East Patterns: Places, Peoples and Politics*. Boulder, Colo.: Westview Press.

Herb, M. (1999) *All in the Family: Absolutism, Revolution and Democracy in the Middle East Monarchies*. Syracuse, NY: State University of New York Press.

Hersch, S. M. (2003) ' "Selective intelligence". Donald Rumsfeld has his own special sources: are they reliable?' *The New Yorker, May 12*.

Hersch, S. M. (2006) 'The Iran plans: would President Bush go to war to stop Tehran from getting the bomb?' *The New Yorker*, April 17.

Hinchcliffe, P. (2007) *Conflicts in the Middle East since 1945*, (3rd edn. London: Routledge.

Hinnebusch, R. (2001) *Syria: A Revolution from Above*. London: Routledge.

Hinnebusch, R. (2003) *The International Politics of the Middle East*. Manchester: Manchester University Press.

Hiro, D. (1990) *Holy Wars: The Rise of Islamic Fundamentalism*. New York: Routledge.

Hodgson, M. (1974) *The Venture of Islam*. Vol. 3, *The Gunpowder Empires and Modern Times*. Chicago, Ill.: University of Chicago Press.

Horowitz, T. (1991) *Baghdad without a Map and Other Misadventures in Arabia*. New York: Penguin Books.

Hourani, A. (1991) *A History of the Arab Peoples*. Cambridge, Mass.: Harvard University Press.

Hudson, M. (2001) 'The Middle East'. *PS: Political Science and Politics*, 34: 801–4.

Humphries, R. S. (1999) *Between Memory and Desire: The Middle East in a Troubled Age*. Berkeley, Calif.: University of California Press.

Huntington, S. P. (1997). *The Clash of Civilizations and the Remaking of the World Order*. New York: Touchstone.

Imber, C. (2002) *The Ottoman Empire, 1300–1650: The Structure of Power*. New York: Palgrave.

International Crisis Group (2004) 'Can Saudi Arabia reform itself?' July 14.

International Crisis Group (2006a) 'Iran: Is there a way out of the nuclear impasse? *Middle East Report*, 51. February 23.

International Crisis Group (2006b)'The next Iraq war? Sectarianism and civil conflict'. *Middle East Report*, 52. February 27.

International Crisis Group (2007) 'Hizbollah and the Lebanese crisis'. *Middle East Report*, 69 October 10.

Kamrava, M. (2005) *The Modern Middle East: A Political History since the First World War*. Berkeley, Calif.: University of California Press.

Kaplan, R. (2007) 'Arab nationalism's last gasp', *Los Angeles Times* (Opinion), January 7.

Keddi, N. (2006) *Modern Iran: Roots and Results of a Revolution*. New Haven, Conn.: Yale University Press.

Kepel, G. (2002) *Jihad: The Trail of Political Islam*. Cambridge, Mass.: Harvard University Press.

Kepel, G. (2003) *Bad Moon Rising: A Chronicle of the Middle East Today*. London: Saqi Books.

Kifner, J. (2003) 'Islamic traditionalists sweep liberals in Kuwaiti elections'. *New York Times*, July 7.

Kimmerling, B. and Migdal, J. (2003) *The Palestinian People: A History*. Cambridge, Mass.: Harvard University Press.

Lapidus, I. (2002) *A History of Islamic Societies*. Cambridge: Cambridge University Press.

Laqueur, W. and Rubin, B. (eds) (2001) *The Israel–Arab Reader: A Documentary History of the Middle East Conflict*, 6th edn. New York: Penguin Books.

Lewis, B. (1990) 'The roots of Muslim rage'. *Atlantic Monthly*, 266: 47–60.

Lewis, B. (1993) *Islam and the West*. New York: Oxford University Press.

Liangxiang, J. (2005) 'Energy first: China and the Middle East'. *Middle East Quarterly*, Spring.

Little, D. (2002) *American Orientalism: The United States and the Middle East since 1945*. Chapel Hill, NC: University of North Carolina Press.

Liu, X. and Shaffer, L. N. (2007) *Connections across Eurasia: Transportation, Communication, and Cultural Exchange on the Silk Roads.* New York: McGraw-Hill.

Lockman, Z. (2004) *Contending Visions of the Middle East: The History and Politics of Orientalism.* Cambridge: Cambridge University Press.

Looney, R. (2005) 'US Middle East economic policy: the use of free trade areas in the war on terrorism'. *Mediterranean Affairs*, 16: 102–17.

Lynch, M. (2006) *Voices of the New Arab Public: Iraq, Al-Jazeera, and Middle East Politics Today.* New York: Columbia University Press.

Maalouf, A. (1984) *The Crusades through Arab Eyes.* New York: Schocken Books.

McDermott, A. (1988) *Egypt from Nasser to Mubarak: A Flawed Revolution.* London: Croom Helm.

MacMillan, M. (2001) *Paris 1919: Six Months That Changed the World.* New York: Random House.

Madslien, J. (2006) 'Economic boom belies Israeli poverty'. BBC News, March 27: http://news.bbc.co.uk/2/hi/business/4833602.stm (accessed 25 July 2007).

Mamdani, M. (2005) *Good Muslim, Bad Muslim: America, the Cold War and the Roots of Terror.* New York: Doubleday.

Manners, I. (2000) 'The Middle East: a geographic preface'. In D. Gerner and J. Schwedler (eds), *Understanding the Contemporary Middle East*, 2nd edn. Boulder, Colo.: Lynne Rienner Publishers.

Martin, J. (2006) 'After the oil …'. *The Middle East*, February.

May, T. (2007) *The Mongol Art of War.* Barnsley: Pen and Sword Books.

Mead, W. (2006) 'God's country?' *Foreign Affairs*, September–October.

Menocal, M. (2002) *The Ornament of the World: How Muslims, Jews and Christians Created a Culture of Tolerance in Medieval Spain.* Boston, Mass.: Little, Brown.

Miles, H. (2005) *Al Jazeera: The Inside Story of the Arab News Channel That Is Challenging the West.* New York: Grove Press.

Moojan, M. (1985) *An Introduction to Shi'i Islam.* New Haven, Conn.: Yale University Press.

Moore, B. (2006) 'Iraq's oil and the Saudi welfare state'. *Energy Bulletin*, March 23.

Moore, C. H. (1970) *Politics in North Africa: Algeria, Morocco and Tunisia.* Boston, Mass.: Little, Brown.

Moore, M. (2004) 'Israeli court orders changes in barrier'. *The Washington Post*, July 1.

Morris, B. (2001) *Righteous Victims: A History of the Zionist–Arab Conflict, 1881–2001.* New York: Vintage Books.

Murphy, C. (2002) *Passion for Islam. Shaping the Modern Middle East: The Egyptian Experience.* New York: Scribner.

Myntti, C. (2003) *Paris along the Nile: Architecture from the Belle Epoque.* New York: American University in Cairo Press.

Nasr, V. (2006) 'When the Shiites rise'. *Foreign Affairs*, 85: 58–74.

National Geographic Education Foundation (2002) *National Geographic–Roper Global Literacy Survey*: http://www.nationalgeographic.com/foundation/news_resources.html#reports.

National Geographic Society (2003) *National Geographic Atlas of the Middle East.* Washington, DC: National Geographic Society.

National Security Council (2002) *The National Security Strategy of the United States of America*, September 17.

Néret, G. (ed.) (2001) *Description of Egypt.* Köln: Taschen.

Noland, M. and Pack, H. (2004) 'Islam, globalization and economic performance in the Middle East'. *Institute for International Economic Policy Brief*, PB04-4, June.

Norton, A. (ed.) (2005) *Civil Society in the Middle East.* Leiden: E. J. Brill.

Norton, R. (2007) *Hezbollah: A Short History*. Princeton, NJ: Princeton University Press.

Oren, M. (2007) *Power, Faith and Fantasy: America in the Middle East: 1776 to the Present*. New York: W. W. Norton.

Ottaway, M. T., Hawthorne, C. and Brumberg, D. (2002) *Democratic Mirage in the Middle East*. Carnegie Endowment Policy Brief No. 20. Washington, DC: Carnegie Endowment for International Peace.

Owen, R. (2004) *State, Power and Politics in the Making of the Modern Middle East*, 3rd edn. London: Routledge.

Owen, R. and Pamuk, S. (1999) *A History of Middle East Economies in the Twentieth Century*. Cambridge, Mass.: Harvard University Press.

Palestinian Center for Policy and Survey Research (2003) 'Results of PSR refugees' polls in the West Bank/Gaza Strip, Jordan and Lebanon', July 18: http://www.pcpsr.org/survey/polls/2003/refugeesjune03.html (accessed September 7, 2007).

Palmer, A. (1993) *The Decline and Fall of the Ottoman Empire*. London: John Murray.

Pamuk, S. (2006) 'Estimating economic growth in the Middle East since 1820'. *The Journal of Economic History*, 66: 809–28.

Pew Global Attitudes Project (2005) 'Islamic extremism: common concern for Muslim and Western publics', July 14: http://pewglobal.org/reports/display.php?ReportID=248.

Pillar, P. (2006) 'Intelligence, policy and the war in Iraq'. *Foreign Affairs*, March–April.

PlanforIraq.com.

Population Reference Bureau (2007) 'Challenges and opportunities – the population of the Middle East and North Africa'. *Population Bulletin*, 62: 2.

Prusher, I. (2006) 'Sharon's legacy of controversy'. *The Christian Science Monitor*, April 12, p. 10.

Qutb, S. (1953) *Social Justice in Islam*. Trans. John B. Hardie. Oneanta, NY: Islamic Publications International.

Ramadan, T. (2004) *Western Muslims and the Future of Islam*. New York/Oxford: Oxford University Press.

Rashid, A. (2000) *Taliban: Militant Islam, Oil and Fundamentalism in Central Asia*. London: I. B. Tauris.

Reid, D. M. (2002) *Whose Pharaohs?: Archaeology, Museums, and Egyptian National Identity from Napoleon to World War I*. Berkeley, Calif.: University of California Press.

Richards, A. (2002) 'Socioeconomic roots of Middle East radicalism'. *Naval War College Review*, 55: 22–39.

Richards, A. and Waterbury, J. (1996) *A Political Economy of the Middle East*. Boulder, Colo.: Westview Press.

Rubin, B. (1999) 'China's Middle East strategy'. *Middle East Review of International Affairs Journal*, March.

Rugh, W. (2004) Comments on Radio Sawa and al-Hurra television. Testimony before the US Senate: http://www.senate.gov/~foreign/testimony/2004/Rugh Testimony040429.pdf.

Sachar, H. (1996) *A History of Israel: From the Rise of Zionism to Our Time*, 2nd edn. New York: Alfred Knopf.

Said, E. (1978) *Orientalism: Western Conceptions of the Orient*. London: Routledge & Kegan Paul.

Scheindlin, R. P. (1998) *A Short History of the Jewish People: From Legendary Times to Modern Statehood*. Oxford: Oxford University Press.

Shlaim, A. (1995) *War and Peace in the Middle East: A Concise History*. New York: Penguin.

Shlaim, A. (2001) *The Iron Wall: Israel and the Arab World*. New York: W. W. Norton.

Shulman, D. (2007) *Dark Hope: Working for Peace in Israel and Palestine*. Chicago, Ill.: University of Chicago Press.

Slackman, M. (2005) 'Anti-Mubarak protesters clash with police in Cairo'. *New York Times*, July 31.

Soueif, A.(2004) *Mezzaterra: Fragments from a Common Ground*. New York: Anchor Books.

Springborg, R. and Bill, J. A. (1999) *Politics in the Middle East*, 5th edn. London: Longman.

Steet, L. (2000) *Veils and Daggers: A Century of National Geographic's Representation of the Arab World*. Philadelphia, Pa: Temple University Press.

Stewart, D. J. (2007) *Good Neighbourly Relations: Jordan, Israel and the 1994–2004 Peace Process*. London: I. B. Tauris.

Tessler, M. (1994) *A History of the Israeli–Palestinian Conflict*. Bloomington, Ind.: University of Indiana Press.

Thesiger, W. (1958) 'Marsh dwellers of southern Iraq'. *The National Geographic Magazine*, February, pp. 205–49.

Tibi, B. (2002) *The Challenges of Fundamentalism: Political Islam and the New World Order*. Berkeley, Calif.: University of California Press.

Tyldesley, J. (2005) *Egypt: How a Lost Civilization Was Rediscovered*. Berkeley, Calif.: University of California Press.

United Nations Development Programme (2002) *Arab Human Development Report: Creating Opportunities for Future Generations*. New York: UNDP.

United Nations Economic and Social Commission for Western Asia (2001) *Economic Diversification in the Oil-producing Countries: The Case of the Gulf Cooperation Council*, January 10.

United States Department of State (2002) 'The US–Middle East partnership initiative: building hope for the years ahead', Secretary Colin L. Powell, December 12.

United States Department of State. Bureau of Democracy, Human Rights and Labor (2005) *Morocco: Country Report on Human Rights Practices*, released March 8, 2006.

Valbjørn, M. and Bank, A. (2007) 'Signs of a new Arab Cold War: the 2006 Lebanon war and the Sunni–Shi'i divide'. *Middle East Report, spring*.

Vatikiotis, P. J. (1991) *The History of Modern Egypt: From Muhammad Ali to Mubarak*, 4th edn. Baltimore, Md: Johns Hopkins University Press.

Watt, W. M. (1972) *The Influence of Islam on Medieval Europe*. Edinburgh: Edinburgh University Press.

Wilson, S. (2006) 'Hamas sweeps Palestinian elections, complicating peace efforts in Mideast'. *The Washington Post*, January 27, p. A1.

Wright, R. (2007) 'US faults detention by Iran of dual citizens'. *The Washington Post*, May 10.

Yergin, D. (1991) *The Prize: The Epic Quest for Oil, Money and Power*. New York: Simon & Schuster.

Zurcher, E. (2004) *Turkey: A Modern History*. London: I. B. Tauris.

INDEX

Page numbers in *italics* refer to items in boxes. Items beginning with the prefix al- are sorted under the main element, eg, al-Qaeda is listed under Q

An Atlas of Middle Eastern Affairs

Ewan Anderson, University of Durham, UK and
Liam Anderson, Wright State University, USA

Cartography by **Ian Cool**

Focussing on flashpoint and conflicts, this new atlas provides concisely written entries on the most important current issues in the Middle East. It contains succinct descriptions and assessment of core background topics, the position of the Middle East in the world and profiles of the constituent countries. Each entry comes with maps and data. This book is a comprehensive reference source and text for undergraduates, as well as providing an invaluable resource for those engaged in the Middle East including policy makers, researchers, journalists and commentators.

- Provides comprehensive coverage to the contemporary Middle East

- Easy to use reference work that gives precise summaries of the most important topics

- Student friendly pedagogical features include further reading, data sets and an abundance of expertly drawn maps

Contents:

Introduction
The Middle East in Relation to the Global Scene
The Middle Eastern Background: Geographical & Historical
The Key Issues of the Middle East
The States of the Middle East
The Influential Rimland of the Middle East

Pb: 978-0-415-45515-2: **£18.99**
Hb: 978-0-415-45514-5: **£80.00**
240pp, July 2009

Suitable for Courses On:
Middle East Geography • Middle East History • Middle East Politics
Geopolitics • Military Studies

TO REQUEST AN INSPECTION COPY OR FOR FURTHER INFORMATION VISIT
www.routledge.com/middleeaststudies

Routledge
Taylor & Francis Group

an **informa** business

available from all good bookshops

The Arab-Israeli Conflict

An Introduction and Documentary Reader

Gregory S. Mahler, Earlham College, Indiana, USA and **Alden Mahler**, Emory University, USA

This book focuses upon the foreign policy context of the peace process and the progress made in the peace process. The book describes the diplomatic and historical setting within which the conflict developed, the Israeli and Palestinian perspectives, and a historical overview of the process itself. It includes over six dozen key documents related to the conflict, going from documents related to the creation of Zionism in 1896 through the "Road Map" in 2003 and the most recent peace overtures of 2007.

Pb: 978-0-415-77461-1 **£22.99**
Hb: 978-0-415-77460-4 **£90.00**
May 2009: 248pp

Suitable for Courses On:
Middle East Peace Process • Arab-Israeli Conflict • Middle East Politics

Contents: Introduction

Part 1: Background and Context

1. The Setting
2. The Israeli Perspective
3. The Palestinian Perspective
4. The Peace Process to Date

Part 2: Documents

Theodor Herzl: The Jewish State (1896)

The First Zionist Congress: The Basle Declaration (August, 1897)

Sir Henry McMahon: The McMahon Letter (October 24, 1915)

British and French Governments: The Sykes-Picot Agreement (May 15, 1916)

British Foreign Minister Lord Arthur Balfour: The Balfour Declaration (November 2, 1917)

Emir Feisal and Chaim Weizmann: Agreement (January 3, 1919)

Winston Church, The Churchill White Paper (June 1922)

League of Nations: The British Mandate (July 24, 1922)

The Palestine Royal Commission (Peel Commission): Report (July, 1937)

British Government: Policy Statement Against Partition (November, 1938)

British Government: The White Paper (May 17, 1939)

The Jewish Agency for Palestine: Zionist Reaction to the White Paper (1939)

German Chancellor Adolf Hitler and the Grand Mufti Haj Amin al-Husseini: Zionism and the Arab Cause (November 28, 1941)

The Biltmore Program: Towards a Jewish State, U.N.

Special Committee on Palestine: Summary Report (August 31, 1947)

U.N. General Assembly: Resolution on the Future Government of Palestine (Partition Resolution) (November 29, 1947)

State of Israel: Proclamation of Independence (May 14, 1948)

U.N. General Assembly: Resolution 194 (December 11, 1948)

U.N. General Assembly: Resolution 303 (December 9, 1949)

U.N. Security Council: Resolution 619 Concerning ... the Passage of Ships Through the Suez Canal (September 1, 1951)

Israeli Foreign Minister Abba Eban: Speech at the Special Assembly of the United Nations (June 19, 1967)

U.N. Security Council: Resolution 242 (November 22, 1967)

Palestine National Council: The Palestine National Charter (July, 1968)

Fatah: The Seven Points (January, 1969)

P.L.O. Chairman Yasir Arafat: Interview (August, 1969)

U.N. Security Council: Resolution 338 (October 22, 1973)

Palestine National Council: Resolutions (June, 1974)

Egyptian-Israeli Accord on Sinai (September 1, 1975)

The Likud Party: Platform (March 1977)

Egyptian President Anwar Sadat: Peace with Justice (November 20, 1977)

P.L.O.: Six-Point Program (December 4, 1977)

Camp David Summit Meeting: Framework for Peace (September 17, 1978)

Egypt and Israel: Peace Treaty (March 26, 1979)

Government of Israel: Law on the Golan Heights (December 14, 1981)

Israeli Prime Minister Begin: The Wars of No Alternative and Operation Peace for the Galilee (August 8, 1982)

The Kahan Commission: Report (February 7, 1983)

Lebanon and Israel: Truce Agreement (May 17, 1983)

Hamas: Charter (August, 1988)

Palestine National Council: Declaration of Independence (November 15, 1988)

P.L.O. Chairman Yasir Arafat: The PLO and the Gulf Crisis (December 13, 1990)

Israeli Prime Minister Rabin: Inaugural Speech (July 13, 1992)

Israel and P.L.O.: Declaration of Principles on Interim Self-Government Arrangements ["The Oslo Agreement"] (September 13, 1993)

Clinton, Rabin, Arafat: Speeches at Signing of Israeli-PLO Declaration of Principles (September 13, 1993)

Israel and Jordan: The Washington Agreement (July 26, 1994)

Israel and Jordan: Peace Treaty (October 26, 1994)

Rabin, Arafat, Peres: Speeches Accepting Nobel Peace Prize (December 10, 1994)

Israeli Prime Minister Yitzhak Rabin: Speech at Peace Rally (November 4, 1995)

Israel and Palestinian Authority: Wye River Memorandum (October 23, 1998)

U.S. President Bill Clinton: His Experience with the Peace Process (January 7, 2001)

The Israeli-Palestinian Conflict

A People's War

Beverley Milton Edwards, Queen's University Belfast, UK

An essential insight into the complexities of one of the world's most enduring conflicts between Israelis and Palestinians, this textbook is designed to make a complex subject accessible to all. Key features include a chronology of events and annotated further reading at the end of each chapter.

Contents: Introduction 1. Roots of Conflict 2. Between the Wars 3. Palestine after the Holocaust 4. Israel Reborn 5. The Dispossessed 6. The Occupation Generation 7. The War of the Stones and Guns 8. A Global Concern 9. Moving from Zero

Pb: 978-0-415-41043-4: **£19.99**
Hb: 978-0-415-41044-1: **£70.00**
July 2008: 240pp

TO REQUEST AN INSPECTION COPY OR FOR FURTHER INFORMATION VISIT
www.routledge.com/middleeaststudies

Routledge
Taylor & Francis Group

an **informa** business

available from all good bookshops